To. Hugh

New York 1988 –

with – love –

Marianne Yoors –

JAN YOORS

THE
GYPSIES

A TOUCHSTONE BOOK
Published by Simon & Schuster, Inc.
NEW YORK

TO PULIKA AND RUPA—
WITH NOSTALGIA

Library of Congress Cataloging in Publication Data

Yoors, Jan.
  The gypsies.

  (A Touchstone book)
  1. Gypsies—Europe. I. Title.
DX145.Y66   1983   940'.0491497   83-12050

ISBN 0-671-49335-3 Pbk.

INTRODUCTION

This book is written as a protest against oblivion, as a cry of love for this race of strangers who have lived among us for centuries and remained apart.

The Gypsies, seemingly immune to progress, live in an everlasting Now, in a perpetual, heroic present, as if they recognized only the slow pulse of eternity and were content to live in the margin of history. They are in constant motion, like the waving of branches or the flowing of water. Their social organization is forever fluid, yet has an internal vitality. The inner cohesion and solidarity of the Gypsy community lies in the strong family ties which are their basic and only constant unit. The larger groups of family units, the horde, they call the *kumpania*. It remains highly mobile, constantly scattering and regrouping as old relationships and alliances shift, as new patterns of interest develop. They keep in touch with each other through a web of secret contacts.

Unlike the Jews, they share neither a Messianic visionary cult nor the consciousness of a great historical past. Oral traditions survive only through strong genealogical awareness; their memories do not extend beyond four, or at best five, generations, limited to those ancestors a living person still remembers—and at his death these ancient ones are forgotten, since no one else has known them alive. There are no mythical or legendary heroes, no stories about their origin, no need for any justification of their worldwide nomadism.

In the past, most scholars and writers on the Gypsies have designated them either by geographic area or by their host countries: Nothing could be more misleading.

It is true there are a few groups of Gypsies who are

sedentary or seminomadic, and who have probably lent themselves more readily to the scrutiny of outsiders: Such are the Gitanos of Spain, the Gypsies of England, the Sinti of Germany, the Rudari of Romania, the Musicians of Hungary. Most of these are practically detribalized and well on the way to acculturation, unlike the purely nomadic Rom, who travel extensively, covering entire continents in their wanderings. Members of both the Lowara and the Kalderash tribes can be found anywhere from the U.S.S.R. to the U.S.A., from Oslo to Istanbul, from Malaya to South Africa and Brazil.

The Rom are a unique exception among those nomadic groups adhering strictly to archaic tribal allegiance, in that their nomadism is on a worldwide scale and is superimposed on Western rural, industrial or urban society. In this they are unlike other wandering tribes who cover restricted areas, mostly desert or wasteland, and who were often the original settlers, pushed back or displaced by later invaders. The Gypsies remain by their own definition "hunters," with hunters' privileges. These are the Rom I want to write about.

They possess a significant sense of being part of a larger whole. Their urge to travel is no mere wanderlust. They voyage to meet relatives as yet unknown, and to find suitable brides for their sons, marrying them within the tribe but avoiding inbreeding. They are part of a continuing cultural transfusion and an ever-flowing force of renewal.

Under a thin veneer of Christianity or of Islam their true religion remains a form of ancestor worship. Their legal system or *kris* derives its coercive force from magic based on this concept of ancestry. The main common bond, besides descent from a related ancestry, is their language, Romani, a derivative of Sanskrit, the secrecy of which is jealously preserved.

The Gypsies have protected their cultural continuity and identity by hiding behind an elaborate system of protective screens, so that reality is often the exact opposite of appearance.

It is under this heading that I would class fortune-telling.

Besides being an obvious source of income, it is at least as important as a means of surrounding the Gypsies with an uneasy, magic aura. It gives substance to their use of curses against outsiders who brutally mistreat them, and often prevents such treatment. The Rom never practice fortune-telling among themselves in any form.

In the United States some tribes have developed fortune-telling into a highly organized, full-time racket, and their shady activities are often reported by the press when they are brought to court for their swindles.

The persistent begging of most children and all women is another of the many ways of discouraging prolonged or close contact with them by the Gaje (the Rom's word for non-Gypsies). Their disheveled appearance, to which they themselves attach no importance, serves the same purpose. There is a joy in this unobtrusive defiance. They hardly ever display open hostility. When approached directly, they show a total disregard for consistency and may become totally incomprehensible about any matter they do not want to discuss, without any sense of embarrassment on their part. They scorn the gullible Gaje who are naïve enough to believe that truthful answers can be obtained in such an unsubtle fashion.

By force of adverse circumstances some Gypsies are forced to practice subsistence thieving—that is, taking their minimal daily needs from the land or its lawful owners: grass for their horses, firewood, potatoes, vegetables or fruit, and of course the proverbial "stray" chicken. In a general way they consider the entire Gajo world a public domain.

As with all legends, that of the Gypsies as thieves has been exaggerated. If they were guilty of all the thefts blamed on them, they would have to travel with moving vans or settle down under the weight of their possessions.

They are often surrounded by open hostility, and because of their lack of political power much of the violence and the inhuman oppression they encounter is left unreported. I often wondered at their strange, inexplicable lack of traumatic reactions to their often violent personal persecutions. I observed, and eventually learned to understand, their rejection of hate or personal bitterness as a response to outside pressures. Pulika, my adopted father, said, "Too often the courage about dying is cowardice about living."

This book is written in the first person because my editor, and friend, Michael V. Korda, prevailed upon me to do so and convincingly showed me that, to an extent, the story of my personal involvement with the Gypsies is the key to the truth of my tales. It was because of a unique chain of circumstances (not the least of which was my parents' amazing broad-mindedness in letting their twelve-year-old son run away) that I was permitted to enter their world in the first place. Later on, my thorough mastery and fluent use of their language were an important factor in their acceptance of me. One day I caught myself saying "We, the Rom . . ." and realized how deep my involvement with them had become. Therefore, I can say that everything I talk about in this book, I saw, I heard, I was part of. . . .

My parents and Dr. Frans O. M. Olbrechts, the head of the Department of Anthropology at Ghent University, Belgium, who closely followed my travels, discouraged me from reading what others had written about the Gypsies, at least until my own observations had become settled and partly organized.

Eventually I found out that there was an extensive and steadily growing bibliography on the subject. In 1914 George F. Black, Ph.D., compiled a list of 4,577 published works, many of them repeating previous works, often with more or less fictional embellishments.

In 1888 the Gypsy Lore Society was formed in England and its *Journal* regularly publishes the results of the active efforts of its scholarly members. For the past few years, the Association des Etudes Tsiganes of Paris has also been publishing a trimestral bulletin. Nevertheless I was appalled at the serious lack of documentary evidence in general.

From July to September 1961 I had the opportunity to travel extensively by car through the entire Balkans and Turkey, revisiting territory previously covered in my youth while traveling with the Rom, to verify my observations on the Gypsies.

The lack of adequate records necessitates studies concerned with the observable present rather than the past—with things visible rather than extractable.

In the descriptive essays of the Norwegian anthropologist C. H. Tillhagen, of the Stockholm Nordiska Museet, I find some of my own observations most closely reflected.

According to the authority of Jules Bloch, Professeur Honoraire au Collège de France, the Gypsies made their first appearance, or at least their presence was first revealed, in the archives of the Western world in the fifteenth century. In 1417 they were reported in Kronstadt, Transylvania; in 1427 in Paris; in 1447 in Barcelona.

There exist records of them as early as 1348 in Serbia and in 1378 in Greece, in the Peloponnesus. The various descriptions of them read disturbingly like those one could read more than five centuries later. Even that far back the descriptions read like a negative imprint, like the reverse image seen in a mirror. The same protective system still operating today was already in action, projecting a convenient mirage to foil the Gaje.

Professor Bloch also quotes the great Persian poet Ferdowsi, who in 1011, in his *Shah Namah* (Book of Kings), refers to 10,000 Luri musicians imported from India by Bahram Gour in 420 B.C. Professor Bloch appears to accept this as probably the earliest reference to Gypsies known so far.

Actually we have no record of their wanderings prior to their appearance in the West, no date at which they left a "homeland," no reason for their departure.

As early as 1780 two German philologists, Heinrich Moritz Grellman and Jacob Carl Cristoph Rüdiger, speculated on the linguistic relationship between Sanskrit and the Gypsy dialects. This relationship was later confirmed by the British linguist Jacob Bryant, by August Friedrich Pott in 1884 and by Alexandros Georgios Paspati, who to my knowledge was the only one to have had any firsthand acquaintance with them. The erudite speculations were further developed by

Ritter Franz Xavier von Miklosich, who believed he had traced their origin to the plains of the Hindu Kush, in northern India. In 1915 Alfred C. Woolner brought out what he feels are the important links with central India. Professor R. L. Turner, the noted Sanskrit scholar, who wrote *The Position of Romani in Indo-Aryan,* in 1927, proposed the possibility of a double parenthood and suggested the likelihood of a prolonged stay in the plateaus of Afghanistan prior to the Islamic and Iranian invasions.

For the time being, all this remains speculation. In the present there is still confusion enough for the scholar. There is, for example, no up-to-date or comprehensive census of the Gypsies in the world today. The U.S.S.R. claims close to one million; Bulgaria, Romania and Hungary each claim between 200,000 and 250,000; Yugoslavia nearly 116,000; Turkey and Greece share another 200,000; Czechoslovakia and Poland have about 150,000 each. In the U.S.S.R. and in the Central European countries the Gypsies are under steady pressure to give up nomadism and become integrated into "productive" society.

Close to half a million were exterminated by the Germans between 1939 and 1945. There is a long history of similar repressions against them, as well as efforts toward "bettering the Gypsies' lot," preceded by forced settlement. Notorious among such campaigns were those of Henry VIII and Elizabeth I in England, of Charles III in Spain, of Frederick II in Germany and of Maria Theresa and Joseph II in Austria. The survival of nomadic Gypsies today shows conclusively how unsuccessful these various attempts proved to be.

Thus it is of the nomads that I sing.

—Y.J.
New York, 1966

PART ONE

CHAPTER ONE

I want to evoke a mood: the overwhelming immensity of the sky and the timelessness of the moment, where night is merely the continuation of the day; of mud and discomfort and brackish drinking water; of the challenge of constant change, of swirling dust, of too few trees and moaning winds, of the reassuring night sky; of snorting horses, of clustered covered wagons and cooking fires, of playing children and barking dogs, of raiding parties and posses of mounted police; of the simple dignity of the Rom, of their exuberant animal magnetism; of the lake where carp play in the sun, of approaching twilight. . . .

As I approached the Gypsy camp for the first time, yellow, wild-looking, stiff-haired dogs howled and barked. Fifteen covered wagons were spread out in a wide half circle, partly hiding the Gypsies from the road. Around the campfires sat women draped in deep-colored dresses, their big, expressive eyes and strong, white teeth standing out against their beautiful dark matte skin. The many gold pieces they wore as earrings, necklaces and bracelets sharpened their color even more. Their shiny blue-black hair was long and braided, the skirts of their dresses were ankle-length, very full and worn in many layers, and their bodices loose and low-cut. My first impression of them was one of health and vitality. Hordes of small barefoot children ran all over the campsite, a few dressed in rags but most nearly naked, rollicking like young animals. At the far end of the encampment a number of horses, tethered to long chains, were grazing; and of course there were the ever-present half-wild growling dogs. Several men lay in the shade of an oak tree. Thin corkscrews of bluish

13

smoke rose skyward and the pungent, penetrating smell of burning wood permeated the air. Even from a distance the loud, clear voices of these Gypsies resounded with an intensity I was not accustomed to. Mingling with them, farther away, were the dull thuds of an ax, the snorting and neighing of horses, the occasional snapping of a whip and the high-pitched wail of an infant, contrasting with the whisper of the immediate surroundings of the camp itself.

The sturdily built covered wagons were perched on high wheels. There were three windows on either side, and double doors at the front opening onto a wide porchlike board. The walls were of deep-toned natural-colored oak and heavily varnished, and the roofs were white. Large piles of eiderdowns covered with fading, brightly colored flowered material lay airing in the sun.

It was a late spring day when the Gypsies passed through my town. I was twelve years old at the time, and had gone in search of the wonderful people my father had so often told me about. Since late the night before they had camped in a large vacant lot on the outskirts of town. Tomorrow they would no doubt vanish again, leaving hardly a trace of their presence— a few dark spots where the campfires had burned, some refuse and trampled grass—and only the rumors about them would remain.

Leaving the paved road, I stepped through the tall weeds into the camp. None of the adult squatters paid any attention to me. I had the distinct impression of treading on foreign soil, but nothing about it seemed frightening. Several Gypsy boys my age ran to meet me where the trampled grass marked the borderline of the two worlds.

I addressed them in Spanish, mistakenly believing this to be the most appropriate language in which to speak to them. I associated all Gypsies with Andalucía, with flamenco music and dancing, with sun and manzanilla wine. Over the years I was to discover that many people wrongly associate these nomads exclusively with Spain, Russia, Hungary or Romania.

The Gypsy boys greeted me in broken German. Between very young human beings there sometimes is a feeling of great ease, almost one of having met before. So it was with us. They showed me the horses, casually giving me highly technical estimates of their virtues and defects. They seemed undisturbed by my failure to respond. I was apprehensive about this initial test and dreaded their judging me by my inadequate familiarity with horseflesh.

One of the boys was called Nanosh. His jet-black hair was long and he had a faded magenta silk kerchief tightly wound around his neck. His dirty white shirt was buttonless and showed his bare young chest. Together we wandered all over the wasteland. Between two wagons at the far end of the camp they delightedly showed me an impressive number of small dead animals hanging from a line by their hind legs. They were smaller than rabbits but definitely of the rodent family. They looked like rats. Nanosh relieved my embarrassment by informing me that they were hedgehogs with their quills shaved off. The boys talked briefly in their language. I could guess that they were reproaching Nanosh for having so easily stilled my fears. Nanosh explained to me that hedgehogs were a delicacy among his people and that the boys spent a good deal of time hunting them; they were at their best in fall, when they had accumulated the fat essential for their long hibernation. He promised to teach me to track them down "next time you come back." Picking up a smallish dead hedgehog, which I had not noticed, from a disorderly pile of debris, he crouched down near a fire and motioned me to do the same. Selecting a twig at random, he cut a sharp point at one end and inserted it in one of the dead hedgehog's hind legs. With the stick he skillfully loosened the skin from the thin bone, then, putting it to his mouth and puffing his cheeks, he slowly inflated the hedgehog until its skin was taut. After tying off the diminutive hind-leg air passage, Nanosh shaved the quills with a practiced hand. The little inflated animal was transformed before my eyes into the uninviting replica of a common rat. Nanosh deflated it and hung it on the line with the others, to be eaten later in the day. In a way I was disappointed, but also relieved, at not being offered a taste of this Romany delicacy. This gastronomic experience was only postponed, and repeated exposure to it helped me share the Gypsies' appreciation: the meat is tender and delicate in texture, gamy, and quite fat. It is often seasoned with wild garlic and black pepper.

A sudden outburst of violent abuse directed at me in a harsh metallic voice shattered my enchantment. A very old woman shrieked to me to go home. She stood erect, framed in the doorway of one of the wagons. Her face, with high cheekbones, was deeply lined and leathery. Her eyelids appeared devoid of lashes and gave her unblinking wide eyes the look of a reptile's, not so much mean as distant and cold. Her hair was a dull gun-gray under a yellow kerchief. Nanosh ran to the other side of the camp, dragging me along. Two other boys ran along with us. Panting, they assured me that old Lyuba did not really intend to do me any harm; it was just a habit with her not only to dislike all strangers—they all did—but to openly express her disapproval of them.

Nanosh told me that the Gypsies call themselves "Rom,"* that is, "Man." All non-Gypsies or outsiders are called "Gaje,"† which he translated as "peasants." He looked me in the eyes as he said it, but there was a slight hesitation in his voice and I sensed the pejorative connotation. I was unwilling to let this moment of ambiguity embarrass me. I realized, however, that the Rom might have as many prejudices against us, the Gaje, as we had against them.

Listening carefully to the Gypsy boys calling each other, I learned and memorized the names of two others: Laetshi and Putzina. At times they also affectionately called the latter Pupus, or even Putzi. Putzina wore an unlikely navy-blue riverboat captain's cap, and both he and Laetshi wore bright silken kerchiefs around their throats, as did all members of the band.

That day I played hookey without remorse. I took off my shoes to be barefoot, as were Nanosh, Laetshi and Putzina, hoping to develop a further common bond. To me shoes were a symbol of proper European upbringing and discipline. In the same category I placed compulsory washing of one's neck and ears and the combing of one's hair, neither of which chores, to my great envy, my new companions seemed to be burdened

---

* The singular and plural are the same.
† The plural of *Gajo*.

with. To my surprise, however, I noticed that to them my discarded shoes represented a half-envied luxury. One by one they tried them on with noisy expressions of joy and a touch of mischief. Older boys joined in the fun, but as they were unable to squeeze their feet in, they cut off the front part of the shoes, with my permission but not with my full approval. This made me decide to stay till nightfall and to minimize the chances of being seen barefoot by the neighbors or my school companions.

Nanosh, his cousins, and I lay in the tall grass, playing and wrestling. Later that same day, unasked, they gave me my first lesson in their language. The choice of words and the sequence in which they taught them to me gave me an inkling of their significance to my informants: *mas*, meat; *lowe*, money; *tshorav*, to steal; *grast*, horse; *shanglo*, police constable. Naturally they added a few other basic words of a somewhat special nature.

Putzina and Nanosh shared their food with me, while Laetshi went to eat with his family. After the meal the Gypsies gathered around the campfires. The men drank beer from a huge barrel and sang in their language.

It was then that I committed my one great semiconscious error: I stayed five more minutes. . . .

The hours went by. I could feel the dampness rising from the earth, but it seemed I was the only one aware of it. When the Gypsies retired to sleep under their huge feather beds, spread out in the open, it was too late for me to go home. I gratefully accepted Nanosh's invitation to share his sleeping stead, together with his many little brothers, between two enormous eiderdowns.

I slipped inside the bed fully dressed and rather ill at ease. We lay on our backs and looked up into the starry sky. I felt humble and also a little solemn. I noticed a shooting star and, eager to share this with Nanosh, pointed out to him where it had passed, far away. In a hushed, husky voice he told me never to do this again; for each star in the sky is a man on earth. When a star runs away it means that a thief takes flight, and by pointing a finger at a shooting star the man it represents is likely to be captured. "My cousin Kore," Nanosh went on, "has gone out tonight with Kalia's son and they have not yet come back. . . ." Nanosh turned his back to me, and moments later I could hear his gentle and regular breathing. He was enjoying the calm sleep of those whose consciences are at peace. Far away on a farm a watchdog was barking and I could not help thinking of the falling star and the man it stood for. It was the first time I had spent the night under the starry sky, and I was too full of new experiences to be willing to surrender to sleep. The night was quiet, and for some time I observed the unfamiliar objects that surrounded me. All around us were fantastically shaped mounds formed by the feather beds under which my new friends were sleeping. The hard light of the moon made the faded covers of the eiderdowns look even more unreal. I was dreaming wide-awake.

Little Balo, a boy of five or six, nestled against me. On the other side a young creature with tousled hair had, like a small animal in search of warmth, slipped between my bedfellow Nanosh and myself. I was uncomfortable. Suddenly a little Gypsy boy at the other end of our *dunha* (eiderdown) turned around with a pull, like a carp. He upset his neighbor, who adjusted his position slightly. A third groaned, displeased with the new arrangement. Then from left and right they started kicking. I asked myself how many there were to share Nanosh's *dunha*. The other Gypsies, sleeping within earshot, called on us gruffly to be quiet. And suddenly all was still again. The struggle started anew: the youngsters were mischievously sly and cunning. Whose side was I to take—I, the stranger? One of the small children, Hanzi, suddenly uttered a terrifying yell. It was followed by stillness, which filled me with anxiety. Then the boy started sobbing till his sobs shook his whole plump little body. Hanzi sobbed louder and louder and his weeping sounded tragic in the stillness of the night. Contrary to my expectations, nobody seemed to hear it or feel it necessary to intervene. Soon he was immersed again in blissful sleep, tightly holding one of my feet in his arms, as if it were a doll. My head ached for lack of sleep. The coolness of dawn hurt my temples. At the fringe of the camp the horses were changing their positions and pressing nearer to one another. A laborer passing by on his bicycle on his way to work roused all the dogs of the camp. Far away, sheep leaving their fold were bleating plaintively. I had the impression that in our encampment people were only waiting for a signal to get up, but as yet nobody stirred. I remained wedged between the other boys and did not dare to move.

After a long wait I heard somebody get up. Discreetly turning my head in that direction, I saw old Lyuba standing upright like a candle, in her voluminous dark skirts. The light of the rising sun made her ascetic features seem handsome. Her movements were slow and stately. She looked strong-willed and energetic despite her great age. She crouched down a few feet away from the sleepers, chopped wood and lit a fire. I closed my eyes. Half asleep, I perceived the odor of burning wood and of coffee, the scent of plants and shrubs and, mixed with them, the pleasant smell of the healthy young open-air creatures, the *shavora*, my companions. The gentle rays of the sun warmed my face and I fell sound asleep.

I woke late in the morning. I was alone under the big eiderdown. I was perspiring, devoid of will power, without energy. Most *dunhas* had been removed and stacked away inside the wagons. Chestnut-brown and dapple-gray horses stood out against a deep blue sky and the various shades of green of the meadows and shrubs. Emerging from a state of lazy dreaminess, I remembered that my father was a painter and realized that it was to him that I owed my awareness of color and the joy it gave me. At the same time it occurred to me with an unpleasant shock that for the first time in my young life I had slept far away from home, among total strangers and under the open sky. I had not returned home the night before and my parents must have been worried and waiting for me. I felt dizzy and sick, but my general drowsiness and the snug warmth generated by the feather bed helped to lull my uneasiness. I abandoned myself to the delights of laziness, listening to the unfamiliar sounds of the Romani language; I tried to convince myself, with all the suggestive power of which one is capable at that age, that I always had lived this way, and that the strangers around me really were my own people. I did not dare think of my parents again. I loved them and had no reason to rebel against their authority or to run away from them.

I was hungry and it must have been midday. I wondered how to re-establish my relationship with Nanosh and the other boys after the prolonged silence of the night and the interruption of our conversation. It seemed as if the differences between us grew out of proportion to the similarities. Pretending to be asleep, I secretly hoped that Nanosh or his parents would come to take away the *dunha* and force me to get up.

A shattering noise of wheels and pounding of horseshoes came from the direction of the highway. A procession of caravans neared the camp. The dogs ran to meet them, jumping and yelping. I could hear the shrill cries of the young girls and the roars of joy of the boys. There were ten or twelve wagons. As they rolled across the curb of the footpath, they would lean over to such an extent that I feared they might overturn. The horses were sweating. There were several plain peasant vans, covered with tarpaulins on a superstructure. There also were a few two-wheeled flat carts laden with a miscellaneous collection of chains, hatchets, washtubs, firewood, and clothes that were drying, having been hastily collected—still wet, possibly—because of a hasty departure. Young girls seemed to emerge from everywhere, and there was a festive air. They busied themselves with various household chores while the boys and young men led the horses to the nearest pastures—so far as I could guess, without seeking permission from the pastures' owners. Groups of women, in fours and fives, hastened toward the village dragging behind them small children who clung to their voluminous skirts. A few of the women carried their young babies, perhaps only a few months old, seated astride their strong hips. The men gathered at the nearest inn to celebrate.

I still had not moved. I remained camouflaged under my *dunha*, more and more perplexed. The arrival of the new group made me feel shyer still, but I also knew I did not want to go home. My embarrassment rose and fell like a wave, yet I deliberately severed the ties to my past.

After another long wait, Nanosh's mother came and carefully searched for me under the *dunha*. She smiled at me with such an understanding smile that I knew I could love her. Lala gently touched my shoulder, and like a kitten that only waits to be patted to stretch itself out, I pretended to be just awakening. Lala invited me to the fire near her wagon. She brought a huge, red enameled coffeepot, raked the fire and warmed the coffee that had been kept for me. She set an enormous black iron caldron before me, at the bottom of which were left some fried onions, tomatoes, red peppers and meat. Mala, a girl a little younger than I was, pulled me by the sleeve and gave me to understand that among the Gypsies one washed before sitting down to breakfast, adding, "Aren't you ashamed of being dirty?" Mala took me aside and poured water over my hands from a pitcher. I ate greedily, and once my hunger was stilled and I was reassured by the affectionate reception of both Nanosh's mother and little Mala, all traces of a thought about home or school vanished again. The only tinge of unhappiness left was the introspective knowledge of my possessing blue eyes, fair hair and a light skin, which distinctly set me apart as a Gajo.

Toward late afternoon the children watched the highway, expecting the return of their mothers and big sisters, who would come back from the hunt with their pockets full of treasures. This was the first time I saw Gypsy women return- ing to the camp. They looked only slightly less supple, a little less light-footed than when they left. They walked rapidly with swinging arms, unencumbered by bulky parcels or bags. They carried their spoils in huge pockets or in their aprons, which were folded back and tucked into their waistbands, to hide their spoils from the untrained eyes of the Gaje. The children ran out to meet them, prancing and uttering cries of joy. The festive commotion reminded me of a Flemish country fair painted by Breughel. The dogs freely joined in the mêlée. The fires were fanned and soon the flames were shooting up, licking the heavy iron caldrons on their primitive tripods. Twilight was falling, and it slowly blotted out the outlines of the wagons. The camp appeared much vaster and the scattered braziers gave it an uncanny light. At the bottom of the black caldrons the fat sizzled and the smell of garlic impregnated the air. In the shadow of a van covered by a light tarpaulin a few silent women were plucking chickens. The famished children were playfully begging around the campfires. Women doled out boiling-hot, half-cooked food on upturned lids of cooking pots. Nanosh called me and I was happy to join the crowd of children. Near the fires the women seated themselves comfortably with their legs crossed or with knees drawn up. They were waiting and had enticed their children to sit near them, lovingly searching their scalps for lice, by way of caress. Loud voices and modulated songs announced the return of the men. They arrived in small groups, and the young boys hastened to surrender their places near the fires to their elders. To judge from the animated way in which they talked, the Rom brought back exciting news. They had spent the day in the nearby villages, trading horses or possibly just drinking at the inn. They mimicked the local peasants to the visible pleasure of their audience.

At a sign from Nanosh's father, who was called Bidshika, his wife and their young daughter brought food in large red and blue enameled dishes, the kind used by the local population as wash basins. There were large quantities of bread, sharp peppers and young cucumbers preserved in vinegar.

Bidshika very formally invited his older brother, Luluvo, and the leading members of the camp to supper; among them were the fathers of both Putzina and Laetshi. Some men reclined leaning on one elbow. Bidshika handed out the forks, of which he seemed to possess only a limited number, and the men began to eat. From the other fires women would send large dishes of many different kinds of food, to be eaten in common by all assembled men. The women and children remained around their own fires. After a pause the younger and less important men were invited too. They ate with their fingers and shared the available knives. Beer and wine flowed profusely. After the meal Turkish coffee was served. Young Mala held a narrow, high brass container with a long protruding handle they called a *jezbeh* over the flames of the fire. As the water boiled she added sugar, and after letting it boil a little longer, she put in high-heaped spoonfuls of powder-fine coffee. She let this mixture boil up three or four times in rapid succession, taking away the container from the flames just before its contents would spill over. It was a powerful brew, worthy of the Rom. After eating our fill, Nanosh, Laetshi and Putzina dragged me away unceremoniously and together we visited many family groups gathered around their campfires. I sensed that the boys showed me off at each stopping place. There were prolonged conversations in Romani, obviously about me. Often there was a certain amount of uproarious laughter, which made me feel uneasy and shy. The same question was often repeated, at times in German, at others in broken French: Did I really like the Gypsies and their way of life? My affirmative answer filled them with mirth. Putzina eventually explained that the Rom found it hard to believe that any Gajo would willingly exchange his way of life for theirs. For my edification, he further added that the Rom would be just as unwilling to exchange their ways for those of the Gajo.

It occurred to me that at nighttime the Gypsy dogs were much fiercer than by day. They growled furiously at every distant passerby. They even attacked Gypsies returning to the camp after dark. Unafraid, the Rom would stoop down, pick up any stone or other loose object available and throw it at them. Its effect was that of a magic password. Putzina made this violent gesture just as successfully empty-handed. Shyly I practiced this newly discovered system, to his approving amusement.

Approaching the next fire on our round, I recognized old Lyuba with a shock. She had been the only one so far to demonstrate an open hostility toward me. She was staring into the distance, far beyond the leaping flames, smoking a short-stemmed brass pipe. As if she had sensed my presence, she slowly turned her head in my direction. Not a line in her strange, expressionless face changed. There was a slight pause, which momentarily reassured me, before she again started yelling at me to go home—not to bother them. Then switching to Romani, she grew more violent still. Nanosh looked indecisive and crouched down at my feet, leaving me alone and more exposed. Lyuba shouted at him, shaking both her old fists. The faces around the fire, which so far had retained their amused smiles and were full of mischief, became tense, but not unfriendly. There seemed to be no end to Lyuba's vehement outpouring. I did not dare to move away. Besides, I was conscious of the vicious dogs roaming the site. As soon as Lyuba's voice lost its intensity and slightly dropped its pitch, Putzina, who was standing behind me, pulled me backward out of the blazing light of the campfire into the greater safety of the half-dark. Nanosh remained seated. Slowly Putzina walked me back toward the meadows where the horses grazed. We lay down in the grass and were silent for a long while. Laetshi and two other boys joined us. All around us the horses were grazing peacefully; the sounds from the camp appeared distant; overhead the sky was luminus with stars and looked very far away. The boys talked in their language, in subdued voices. With an air of conspiracy they informed me that this night I would sleep with Putzina. *Phuri* (old) Lyuba, who was Nanosh's grandmother, had forbidden him to have any further dealings with the little Gajo boy, under the threat of violent curses.

When the fires in the distance burned lower, we went back toward the wagon of Putzina's parents. We walked in a wide circle, avoiding the main section of the encampment. Many fires had been left to burn themselves out. Laetshi and the two other boys parted from us as we neared the wagon. They wished Putzina and me good-night in Romani, forgetting for a moment that I was not one of theirs and that I did not speak their language. I repeated after Putzina the sounds I heard him make. In the moonlight the wagon cast a large shadow, where several *dunhas* were spread out. Putzina's mother, who was called Rupa, was waiting for him, crouched by the glowing embers. She gave both of us a drink of cold water before going to bed. We drank directly from the ladle which she dipped in a white enameled bucket. She warned me not to drink from any other container but this one. The water in the other receptacles was "dirty." One was used only for washing. Another was "for the women," she emphasized; still another was strictly reserved for the horses. These were *marhime* or unclean. I did not understand what she meant but let it pass.

The camp was hushed. Putzina motioned to me to follow

him. He slipped in between the two eiderdowns, and with a few practiced movements he undressed. Silently I tried to imitate him, only to get tangled up in the feather bed for a short desperate moment. Then we lay on our backs looking into the sky. Unlike Nanosh, whose bed was inhabited by numberless small children, Putzina shared his only with me. It was more comfortable even though I missed the particular excitement and mood of my first night among the Gypsies. I was exhausted and suddenly became apprehensive again about my insane adventure. My last thought before falling into a deep dreamless sleep was that even in bed Putzina was wearing his navy-blue riverboat captain's cap.

I woke up the next morning, my second one among the Gypsies, to find the whole camp in an uproar. Loud voices were shouting explosively, to be answered by others in anger. The police had come to chase the Gypsies away, as, I was later to learn, happens so often in the life of the Rom.

We dressed hastily deep under our eiderdown, while Rupa and several young girls, Putzina's sisters, gathered the voluminous bedding and piled it inside the wagon. The heavy iron tripod, which had been placed astride the wood fire to support the cooking caldron, was lifted, still red-hot, with a sturdy piece of wood and was suspended from a hook underneath the wagon. The men rounded up the horses from the meadows to harness them and hitch them up, one on either side of the long wagon shaft. Nanosh, his hair uncombed, ran to inquire about me and to help Putzina hide me in a stack of feather beds. Children screamed and dogs howled. There was a sudden jerk followed by the violent pitching of the wagon: The caravan was on the move again. We passed other wagons waiting to get in the single line. As we reached the paved road, police officers would indicate which direction each driver was to take. They were breaking up the large concentration of wagons. Under the sneering supervision of the officers, the Gypsies were compelled to travel in the directions of the four winds, with total disregard for their family allegiances. The police used obscene language. It struck me that the Rom departed without taking leave of one another. In time I found out that after a few days they would change their courses, stray for a while, and then one day they all would converge and meet again, in numbers too large for the local police force to cope with. They were like the quicksilver that constantly merges and divides.

The cover of the eiderdown under which I was ensconced was of crimson silk, with a large design of stylized marigolds outlined in black. I spent hours in formless daydreaming, rhythmically rocked by the swaying of the wagon and lulled by the hypnotic sound of the horses' hoofs on the paved road. I had lost all sense of time and place. I was numbed to reality and let myself be carried off farther and farther from my parents' home. I stayed six months with the Rom, during which time I failed to communicate with my parents. Several times older members of the group tried to chase me away, but boys my own age found ways to hide and feed me until the danger was over.

During the day the family rode in the wagon. Passing through a village or hamlet, some of them jumped out to go on errands, to catch up with us again and climb back in the *vurdon* (wagon) without ever slowing down or stopping. Firewood was gleaned on the way, as was fresh clover and some other necessities. At all times an adult or child would watch the road behind, through the rear window.

The three girls, Putzina's sisters, were silent, quick and watchful. The older one was called Keja. She was a sturdy and energetic girl with an open face, bold eyes and a smooth golden skin. She had a long, strong neck and high, full breasts showing through her low-cut yellow-and-white blouse. She wore small rings in her earlobes, unlike the other Gypsy women, who wore heavy pendants made of gold pieces. She must have been only a few years older than I, but she was already a full-grown woman, with authority and great dignity. The youngest one, Mala, was still almost a child, but earnest and collected. She was pleasantly plump and gentle. Tshaya, the middle one, was my own age. She was darker than her sisters and dressed in somber colors. She was strong-willed and unruly. I was to develop a happy relationship with Keja, but the one with Tshaya was to remain awkward and trying.

Toward late afternoon the wagon stopped in a deserted spot

and Putzina came to drag me from my hiding place. There was only one other wagon besides our own. It belonged to Yojo, Putzina's older brother. He was married and had a large number of small children. He was tall and good-humored. For hours we sat by the smoky fire. The conversation was in Romani and little attention was paid to my presence, though I was not treated unkindly. Food was served in generous portions. Putzina and I shared with Kore, another brother, about two years older than I. We ate with our fingers, lying down, from a deep-blue enameled bowl. Having spent the two previous days and nights in a large camp, I found this family life lacked somewhat in excitement, yet it was bringing me much closer to the Rom. Shortly after our arrival, Putzina's father, Pulika, had gone to the nearest inn with big Yojo. I awaited his return with some apprehension, as I feared he would not encourage my staying with them. Rupa, Putzina and the rest of the family certainly did not seem to object to my presence. I dreaded Pulika's breaking off the present enchantment and the inexplicable budding sense of belonging. I was fully conscious of the distance, both in miles and in time, which separated me from my immediate past and made my turning back impossible, nor did I underestimate the problems of my still being barefoot and my clothes being rumpled and not very clean. This was the third day with the Rom.

Upon his return Pulika teased me about my fears, but his eyes were smiling and he let me stay. He gave me a pat on the back of the neck with his open hand. He did not ask any questions, nor did he feel the urge to lecture to me. The only thing he asked of me was that I remain out of sight whenever police would visit the camp. He said that the police officers often searched the wagons; I should therefore move outside the camp and turn around to face it, in this way clearly indicating that I did not belong to it.

Pulika was a rugged, aristocratic-looking, imposing man with a strong face, challenging eyes, and a very impressive drooping mustache. He wore massive gold rings on his small powerful hands. Dark-brown riding boots showed under his wide gray corduroy trousers. Across his chest, from one waist-coat pocket to the other, hung a heavy watch chain from which gold pieces dangled. The silk kerchief around his neck was purple, and had a fading Kashmir motif. In time I was to learn that under his exterior of virile authority he was kind, generous and wise; and that he had a subtle sense of humor.

I wondered where Nanosh and his parents were at this moment. I worried about Laetshi and all the others. I was indignant and angry at the way the gendarmes had behaved toward the Gypsies, and at their abusive and obscene language toward those who I felt at that time were the victims of official persecution. At the same time, questions formed in my mind about the source of the freshly cut clover, and of the generous quantities of firewood that kept the fires burning for days on end.

Our group consisted of Pulika and his wife Rupa; Kore, who was a few years older than Putzina and still a bachelor; Putzina; the three girls; and two young children: Boti, a dark wild-looking little girl of about seven, with unkempt and still-unbraided hair, who wore unbelievable rags, and a small boy, Tina. In the other wagon there were big Yojo and his wife and four small children, the oldest barely five. This little girl was dressed in ankle-length skirts and bravely tackled household and baby-watching chores well beyond her age. There were fifteen people in our group, not counting myself.

For a while Putzina's family traveled leisurely without meeting any of the other Gypsies. For me the relaxed pace and the mood in general were those of the happiest summer vacation ever spent. The initial excitement about my strange adventure was wearing off. Slowly I was becoming more accustomed to the smells, sounds and colors around me. I was also losing all sense of time. The days started at breakfast, for which there was no fixed hour, and ended after a late evening meal, at an hour equally unpredictable. The day had no more specific divisions. It was either before or after breakfast, before or after the evening meal.

Since no Sundays, or for that matter any other special days of rest, seemed to be observed, days and weeks simply flowed into one another without punctuation. None of the children around me differentiated between the successive months of the year, nor did they care what month it was. It was either summer or winter to them. Summer was obviously much longer than winter. The distinction between these two seasons was that during one the Rom traveled widely while during the other they were immobilized by climatic conditions. Unaware of the historical years recording the Christian era, they designated the passing of time only by referring to "the summer Pipish died," "the winter we almost perished of cold and hunger and were attacked by wolves," or "the year Zurka was born and we sold the three stallions."

To each overnight camping site police officers came in the morning to inspect the Gypsies' identity papers and remind them not to overstay the twenty-four hours during which they were tolerated, reluctantly, to camp within the village boundaries. A stern warning for them to stay away from the barnyards was traditionally included.

The countryside was beautiful, and the constant, if forced, moving ahead appealed to my imagination. Only a small part of the time was spent at such camp chores as watering and caring for the horses, or cutting firewood. Putzina, Kore and I roamed through the woods together, fished in the streams, bathed and rode horses bareback. There existed an implicit division between our occupations and games and those of the young girls of the family. For the most part it was they who looked after the smaller children. I noticed with curiosity that they had no toys or formal games of any sort. The girls helped in the washing, cooking and tidying up, such as it was. Instead of brooms Keja and Mala used short bundles of twigs which they threw away after one sweeping, only to gather fresh bundles the next time they deemed cleaning up was necessary. They had to bend far forward, and worked with rapid, short strokes.

Sitting on their haunches, they scrubbed the plates and cups with a pinch of earth, and then rinsed them afterward. The heavy cast-iron caldron they only wiped clean with pieces of bread. I do not remember ever seeing any of them wash it.

The few notions of conventional propriety and basic hygiene I had at that age were put to a severe test. At every meal Keja and Rupa forced overwhelming quantities of rich food on me until one day I discovered that because I never belched loudly and proudly, to indicate my state of satiety as did the other Gypsies, both of them feared I was constantly hungry. The Rom belched and said ritually, *Tshailo sim* (I am replete). Promptly I decided to learn to be more polite, in Gypsy society.

The children ate with their fingers, and after the meal they wiped their greasy hands on their own hair, "to give it added shine," or on the aprons of mother or little sister if they happened to be near at hand. However, the Rom were fastidious about certain other matters.

One evening, early in my first stay with them, while I was perhaps somewhat thoughtlessly standing against a tree urinating in the typical, if permissive, French manner, I was cursed out with unexpected vehemence by some women passing by at a goodly distance. Putzina and Nanosh scolded me solidly for my lack of manners and respect. I learned then how strictly the separation between the sexes was to be observed in everything, and at all times. From that day on I never left a mixed group alone, as this could give an indication, however slight, of the private nature of my errand. I would ask several other boys to join me in "going to look at the horses," or else I would eagerly follow any group leaving the camp for any alleged occupation that would provide me with an excuse. The boys of my age questioned me about the Gaje's habits and were shocked to learn that in our houses we had a special room reserved solely for this purpose and with *ad hoc* installations. "But," they objected, "how can you possibly be respectful and polite and still go to this one obvious place when everybody present knows the purpose of your going there?"

Nanosh wanted to find out about some of the other strange practices of the Gaje. He had heard it said that they filled large containers with boiling water in which they sat down to soak. In this "extract" they later washed their faces and hands. The Rom only used running water and certainly would never wash the lower parts of the body and the face and hands in the same stagnant, dirty water. The idea of using a handkerchief appalled them: "Why on this sweet earth would the foolish Gaje want to preserve the dirt of the noses?" But then, as everybody knew, Gaje were strange and totally unpredictable. . . .

Every day, usually around noon, the Gypsies moved their wagon camp before being actually chased away. For a very long time I was unaware of the actual hardship this entailed for them. I fully lived this fabulous boyhood dream and avoided marring it even by asking myself certain simple questions. I could not help noticing the hostile faces of the farmers we met daily on the road, or their distrustful and hate-laden eyes.

The growing wheat was swaying peacefully and promised a rich harvest. Nature was appeasing and bountiful, in startling contrast to the nasty peasant women hurrying to take down the clothes drying on the clotheslines wherever we traveled. I resented their ostentatiously chasing chickens and geese off the dirt tracks and into the barnyards, scolding and cursing. Anger welled up in me at these constant insults.

None of the Gypsies seemed to notice it. Instead of sulking they were defiant and their eyes sparkled.

The Gypsy women told fortunes by the roadside and sold charms. They created an aura of fearful superstition around their race, convincingly pretending to possess mysterious powers. At times the men acted overly fierce and spoke violently. Both the Gypsy men and the women were conscious of the image they projected, and among themselves they joked about the fear they inspired in the Gaje.

As time went by we caught up again with the other small traveling units of Gypsies. We were joined by Bidshika and Luluvo and their brother Kalia. At various times small family groups of three or four wagons would simply leave us at a fork in the road to go their own way, to meet us again a few days later in what seemed to me an unpredictable pattern.

At nightfall, one hot summer day, an unusual commotion attracted my attention. The police were coming to the camp, followed by a noisy crowd of local peasants. I retreated to the nearby underbrush and waited. As they aproached the wagons, they kicked aside the barking dogs and spread out through the entire site. The peasants carried flails and pitchforks. A few had shotguns. The haughty police constables encouraged the vindictive mob. Frightened little Gypsy children shrieked fiercely. The Gypsy men huddled near their horses with weary, self-imposed patience. The older women were prepared for violence. From where I was I could see Rupa standing with one fist on her side, the other holding the handle of the boiling caldron. She looked determined to empty it on anyone who approached her. Old women, crouched by the fires, muttered maledictions in Romani, gesturing wildly in the direction of the self-appointed vigilantes. Under the scornful supervision of the police constables the villagers ripped away feather beds under which children were sleeping, poked through piles of women's clothes and heaps of horse harnesses, turning over cooking pots and buckets of drinking water.

Young girls screamed and bit as they were searched with lecherous brutality. The implacable search continued as night fell. There were isolated scuffles at the far end of the camp. I heard the din but could no longer clearly see what was going on. The fires were burning low: they had been neglected or had been snuffed out by the Gypsies themselves by pouring kettles of food over them.

Flashlights cut into the darkness. The confusion became general and the cursing of the peasants grew louder, indicating their mounting frustration.

The dogs stayed out of range of the invaders, baying furiously, ready for renewed attack. The horses were becoming skittish from the noise. I remained squatting in the nearby underbrush, deeply troubled by what I considered cowardice on my part, at the same time painfully aware of my helplessness. The consciousness of absolute impotence, under the present circumstances, was the most painful sensation I had ever experienced. I vaguely sensed, but could not understand, that this same powerlessness applied to the Gypsy men. Any aggressive action on their part would certainly have brought disaster.

I came out of hiding, or perhaps unconsciously I felt protected by the darkness. I circled the camp and remained standing near the dirt track which led to the nearby village. Unthinking, I wanted to see the mob on their way home at close range. The gendarmes had arrested a Gypsy woman and were taking her away handcuffed. I knew her by sight but did not remember her name. Her eyes were glassy and she was very quiet. The peasants, having spent their anger, were in a jubilant mood and talked excitedly about their exploits. The police officers needlessly pushed the arrested woman around like a sack of wheat. I followed them for a short distance, unable to tear myself away from this ugly scene. As I fell behind, they were lost in the night. From the camp far behind me now arose the sounds of wailing. I was shattered by the unexpectedness of the events of the last hour, overwhelmed by a sense of outrage. For the first time in my life I cried out into the empty night the angry expressions I had heard my companions utter against the Gaje: expressions explicitly criticizing the potency of their men and the virtue of their women, and which—beyond being able to repeat them—I only partly understood. In my unstilled anguish I groped for still more passionate maledictions I had heard the Rom use.

The night air and the passing hours soothed my bitter resentment. Anger gave way to perplexed sullenness.

That night the fires burned low. The Rom huddled around them were moody and subdued but they also seemed to resign themselves to the inevitability of what had occurred. The small children of the woman who had been taken away were sobbing inside their dark wagon. Her husband was talking with Pulika and Tshukurka about steps to take come morning. The local police could not keep her locked up here in the village but would have to transfer her to the jail in the district capital to await trial. He must go there at once with his children, wagon and horses. Pulika promised to call a lawyer he knew in the big city, who was willing to handle "Gypsy affairs." He would guide them through what they could only construe as the elaborate legal fictions of the Gajo universe. They talked until dawn.

I went to sleep fully dressed, ready for any emergency. I was obsessed with the savagery and inhumanity of the Gaje— of whom, by birth and background, I was one—but also with an unexplained eroding bitterness toward the victims for their apparent failure to protect themselves adequately and hit back at those who hurt them. I was not yet thirteen years old.

It was two or three days later that Kore told me that Pesha,

Shandor's wife, who had been arrested "for stealing chickens," had been taken to the city prison and that his father's (Pulika's) lawyer would handle the case. She might be with us again before the first snow fell. Kore wanted to reassure me. He wanted to make me stop sulking pointlessly: "It was not your mother who was caught, was it?"

Upset as I was by my first violent experience with the other side of the law, I had, naïvely, not given a thought to the cause of Pesha's arrest. I had simply seen a senseless injustice done to the people I loved. It had never dawned on me that they, my friends, really stole chickens. Being their guest, I had never questioned the source of their lavish hospitality. In assuming that their defenselessness alone was what had tempted their tormentors, I had made my renewed allegiance to them uncomplicated and direct. The pitiful discovery of their thieving, by Kore's untroubled admission, showed me the fallacy of this uncritical loyalty and shattered my illusions. I was bitter and amazed. When I asked Kore if anybody in our family "caught" chickens in "this way," he said unhesitatingly that Pulika would not have it because he did not like chicken meat and therefore felt the consequences were not worth it. He added boastfully, "Keja is very good at it, almost as good as Liza le Tshurkinaski."

Putzina explained to me that stealing from the Gaje was not really a misdeed as long as it was limited to the taking of basic necessities, and not in larger quantities than were needed at that moment. It was the intrusion of a sense of greed, in itself, that made stealing wrong, for it made men slaves to unnecessary appetites or to their desire for possessions.

Gleaning a little dry wood for the fire, from the forest, was no misdeed. There was so much of it, and anyway if they did not take it, it was left to rot. Putting a few horses to pasture overnight in someone's meadow was not that bad. Grass grew without the owner's active contribution or effort.

Because I was a Gajo the Rom would not allow me under any circumstances to take what was not mine. This too was the law.

CHAPTER TWO

Pulika's band traveled every day on and on toward boundless, ever-changing horizons. The environment and the circumstances of our vagrant life were never the same two days in succession. The monotony of constant moving contrasted sharply with the total lack of routine and the sort of security we somehow derived from it. I faced each new day with expectation and apprehension, identifying ever more deeply with the Rom. On a few occasions I was distressed when we left a particularly pleasant or convenient camping spot. These regrets were due to the conservative streak of a nature basically more sedentary than that of the Rom. Rupa chided me for this, in her gruff way; she said I would, by losing it, cherish the memory of this place even more, with the tenderness reserved for incompletely satisfied longings. She said in time I too would learn to possess the single passing moment more passionately, more fully, without regrets. She tried to tell me that the Rom lived in a perpetual present: memories, dreams, desires, hungers, the urge toward a tomorrow, all were rooted in the present. Without *now* there was no *before*, just as there could be no *after*.

She said that "to the Lowara a candle is not made of wax, but is all flame." In the stories they told, the Rom praised extravagant lavishness and most of them practiced this all-consuming generosity, at times to the extreme of outright squandering. In their language thriftiness, or any other word denoting carefulness, was translated as stinginess. They strongly disapproved of saving, with the result that between red-letter days, worthy of legend, there were hollow ones, more frequent than bargained for.

When I was hungry, cold or tired, I had a tendency to

become silent and withdrawn. And I was often hungry because there were only two meals a day; and between the elaborate breakfast and the very plentiful and heavy late dinner there were many long hours of active, open-air life. Secretly Keja saved lumps of bread for me, which she dipped in chicken fat for me to devour, sprinkled with pepper or salt. Tacitly we both kept this a secret from the other members of the family in order to save my pride. I was in awe of the Gypsies' physical endurance, their resistance to fatigue, cold and hunger. I envied them their resourcefulness and their adaptability, which I proudly tried to emulate.

Life with Pulika's band was a forever-recurring series of encounters with their kinfolk at innumerable crossroads. We, the young people, often ran alongside the wagons to spare the horses. For a short rest we would hitch a ride in one of the long row of wagons; then we would resume hours of running along the hot country roads, our bare feet half buried in the dust. My feet were tender, and in the beginning they blistered badly, but I limped on, I hoped not too noticeably, insisting on doing as the others did. By now my face was burned a vivid red by wind and sun. My hair had grown long and by contrast appeared fairer than its actual color, emphasizing even more the distinction between me and my hosts. Wound around my throat was the *diklo,* kerchief, Rupa had given me. It was a piece of yellow material with white flowers, which had been torn from a blouse and left unhemmed.

For weeks at a time we boys and also the men lived exclusively in the open, unlike the women and the older girls who occasionally retired to privacy of a kind inside one of the wagons. Especially in the beginning of my life with the Gypsies I would suddenly feel an overpowering need for physical shelter, for enclosed space, for actual shade and for privacy in the Western sense, to be able to close a door, yes, even to turn the key and lock the door. With her uncanny sensitiveness and her unobtrusive affection Keja would then intone a monologue seemingly coming from a clear blue sky. Her voice had a honeyed quality, if slightly husky, and she spoke with a hypnotic intensity. She said privacy in the first place was a state of mind; perhaps the clever Gaje erected walls to create secluded privacy. In the walls there were doors and in the doors keyholes, the better to pry. To the Rom privacy was first of all a courtesy extended and a restraint from the desire to pry or interfere in other people's lives. However, privacy must not be the result of indifference to others, but rather a mark of respect for them and of real compassion.

Most of the time the Gypsies lived together in fairly restricted quarters. In summer and in fair weather they all slept in the open, but even then their sleeping steads were at the most ten to fifteen feet apart without partitions of any kind between them. Privacy therefore was a concept that worked two ways: not only to avoid prying in the affairs of others, but also to keep from giving offense to others nearby who could not possibly avoid seeing what you were doing. In this same spirit of tactfulness and restraint one did not address another person in the morning before he or she had washed and was prepared for social intercourse. The same delicacy of feeling and extreme sensitiveness existed in relation to the functions of nature; neither were there jokes about the subject. Relating these observations about the Gypsies, I hardly want to imply that they were Victorian in any sense; but the fact that they constantly lived at close quarters with an ever-changing assortment of strangers, even if these were Gypsies too, made it mandatory that certain specific restrictions be observed. I often wondered at their delicacy of feeling and respect for others. These various restrictions, broadly speaking, applied only from puberty onward; by contrast there was more than a certain laxity about the behavior of small children, though little boys certainly had far greater leeway than little girls at any age. In the presence of Gypsy adults, respect and a minimum of decorum were demanded, whereas in the presence and at the expense of the Gaje almost anything was allowed. Not infrequently the Gaje were the horrified targets of exhibitionistic performances by the small children. These games were frankly intended to be insulting, and as such were slyly encouraged by some Gypsy adults. No such untoward familiarity would ever be tolerated by the Gypsies themselves.

When I sat by a campfire, the wind would change direction and the acrid wood smoke stung my eyes, filling them with tears. Putzina never understood why I disliked smoke so much and wondered at my tender Gajo nature. It was with some difficulty that I became accustomed to the ever-present ammoniated reek of horse urine and the pungency of horse sweat.

The first time I saw Pulika bleed one of his horses or force a massive dose of purgative down its throat, my gentle city upbringing left me unappreciative and even squeamish about these skills. Pulika took hold of a fold of skin of the horse's neck, holding it firmly between his left thumb and forefinger, while with the other hand he pierced it with a large crooked needle used for sewing burlap bags. Kore held the horse's head. A shiver rippled its shiny skin over the protruding ribs and its hind legs danced nervously. Pulika punched a quick incision where the needle protruded on both sides. Dark blood spurted violently, staining the earth. The horse quieted down, baring its teeth as the blood flowed with rhythmical jets. After a while Pulika tightly wound a piece of twine around the slightly raised piece of skin through which the needle was sticking and which prevented the string from slipping off until the blood stopped flowing and the cut was closed. Pulika's hands were black and glistening.

Many of my memories of that early period among the Rom were visual or tactile, as at that time I was still not in full command of their language. At night around the fires I sat mute, observing, absorbing the uncomprehended words and sounds. During the day spent among the young boys my own age, I could ask for translations of sentences or words I repeatedly heard and could remember. I was at least at liberty to ask for explanations, if not always certain of receiving a correct answer. From nightfall on we sat together by the fireside with all the other Rom, and by tacit agreement no questions could be asked. The adults merely tolerated me at best and I had learned to be as quiet as possible and make them forget my intrusive presence.

The Rom talked animatedly through whole nights. They never seemed to be short of subjects of conversation. When certain family groups met, they often celebrated their happy reunion with profuse and joyous drinking, which in turn led to nostalgic songfests. The more important heads of families would then sing wild sad songs to each other in Romani, their eyes closed in deep emotion, while their listeners silently nodded their heads with approval, lost in contemplation.

When I asked Putzina what the Rom were singing about, he would grope for adequate words or he would say, "They sing about us."

Occasionally young girls were asked to dance to "honor" an important guest. Everybody joined in the boisterous singing, clapping their hands, until the pale predawn light scattered them. In the distance the cattle were lowing mournfully. The feather beds were spread out in the open, throughout the camp, around the individual wagons. Before retiring for what was left of the night a group of us would for a last time "go and look at the horses."

Waking up after a night's deep sleep, I stared into the infinite, vacant sky. I could not focus properly and failed for an instant to make the association with height or depth, so that I was overtaken by a violent sensation of vertigo. I grabbed at the weeds growing beside my sleeping place, to hold myself back and avoid dizzily falling into the shimmering blue sky above me. I closed my eyes violently, trying to subdue this flash of senseless obscure agony and quietly absorb the affirmative touch of the earth. Several times, as a child among the Rom, I had had the overwhelming sensation of awe that comes from exposure to too much sky, and I had wondered about my companions, who felt no need to be protected by enclosing walls, always exposed to voiceless fears and sudden violence.

To tease me, Tshaya, Putzina's older sister, would repeat

the Romani saying that "both the Gajo and the fish smell badly after three days," reminding me that I did not belong, despite what I sensed in myself as a strange pre-existing readiness to share their way of life. They called me *Raklo,* which simply described my actual status as a non-Gypsy boy, as opposed to the term *Shav,* which designated any still-unmarried Gypsy youth. This term was used from early puberty up to the day one took a wife, when one became a *Romoro,* a little man.

I dreaded the long rainy days when the whole family would have to share the limited space inside the wagon. Our clothes were damp and the temperature inside grew unbearable, the air painful to breathe. The potbellied stove snored viciously, turning red-hot, and, depending on the direction of the wind it could be nearly impossible to control. Rupa took off the lid and the wagon was lit only by the flames of the fire while coal fumes would thicken the atmosphere. The campsite became ankle-deep in mud. Kore and Putzina put branches, stones or ashes under the wheels to prevent them from sinking too deeply into the mud. We covered the horses with army blankets and pieces of tarpaulin. The dogs took refuge under the wagons and whimpered. Everybody laughed and joked and reacted to the drenching rain as only playful children possibly could. At night I fell asleep listening to the rain drumming loudly on the thin wooden shell of the wagon as violent wind gusts rocked it on its high wheels. These rainy days, which to me at times seemed without end, made me fearful of the winter months to come, though I loved the smell of rain. Only under those circumstances could I be grateful for the old pair of hunting boots, which I haughtily ignored when the weather was fair. One day I was told Keja had begged them from some Gajo; she had claimed she wanted to wear them herself. At the first rainy day that followed, however, she threw them at my feet, claiming they hurt her. She had never tried them on.

With abrupt suddenness Pulika told me one day we would pass within a few miles of my place of birth, where my parents lived, and the actual place from which I had run away to join the Gypsies months ago. My flight from home had been unpremeditated and unintended. My hiding in Pulika's wagon during the scattering by the police of the various members of the mobile group had been without forethought, and if it had not actually been the cause of my running away, it certainly had made it easier.

Pulika sent me away with a solid hug, saying in a low voice that surely we would meet again after the winter months. He gave me some small change to take the bus. I wanted to protest, to refuse to be sent away so arbitrarily, but I could not; all my pent-up apprehensions of the approaching winter almost made me grateful for so easy a solution, especially because I was so close to home.

I came back to the house of my parents after an absence of nearly six months, which seemed like a lifetime. I arrived there at dinnertime and as usual they had a number of guests, painters and writers. Nothing was said in front of them about my long absence, nor was my disheveled appearance explained. I was sent to bed early. I waited tensely for the scolding and punishment I knew I well deserved. After the guests left, I could no longer bear to wait, and after some understandable hesitation I went to my parents rather than wait for them to come to me. I found them already asleep—or perhaps they were just pretending; I never found out. Even today this subject is for some unknown reason kept in a mythical haze, by all concerned. In the morning, I confronted them with my prolonged absence and emphasized the fact that I had run away with the Gypsies, possibly to make it even more provocative. With rare psychological insight and wisdom they replied that although of course this had caused them sorrow, since they loved me, they nevertheless wanted to respect my personal choice and they trusted me to know my mind even at the age of twelve. I was shocked. It was so entirely unlike my anticipation of the event. My father added he had hoped I would become an artist like himself, but if I preferred to become a full-fledged member of a band of nomads, he wanted the choice to be entirely mine. I kissed my father and my mother and shed tears, long and bravely held back. During the following winter months I applied myself to my studies at school. My six months' interlude receded into an unbelievable past.

As far as I could remember I seemed to have been aware of the Gypsies, perhaps not distinctly but in a dreamlike way, typical of childhood. My father, who was a designer of stained glass as well as a painter, had grown up in the south of Spain, though born of Flemish stock. He spoke of Andalucía the way he would have about the Garden of Eden, and the Gypsies were always part of it. He called them Gitanos, and I grew up with their music, the *cante hondo*. Our house in Antwerp was a very happy and sunny place, and I remember my early childhood as one persistent illumination of happiness and fulfillment. In his huge-scale designs for church windows my father used vibrant reds, flaming sunlike oranges, intense ultramarine blues, royal purples, luminous golden yellows. My father had a way of making them sing in unison.

As a small child I grew up in my father's two-story skylight studio, drawing, painting and dreaming. After long hours of intense work my father would reward my silence with stories about Greek mythology, the Finnish Kalevala, the Ramayana, Mahabharata, the Bhagavad Gita or the Knights of the Holy Grail. They awoke in me a great longing for faraway places. His concept of life was Homeric. The day was always at dawn. All men were heroes and the sword decided for the just. He taught me to share his love of sun and freedom.

My mother was of German and Cuban descent. She was much involved in social reforms, and her focal points of interest at this time were Russia, India, which she visited, and China.

At home I spoke French to my mother, Spanish to my father, German to the exchange students who helped in the household, and since we lived in the northern part of Belgium, I learned Flemish and eventually went to a Flemish school. I spoke all four languages fluently, but with a slight foreign accent. I never had the feeling that a specific one of these might be my mother tongue; neither did I identify consciously with the culture any one of these languages reflected.

One day at lunchtime my father casually mentioned that a band of Gypsies was camping on the outskirts of town. What I secretly feared most was happening once again, and I was faced with a decision for which I felt I was unprepared. I was drawn to the Gypsies as by a magnet; at the same time, I was fully aware I ought to shake off the spell but was strangely unable to. My father solved this dilemma by telling me I should join the Gypsies if this was my desire, but he insisted on one condition: that if ever I was in trouble I would remember my parents and that I would come to them for help under any circumstances.

I joined the Gypsies again. The chief of this group was called Butsulo and he let me stay with them until we caught up with Pulika's band. They let me sleep in the hay in the manger-like arrangement at the rear of the wagon. I slept wrapped up in horse blankets. They fed me well and were good to me. In return I amused them with the bits of knowledge of Romani I had retained and was only too eager to show off. They told me they had heard about me and that Pulika certainly would be glad to see me. We traveled many weeks before catching up with him, and I was beginning to regret my adventure as I felt much less at home among the people of this particular band. I felt a great affection for Pulika, Rupa, Yojo, Kore, Putzina, Keja, Mala, Boti and Nanosh. Finally we met. The horses I remembered from last fall had been sold long ago. Many of the other things I thought I remembered were now different. I knew I could not expect to find unchanged what I had left behind; I too had changed. Several other families that I did not know had joined the group. For a short while I was the center of interest, but then, with a mixture of both regret and relief, I again became just one of the many young ones.

Within days my clothes were ragged and my general appearance closer to that of the other Gypsy urchins. To my regret nothing could be done about my blue eyes and my fair hair. Using a typical Lowari phrase, Pulika told me not "to try to jump over your own shadow" (*te na khutshos perdal tsho ushalin*). I felt sunburned, healthy and often hungry. The smoke of the wood fire once again stung my eyes and filled them with tears.

Then, after following the horse-drawn wagons for a long period, I would quite suddenly one day feel the impelling eagerness to go back to the world of the Gaje. This would come over me like a spell, and I left the Rom as impulsively and as unpredictably as I had come to stay with them in the first place.

For endless months I had been spellbound, intensely happy, living in the world of the Gypsies, so utterly different from the one I now yearned to return to. It seemed inconceivable to me that I could have turned my back to it and for so long stayed away from it. It was like waking up from a strange, wondrous dream, and I had the urge to share it, to talk about it. The wagons were rolling on over the hills in one long row. As far ahead and as far back as I could see there were Gypsy wagons moving peacefully with the reassuring sound of horses' hoofs. I felt detached from it all and I wondered, without understanding, what could have fired my willingness to share this strange, vagrant, primitive life. My feet were bare, my clothes colorful and in absolute rags, my hair unkempt and long; I felt healthy, sunburned, hungry; I knew I wanted to be alone to think, to think and . . . to run away, this time, for a change, from the Gypsies.

Pulika, Rupa, Bidshika, Yojo, Kore and Pulika's brother Tshukurka, all were the same as ever. I was changing. Everything about me had suddenly assumed an unfamiliar look and appeared senseless. I knew this was not the effect of a sunstroke or of swamp fever. I could not understand how I had been willing to live all those months without the accepted forms of comfort and ease I had been brought up to consider normal, desirable, even indispensable. I did not understand how I could have trekked wildly across many countries, as part of a band of human beings who were unwanted, misunderstood, without apparent goal outside of plain survival and self-perpetuation, and were devoid of the feeling of security that grows out of routine, the accumulation of material possessions and the delusion of being part of a majority.

For months I had slept under the open sky; I had eaten irregularly: meager fare and overabundant feasts. I had been scorched by the sun, drenched by rain, but at the same time deeply grateful for being alive. I had been part of the dream of all normal, healthy boys my age in an established society: to run away and participate in the hard adventurous life that had supposedly been lived by pioneers and early settlers. But there was no end to this trail: no greener pastures, no peace or work to hope for, on the other side of the horizon. These people were doomed to live a strange fate as eternal wanderers.

I left the traveling caravans. I said farewell to Rupa and I wondered at the understanding she and Pulika showed me. They asked no questions; they only said I was the *vadni ratsa,* the wild goose of Romany legend. They said they had known I would have to leave. They also said they knew I would come back.

I stood by the wayside and watched the wagons pass one after the other, until the last one faded away in the distance and the familiar sounds died away. Once again the countryside was hushed, without the noise of rattling wheels, neighing horses, yapping dogs, crying babies and singing boys. A great silence filled the air.

I remained while they traveled onward. Taking a shortcut through the fields, I walked to the nearby village. Approaching the non-Gypsy world again, I decided to put on the shoes I carried hanging by the shoelaces and slung over my shoulder. I took off the faded purple kerchief, which was knotted around my throat, Gypsy fashion, and stuffed it into my pocket. I brushed back and smoothed my hair, and washed my face, neck and hands at a running brook.

I could feel the expression on my face change as if my sun- and wind-burned skin was stretching in places, shrinking in others, in an accelerated process of aging. The red-roofed houses once again became pleasant homes in my eyes, instead of the dreary prisons the Rom had momentarily made me believe them to be. What might have made them prisons was only the spirit of those living inside. Nearby the cattle were lowing and bleating. I expected life among the Gaje to seem stale by comparison, but I was deliberately turning my back on the magnetism of the Rom. I started thinking about the reception my parents would give me and about going back to school, college, an eventual profession and the future. I no longer would express myself in the wild, archaic "Romanes," unfit for small talk. I would no longer use the forceful, poetic, plastic descriptions and ingenious parables of the Rom or indulge in the unrestrained intensity and fecundity of their language. Old Bidshika once told us the legend about the full moon's being dragged down to earth by the sheer intensity, weight and witchery of the Romany tongue. And it almost seemed that it could be true.

My homecoming was always made to be a joyous one. The house in Antwerp, with the large skylight studio, was sunny, comfortable, happy, permeated with the familiar smells of beeswax and freshly baked bread and cakes. There were books everywhere, paintings, Oriental rugs and classical music.

I made a feast of the rediscovered luxury of a hot bath, clean clothes and a thorough haircut. In counterpoint to this I would at the most unexpected moments wonder how young Kore or Nanosh, the son of Bidshika, would react to all the physical comforts of my present life. At the same time this world of covered wagons and tents, of the dark-skinned people who were my exuberant, joyous, barefoot companions of not long ago, seemed so far away that the thought of them made me smile. It seemed as totally unreal, but as distantly desirable, as a strange half-forgotten dream.

My parents seldom spoke about the Gypsies and certainly never against them. Somehow the Rom remained my very own and secret domain. Because of the doubtful social status of the Gypsies and my circumvention of the laws concerning obligatory education, very few people were aware of my extra-curricular activities, and this prevented me from telling anybody about my life with the Gypsies. Because of this I was given to telling supposedly made-up stories about my life with the redskins. To my schoolmates and to my teachers alike these must have sounded like the fantasies of an imaginative inveterate liar. Nobody ever realized all the adventures I talked about had really happened to me and that the people I named were real if not necessarily the redskins they were said to be.*

As each year passed I became more of a Gypsy, less of a Gajo, though I still faithfully visited my parents every year in Antwerp and later on in London. I was torn between two worlds and unable to choose between them, despite the Romany saying that *yekka buliasa nashti beshes pe done grastende* (with one behind you cannot sit on two horses).

---

* One of the very few people who did know was the late Professor Olbrechts, at the time head of the Department of Anthropology at the University of Ghent, who gave me a great deal of encouragement, besides giving direction and purpose to my curiosity. He taught me to take full advantage of my unique position, that of actually living with the Gypsies as one of them.

CHAPTER THREE

Only too often was I made aware of the breach dividing the Rom and the Gaje: It was a basic, ever-present belief that they were of two different breeds with little, if anything, in common, and would never meet. It was only after I had accepted this concept of theirs that I found the Rom. I had to stop feeling incriminated each time the word Gajo was used disparagingly—which, of course, it was most of the time. The civilization of the Gaje could have no meaning for them. All they were allowed to see of it was the failures, the dirt, the injustices, the aberrations, the dregs. Their contact with the world of the Gaje was all too often limited to persons seeking their services as fortune-tellers or as practitioners of black magic, who revealed to the Rom their frustrations and exposed their own ruthless desires and petty hates; the gendarmes who self-righteously went beyond the letter of the law, the deviates in search of cheap thrills. It was this exposure to these aspects of Western culture which made it easier for them to resist the desire for integration and counterbalanced the temptations presented by the superior material standards of Gajo life. The moods the Rom displayed to the outside world were unpredictably volatile, and they switched from conciliation to menace and back without forewarning. They reveled in the bewilderment their inconsistency caused the Gaje. They could suddenly become almost excessively meek, which in fact was only one more common device for ridiculing the Gaje, who naïvely accepted the meek behavior while the Rom secretly would be laughing at his easy gullibility.

In any Gypsy camp the most aggressively anti-Gajo element were the older women and the very young children. Whenever the Rom assembled in large numbers and festive moods prevailed—and the one always flowed from the other—the children tended to get out of hand, terrorizing the Gaje bold enough to stray too close to the wagon camp. They aggressively assailed them in large numbers with competitive begging, in turn defiant, tearfully convincing, exuberant or insolent. They exerted great charm, flashing the sweetest, most innocent smiles, or they used the stark, direct appeal of the distressed, of the starveling. Occasionally they tried the entire scale in such rapid succession as to unwittingly spoil the effectiveness of all by the self-contradictory exuberance of it. These performances were staged for sheer roughhousing fun rather than for gain. The children closed in on the unaware, poking, pulling, grabbing and shoving. It was of no use for the Gajo to become angry; this only made the children answer with impertinent jeers. Depending on their mood, the children might even throw stones, inaccurately but convincingly. I soon discovered that the constant begging practiced by the *shavora,* the small fry, was intended to discourage curious observers from invading the campsite. It was not only fun—it also created an effective, invisible screen for the privacy of the entire Gypsy community. This eager, persistent begging by Gypsy children everywhere gave the onlooker a totally false picture of the real condition in which they lived, unless one was also aware of their vivacity, their health, their cheerfulness and their theatrical skills, and overlooked the ragged state of their clothes.

I remember the awe and the excitement I felt when, one day, I came upon Rupa inspecting a hoard of gold pieces, which she referred to as *sumadji,* or family heirloom. Spread out on the trampled grass next to our wagon were several big stacks of gold pieces of different sizes and denominations, piled on wrinkled, slightly soiled pieces of colored material in which they had been wrapped. Unconsciously I was surprised that she made no effort to hide them from me. Quite unconcerned, she counted them before putting them away again. I had grown used to seeing the many gold pieces worn in necklaces, earrings or bracelets by the women of the family without ever before paying any attention to their possible monetary value. I had the exhilarating impression of having been allowed to share a great secret, the knowledge of how rich Pulika really was—and I was—and I was grateful without knowing why. Shortly after this, on the same day, I watched Keja, equally fascinated, as she swiftly approached a Gajo passing by the dirt road leading to our camp. She talked to him as only she knew how when she wanted something passionately, intensely proud and humble at the same time. She followed him until he stopped, searched himself slowly and self-consciously, and gave her money. As she sauntered back to the camp, she was met halfway by several giggling Gypsy girls. It appeared they had made a bet with her, challenging her abilities to rouse the Gajo's pity and wheedle a "donation" from him. The bet was ten times the contribution obtained. Money was not the object at all, but rather a professional pride of sorts. I watched this game being played by several girls until they had nothing more to prove and stopped begging for the day.

When the Rom traveled in small units they displayed a greater tolerance toward the Gaje. Occasionally they even sought out such contacts and enjoyed being entertained by the unsuspecting Gaje. Sitting around the blazing campfire, they played a more subtle game of mystification, leaving the Gaje totally unaware of their ridicule, never betraying themselves by so much as an amused smile. Many of the wilder stories about the Gypsies were told in this spirit to unsuspecting Gaje, to be repeated or even published in complete good faith. With more alert and inquisitive Gaje, such as two purposeful anthropologists who visited a Gypsy camp, a different technique was used. The Rom affected a childlike admiration for them and any object they possessed—shoes, clothes, watches, eyeglasses, rings. This was followed by unending and detailed questions about these, worthy of a good fieldworker. Several Gypsies took turns at this eager interrogation, often repeating the same question. The Gaje replied willingly, only too happy to be able to establish a working base so rapidly and easily. They relaxed their initial suspicion. The Rom saying is "Admire him profusely and let him talk long enough and any Gajo will lose himself." Several hours of this persistent treatment left the inquisitive Gaje exhausted but happy—until it occurred to them that they had been prevented from asking any questions themselves. When they returned to follow up the initial contact with the Rom, they found the Gypsies had left.

On the rare occasions when the Rom chose not to avoid an actual dialogue with the Gaje, their answers were almost as inconsistent and bewildering. If one question was asked of twenty different Gypsies, all the answers, as might be expected, were contradictory. If the same question was asked twenty times of the same informant, there was an equally wide diversity of answers. Pointing out to the Gypsies their lack of consistency did not embarrass them in the least. In Romani they said, *"Tshatshimo Romano"* (The truth is expressed in Romani). It was the Gaje who, by forcing the Rom to speak a foreign language, made the Gypsy lie. The Rom said, *"Mashkar le gajende leski shib si le Romeski zor"* (Surrounded by the Gaje the Rom's tongue is his only defense). Often they simply pleaded ignorance or, by interrupting him in mid-sentence, refused to allow the Gajo to pursue his line of thought. An old woman might turn on him begging, urgent, demanding; unsettling in the stark, almost brutal simplicity of her approach. His attention might be distracted by a sudden violent quarreling among his listeners, or a young woman might start a provocative flirtation, not easily ignored.

The Rom sometimes resorted to scratching themselves persistently in the presence of unwelcome Gaje. With the strangers' departure all scratching ceased. A number of times I have seen old people, who disapproved of what they felt was the undue interest of outsiders, start coughing violently, driving the Gaje away by the implication of some contagious, dreaded lung ailment.

In accordance with Gajo law the Rom had to have family surnames and first names. These were the ones which appeared on their identification papers. These names had been acquired more or less at random during their long migrations and had no real meaning for them. As opportunities to improve their legal or residential status presented themselves, they would try to change their surnames, preferably adopting names of the host country in which they resided. A given name changed in spelling, eventually even in actual sound, as it was transliterated by border officials from the Cyrillic alphabet into Roman characters, or from Greek into Turkish. Often names were simplified or summarily replaced by nicknames, especially among those Rom who had lived in the United States. Besides these official or Gajo names the Rom had their Romany names, which were the only ones they themselves would answer to. Kore, son of Pulika, son of Yojo, son of Barfko of the Lowara, was thus known as the *Yojeshti*. Three or four generations of descendants of an important Rom used his name as a patronymic, which changed as the generations advanced and other important men arose in the genealogy, whose names in turn replaced the older ones as the group split into smaller but growing subunits. Among the Lowara many a Rom used Gajo surnames of Romany derivation and origin. Pulika's most currently used surname (he used a number of aliases) was Petalo, or Horseshoe. Most Lowara surnames, however, were of a more ribald or obscene nature, such as Karbaro, Mijloli, Porado, all variations of the term erection. Every time a police officer, court official or administration clerk called a Gypsy by his surname, which in itself often spelled trouble of some kind, the Rom felt the joke was on the Gaje—which, in a minor way, helped to sweeten life.

There also were times, of course, when the Rom did establish lasting relationships with Gaje. These voluntary contacts were always of a practical nature, in keeping with the saying Rupa was so fond of repeating: *Na may kharunde kai tshi khal tut* (not to scratch where it did not itch). Not infrequently these friendships stemmed from unselfish services rendered to the Rom in an emergency, for which they showed gratitude. The Rom saw to it that "their" Gaje were never bothered or taken advantage of by other Gypsies, which gave rise to purely mythical stories of their mysterious loyalty. In fact it was not because of a sense of moral obligation on their part, since a Gajo is always just a Gajo, but rather because any protector must be spared for possible emergencies—for as the Rom said, *"May mishto les o thud katar i gurumni kai tordjol"* (It is easier to milk a cow that stands still). It was essential that he was not an outcast or a misfit in his own society and that he did not display undue curiosity about the Gypsies in general. These people became "points of contact" for the Rom, where mail could be forwarded. They served as relays for long-distance telephone calls and became part of a well-organized network of communication, often covering a large number of countries. Each important Rom had his exclusive personal contacts, and those made by other members of his family, which were jealously guarded. A scrap of paper with the telephone number as the only identification was carefully folded many times over and kept in a separate compartment of the billfold. It was by the color of the piece of paper or by its quality or by the way it was folded that they remembered the identity of the person involved and the place where he resided, in this way adding extra secrecy to the number. The actual degree of fading or wear of the piece of paper, sometimes reducing the number almost to illegibility, was also a guide. I remember one instance when Tshukurka stared at me in utter disbelief, reproving me for what he misconstrued as my inability to read, when in fact there was nothing left to decipher on the precious scrap of paper he offered to my scrutiny.

Occasionally priests or people connected with social work became "Romane Gaje." It also happened that wealthy landowners, whom the Rom called *raya,* took a fancy to a particular Gypsy child and acted as protector for the entire family. The Gypsies honored selected Gaje by asking them to become godfathers to their children, thus establishing a more formal, if illusory, bond. Pulika told me how he himself, his brother Tshukurka, several of their married children and a number of cousins had been befriended by the late Cardinal Mercier of Belgium, the legendary figure of World War I, and how, to please him, they had welcomed his offer to marry them according to the rites of the Catholic Church they were supposed to have joined. This eventually took place in great pomp at the basilica of Koekelbergh. So at least Pulika told me, adding with a chuckle of visible satisfaction, "We made the Bishop very happy."

The stealing of chickens was the cardinal sin with which the country population often rightfully reproached the Gypsies. Sometimes the Gypsies were violently denounced as the abductors of Christian children. At the same time the country population and also city dwellers consulted Gypsy women about their most intimate family problems, their fears, failures and secret longings. Fortune-telling was practiced by Gypsy women the world over. A remunerative occupation, it also served as a convenient source of information, a sounding board for the moods of the particular region. Rupa and the girls read palms by the wayside, with quiet conviction, earnestness and an air of mystery. The first time I showed interest in this, Rupa, with a voice that turned hard, gave me to understand, once and for all, that for the Rom this activity carried a double taboo; it was intended for the Gaje, and it was exclusively practiced by the women, "never the Rom." Rupa stood very erect, had deliberate, measured movements and was thin by Lowara standards. Her complexion was dark, and when she spoke to the Gaje she had a wild expression in her eyes, an abrupt manner and a low, almost whispering, husky voice. Kore, Tshaya, Boti and little Tina resembled her, while big Yojo, Keja, Putzina and Mala were much more like Pulika. In referring humorously to her dark tone of skin, Rupa said, *"May kali i muri may gugli avela"* (The darker the berry the sweeter it is).

The Gypsy women stopped passersby and, gripping them by the wrist, insisted on reading the Gaje's futures in the lines of their hands. The suddenness and the dark intensity of their approach made it difficult to deny them. Some Gaje were amused, others intrigued, but most were apprehensive and disturbed by this.

I was too young and too full of imagination to be attracted to divination or to be in search of its solace. Daily I saw the women of our group practice it, and because of this I was taken aback by Rupa's angry, emphatic refusal to answer my questions about it. Keja also rebuffed me when I approached her about the subject. She shrugged her shoulders and smiled with just a trace of disdain. Without Rupa's bitterness, however, she told me, "This is not for the Rom. Leave it to the foolish Gaje." Whenever I saw Rupa tell fortunes, she looked so convincing that I thought to myself she might very well have second sight.

A few days later we were driving through a vast sandy plain covered by heather, at the edge of a pine forest. Swallows dived low to the ground crossing the dirt track along which we traveled at a lazy pace. Pulika and Rupa had joined Yojo in the wagon ahead. Tshaya and Mala and Yojo's young wife had left our wagon as we passed the farmhouse with the low-hanging thatched roof. They would take a shortcut across the fields and do some errands and would be waiting for us farther ahead. Kore sat on the wide board at the front of the wagon, loosely holding the reins in his hands as the horses followed the lead wagon without needing attention from the driver. Putzina sprawled in the feeding rack at the rear of Yojo's wagon, staring up at the sky and smoking hand-rolled cigarettes of black tobacco. Keja sat on her haunches in Gypsy fashion, rocking her brother Yojo's youngest child and pacifying his persistent cries for his mother by giving him her breast. Her breasts were round and full, but she was still a young unmarried girl and had no milk. Without turning her head she intoned in a soft voice a monologue about fortune-telling, for my attention. It surprised me that she should be sensitive to my concern about this. She talked without reticence. In essence Keja said that the avidity for fortune-telling came from an inability to cope with one's anxieties. Instead of satisfying, it created a self-perpetuating greed for prophecy, akin to compulsive gambling, only more harmful since one lost not money but insight. It blinded one to the causes of one's problems, and this was "madness." It was a vain and self-defeating search for expedient solutions to problems of moral integrity, and was caused by an unwillingness to face life as it was. Most people consulted fortune-tellers primarily to seek the confirmation of their fears, more often than of their hopes. Fear could become father to a wish, for many subconsciously wanted to have happen that which they said they feared most. Keja said that fear impoverished, while the acceptance of sorrow could enrich. The Lowara said, "Without wood the fire would die" (*Bi kashtesko merel i yag*), disclaiming guilt. Seen from a practical point of view, the tangible substance of fortune-telling was the ability to listen with endless patience to every human folly. To this they added some vague generalities into which specific and personal meanings could be read. Keja talked for a long time and with great openness.

She told me about a country squire in Serbia, long ago, who imagined that he had a dreaded, incurable disease. He consulted a physician in Sarajevo who reassured him and emphatically denied his fears. The squire rushed to see other physicians, all of whom agreed with the first doctor. He went to Nish and to Belgrade and to Sofia in Bulgaria. In despair, he went to see a soothsayer, who immediately confirmed his fears, proving the medical authorities wrong in the eyes of the squire. After a protracted and costly treatment he managed to save the squire—from an imaginary illness!

There are times in people's lives, Keja conceded, when consulting a palmist might relieve their loneliness, provide a confidant, or allow them to project their anxiety or hostility. It could relieve boredom, add salt and exoticism to life. It might satisfy a passing need for dabbling in the mysterious, with just enough of a suspicion of the satanic. The promise of a hypothetical better tomorrow might, if not taken too seriously, help break the habit of unhappiness and of material misery; otherwise it became a crutch that crippled.

With witchery in their eyes the Gypsy women practiced this art for a modest price. It was rare that they went beyond this and tried to gain a personal and more permanent power over their willing victims. The legend of Gypsy divinatory faculties, like all legends, was simply an exaggeration. It was spread and magnified largely by the half-believers, those who sought sensation and were more vocal than the truly addicted. Coincidence often seemed to substantiate the accuracy of what was in reality daring guesswork, and people remembered only those predictions that came true. They tended to forget the errors. The Rom spoke of a general practitioner in Moldavia,

Romania, who predicted the sex of an unborn child many months ahead, without ever failing. His system was based on pure guesswork, complemented by a clever device. If he announced that the baby would be a boy, he wrote down in his notebook a girl. If it was a boy he was proved right and no questions arose. If, on the contary, it was a girl, and the parents, disappointed in his ability, confronted him, he simply claimed not to remember and checked his book, which contained written proof of his having made the right guess originally.

The Rom certainly gained a degree of self-protection from the Gaje's fear of the Gypsies' curses and spells. In a subtle way it could limit the brutality and the repression inflicted on a minority without adequate defense. The legal status of the Gypsies was at best that of a tolerated minority, at worst that of undesirables to be extradited or eliminated, and at the mercy of all. By fortune-telling they imposed on the credulous a certain fear and respect: a slim defense but better than nothing.

CHAPTER FOUR

Sometimes the Gaje were intrigued by my fair skin, blue eyes and blond hair. Occasionally one of them, well-intentioned, offered to help me escape from what he assumed must be a miserable captivity. The people who stopped me on the roads to question me about my origin were confident that I was the stolen child of legend.

Kore, Putzina and even Keja were much amused, and out of sheer mischief they themselves sometimes talked to the Gaje of my "captivity." To them the notion of *stealing* Gaje children was farfetched and pointless. Did the Rom not have a profusion of children of their own? One of the games we played was for me to pretend ignorance of the local tongue of the Gaje and ask the Gypsies to act as my interpreters. For a short while we developed variations on this theme, until one day it came to Pulika's attention. He was having a quiet beer at a tavern not far from our encampment when the local veterinarian bluntly accused him of kidnaping and detaining a child. Devoid of any real guilt or a sense of wrongdoing, but ever aware of a good opportunity to ridicule the Gaje, Pulika calmly replied that it was none of the man's business. As an afterthought he warned the man to keep away from me. He warmed up to his role and in convincing detail described the cradle snatching that had never occurred. The Gaje were baffled and disarmed by his simple confirmation of their worst suspicions and by his complete cynicism. Pulika winked broadly at them, paid for his beer, and left before they had recovered their breath. Pulika relished his success of sorts as a teller of tall tales. At every opportunity he repeated his story, embellished it, embroidered upon it, changing the country, the social status of the stolen child's parents, the age at which he supposedly had been abducted by the Gypsies. Pulika did his best to live up to this legend of notoriety. Unknown to us, the rumors grew and changed and further multiplied. Then one day, to the consternation of all involved, the camp was surrounded and raided by the mounted police. They were accompanied by several indignant witnesses: the people Pulika had told the story to and, it suddenly became obvious to him, had been too thoroughly taken in. I was soon found. However, on checking my identity, all concerned were much relieved to find that I was not the son of a certain well-to-do figure of the Austro-Hungarian nobility whom Pulika had made me out to be. I heard the police officers and the Gaje talk about all the other little boys that had been stolen by the Gypsies, and I suddenly realized these were only my numerous alter egos, innocently made up by Pulika's fertile imagination. I bravely assured them that I was living with the Gypsies of my own volition. I was taken away from the Rom. That afternoon the sky fell, and I was sure I would never be able to smile again.

As we were leaving, Keja came up to me to say goodbye; unseen by the police, she pushed a small wad of crumpled banknotes down my open shirtfront.

Passersby stopped to stare at us as we made our way to the Gendarmerie headquarters. I left Pulika behind at the mercy of the witch-hunters, a target for automatic denunciation. I was taken into custody to spend the night locked up, for the first time of my life. My few and useless possessions were taken away and registered, including Keja's money. My mouth and throat were parched; my heart was beating furiously and I felt sick. The cell in which I was temporarily confined smelled of stale tobacco, shabby deprivation and of fresh human excrement. With shattering suddenness I had become aware of my vulnerability and powerlessness. I wanted only to lie quietly and turn my face to the wall, instead of which I was interrogated at length again by an inspector. He was blindly prejudiced against the Gypsies. He used many loud but irrelevant words and his eyes were unseeing. I realized then what the Rom must have known from long experience—that it was impossible to talk to a man with power over you—and the awesome disparity between us grew. He cursed volubly and subjected me endlessly to his tough language and his vulgar assumptions about the Gypsies' criminality and debauchery. I was too stunned and disgusted to react. He typed up a statement which I was made to sign. I never read it but I knew it would have made little difference if I had. I felt alien to the whole situation.

In view of my age I spent the night on a grubby, straw-filled pallet in a reform school run by friars, rather than in the city jail, pending further developments. There I fell asleep with the paling darkness of the gray dawn, thinking with extravagant tenderness of Pulika and his people; and I knew I was now willing to accept and share their life as my own. It was true that, as Pulika said, "it was in the water that one learned to swim" (*feri ando payi sitsholpe te nayuas*).

I stayed there only a few days, an abandoned orphan, while contact was established with my parents in Antwerp via the consular authorities. Eventually I was released and sent home. I was given clothes slightly better than those I had been wearing, and I traveled in the company—or rather the custody—of a Belgian lawyer who was going back on business. He was what was described as "fatherly," condescendingly forgiving of my mistakes but anxious to give advice. He understood, even slyly approved of, what he thought must be my precocious interest in Gypsy girls. He kindly advised me to turn to professionals, who, as he explained, had "all the prerequisites and none of the drawbacks." Noticing my lack of enthusiasm, he winked conspiratorially, as one man of the world to another, suggested perhaps I was more interested in little boys. I closed my eyes and pretended to sleep.

My parents were most understanding and did not immediately press me for explanations. There were some minor complications as a result of my being a truant. When I briefly returned to school, my fellow students seemed young and out of touch with reality—the reality of things I had known during my time away from "formal learning."

My parents managed to obtain some kind of pass for me from a highly placed person they knew at the Aliens Department of the Belgian Sécurité Publique, who agreed to keep an eye on me and to minimize future misunderstandings with the Belgian police. This made it unnecessary for me to leave the camp whenever the police came. Obviously the pass did not explain my presence among the Gypsies. It just gave notice that in case of trouble a certain Inspector D. S. should be informed immediately; this gave the false impression that I was there on his account, as an informer of sorts. But who cared what the constabulary thought? And the Rom merely congratulated me for so cleverly outwitting the authorities.

A short time later, I rejoined Pulika's *kumpania*. They had fled the Rhineland, driven by the rising tide of Nazi xenophobia, and crossed into the Netherlands. Now they were making their way to France through Belgium. The new camping ground was a sandy clearing at the edge of a sparsely grown pine forest. A slight haze softened the extended purplish patches of heather in every direction around us. Clouds of huge, angrily buzzing blue-black flies descended on leftover food and on the yet unwashed plates and cooking caldrons. Flies in search of moisture crawled on my face and on those of the other Gypsies. Many smoldering fires of pinecones and peat studded the site. It was one of those indescribably peaceful moments in perfect accord with the equal peacefulness of the surrounding landscape, typical of the Flemish *Kempen* of northern Belgium and southern Holland. The small whitewashed peasant dwellings had enormous, overhanging thatch roofs, out of proportion to the dimensions of the houses themselves. The doors and windows were exceedingly small. The houses and the sprawling, low-built barns and sheepfolds were in perfect harmony with the landscape, and from a distance the thatch roofs suggested giant moss-covered toadstools. There were pear trees and carefully tended vegetable gardens everywhere. There also seemed to be an abundance of calico cats. At first sight it all gave one an impression of gentleness and friendliness.

At the edge of the camp, behind our massive yellow-oak wagon, Pulika and Yojo were leisurely shaving. Yojo had wedged a shard of half-blind mirror between the broken, withered branches of a sapling pine. Pulika trimmed his fierce, bushy mustache and his long sideburns. Earlier in the day Kore and another boy had gone to the nearby hamlet, offering to whet knives and sharpen and adjust scissors. They had no equipment with them, and the farmer's red-cheeked daughter had been distrustful, unwilling to let them take away any knives or tools. Rising to this challenge, the Gypsy boys had used all the charm and persuasion at their command. She had relented and given them one pair of old scissors to adjust. It was this pair of scissors that had prompted this open-air *toilette*. Kore bargained for the use of the Rom's open razor and carefully shaved the dark fuzz off his cheeks, sparing that on his upper lip. Putzina and I in turn begged Kore for the razor, but he refused to let us use it. When Pulika and Yojo were finished with the scissors, Yojo volunteered to cut our hair. He teased us, saying that no village barber would be willing to render us this service. And he was right, though the need for a haircut rarely occurred to us, or for that matter to our elders.

Overhead, schools of small gay white clouds drifted slowly across the lofty blue sky.

After some prodding from me, Kore relented and we returned the scissors to their rightful owners even though he saw no reason to do so. He had no intention of *keeping* the scissors, since we would not need another haircut for a long time, and then, no doubt, other scissors could just as easily be had. He simply felt that the scissors could take care of themselves, that they would "get lost," or be borrowed by other Gypsies in need of them. It was certainly not out of an acquisitive instinct that Kore hesitated to take them back. He just failed to see why this was of any consequence. The Rom often surprised me with this typical indifference to material possessions, toward "mere objects."

On the way back to the hamlet it occurred to me that Kore had not done anything about sharpening the scissors, apart from using them himself, and I realized that this might be the reason for his original reluctance to take them back. As if he had read my thoughts, Kore casually stopped by a rusty barbed-wire fence and began cutting it. I failed to see the point. It would have been impossible to cut the heavy wire with simple sewing scissors; nor could he have any possible use for a piece of rusty wire. After sawing away, Kore looked at the blades with visible satisfaction, and to prove his point, he snipped at his shirt-sleeve. After this operation he crouched at the side of the dirt road, laid the scissors on a large pebble, and with another one, picked up at random, he banged a few times at the screw to tighten it, as if it were a rivet. The Flemish peasant girl came to meet us at the Dutch door. In this particular region the farmers had doors that opened in two separate sections, an upper and a lower one. Often they left the upper part open, especially in hot weather. This permitted them to look out, and the lower part formed a kind of counter. In the house there was a strong smell of sour milk. Before anybody could say anything, Kore explained that he would be unable to handle their order since we were moving on. He added that he would not charge anything for the sharpening of the scissors, but would the peasant woman, the girl's mother, consider selling us some food? I knew he had no money with him, nor had I. His offer to pay mollified the woman and she invited us to sit down at a corner of the large, clean-scrubbed kitchen table. She cut some thick lumps of fresh bread and served us large cups of coffee from a red enameled coffeepot that was simmering at the back of the stove. As an afterthought she made us bacon and eggs. It was hard to follow her conversation because of the dialect she spoke, even though I spoke Flemish fluently and Kore's speaking knowledge of it was fair. He did not even try. She explained it was the time of the local country fair, and she guessed that we must belong to the traveling merry-go-round—or were we connected with the troupe of wrestlers that was traditionally part of the festivities? We gulped down the food and I noticed that Kore ate only the fried bacon and left the egg untouched. He told me in Romani that eggs, like milk and other slippery or weak substances, were debilitating and he firmly advised me against eating mine. The woman offered us some pieces of pie filled with rice, which Kore sniffed at and then also refused to eat. Who ever heard of rice with sugar? he asked disdainfully. As we left, I heard the puzzled woman wonder out loud about our peculiar eating habits. She felt strongly that poor hungry children should eat whatever was put before them and she said so loudly. Besides, these Gypsies, *barakkenvolk,* did not even take off their hats to eat and had said no prayers. In Flemish *barakkenvolk* literally means "people living in covered wagons," but it implied "scum of the earth." Kore pointed out to me that what had spoiled his appetite was the numerous cats drinking milk from a plate on the kitchen floor. He insisted that after the cats were through the woman had given me the plate. In a corner of the kitchen there had also been a small rosy baby girl with abundant blond curls who sat on a potty, to Kore's indignant disapproval. The Gypsies certainly would never have done such a thing; what was the matter with these Gaje? And what about that awful, sticky flypaper the peasants had hanging over their table, black with the flies that had stuck to it?

As we were leaving, Kore said a few very derogatory words to her in Romani, which I only hoped for her sake she would interpret as "Thank you."

On the way back to the camp we came across several small groups of Gypsies, either going toward the hamlet or, like ourselves, returning from it. Some girls had gathered pinecones and branches for fires. Half-naked young children were playing and running along the dirt track, straying too far from the camp. We noticed that the numerous horses grazing about were getting frisky. They had been left untethered because the grass was sparse and this left them more field to graze on. They lifted their heads, twisted their ears and snorted. Without any hesitation we ran over to them to investigate. Kore caught two of them by the manes and brought them to me to hold by the braided rope halters while he tried to get another one, while several other boys and men ran to catch their own, sensing trouble but still ignoring the reasons for it. The horses breathed heavily, and Kore, who was with them more than I was, held on to the frisky stallion, which danced in a half circle around the barefoot boy. Its legs quivered with excitement and the taut veins stood out noticeably on the buttocks. As the wind shifted slightly, the horses pulled away in one direction like a frightened herd, pulling us along with them.

They stopped to look back again and milled around in disarray while we hung heavily on the halters or onto the manes, trying to subdue them. Shading our eyes, we peered in the direction the animals seemed to be fleeing from, and they turned their heads toward the danger. Then a crackling, hissing sound caught our attention. It was immediately followed by a more ominous rumbling as of an oncoming storm but at ground level instead of in the sky. A brush fire was suddenly rushing toward us. We swung onto the horses' backs and with wild yells encouraged the herd to flee, directing it toward the camp instead of letting them simply scatter, which in their fear was their tendency. Our distant yells echoed throughout the entire camp, where most Gypsies had also seen the signs of danger. We hurriedly gathered all small children within easy reach and bundled them off with several young women, babies astride their hips or still nursing. Everywhere women hastily gathered their belongings and threw them into wagons already on the move. Pulika stayed behind and so did Keja. When we were a fair distance up the road, Kore and Putzina tried to ride back, straddling the stallion, but they could not force the frenzied animal in the direction of the fire. There was little smoke, but the heat could be felt even at a fair distance. Hordes of frightened game ran out of the brush, and loudly shrieking pheasants and partridges shot by in their uproarious and heavy flight.

We drove on for a few more miles and stopped to wait for the others. There was no time to go back on foot to help. We waited and smoked hand-rolled cigarettes, ready to flee on. The fire was spreading rapidly. It would unexpectedly flash out far ahead to one side where no one had expected to see it. Several wagons came hurtling down the unpaved road, leaving the deeply churned sand as evidence of their haste. Fortunately there had been no mishaps among the Rom, and soon all the wagons had caught up with us and we fled together. Ahead of us the road was becoming obstructed by fleeing villagers who drove their lowing cattle ahead of them. Some of these people traveled in small carts, which resembled crates on wheels, pulled by dogs. We slowed down as it was impossible to pass them. The sheep and the cows were difficult to manage and ran in all directions. The church bells sounded the general alarm; we could hear the muffled roaring of the fire and the intermittent crash of falling timber. Far behind us a chained watchdog left behind howled shrilly its hysterical cry of agony.

The children were unnaturally silent as the crowds of refugees fled onward. After some time we crossed a magnificent paved highway, the Route Nationale. We could relax somewhat in the knowledge that this treeless space might slow down or possibly even stop the spreading of the wild fire. As the urgency of the flight lessened, the peasants, some traveling ahead and some behind us, suddenly became conscious of our foreignness. There were hateful stares. The anguish and anger of their impotence in the face of the catastrophe turned into hate for us. They whispered urgently among themselves. Some looked significantly in our direction. Some women and older people had been invited by the Gypsies to sit on the driving boards of the wagons and had been grateful for the considerate if normal assistance and had thought no evil of us. Now peasant children who had shortly before cowered in fear stuck out their tongues at us. We soon found out that the peasants suspected us of arson. It became clear that it would be safer for us to break away as soon as this was physically possible. The pace of travel was exasperatingly slow and the peasants willfully prevented us from passing them. Eventually they stopped at a fairly large homestead. Some of them swung off the road. They pumped fresh water and let their children drink. They turned to the direction they had come from to weigh the situation. They exchanged opinions with the farmer whose homestead they had arrived at. The men swore and the women sobbed quietly while they forgot about us momentarily. We kept moving, slipping off without unpleasant incidents, with the exception of a few towheaded farm boys who threw stones at the last wagon of our column when it already was out of reach. It seemed wise to move as far away from the present locality as the tired and overheated horses would permit. The men and the boys walked alongside the wagons to spare the horses. The Rom were feverish and flushed from the excitement and from exposure to the heat; we were thirsty, our throats were parched, our lips flaky and cracked. Small children cried but we had no immediate access to water.

That night we camped along the roadside and kept the horses tied to the backs of the wagons, just in case. Fires were forbidden, to prevent our attracting attention to ourselves. All night long we could see in the distance the afterglow of the great fire lighting up the sky with its incandescence. The wind was stifling, hot and reeking of carbonization. At intervals a geyser of sparks shot up briefly to rival the stars.

The next day we moved on. Stopping at village taverns by the road, the Rom inquired about the fire, careful however not to admit to having been in its vicinity, afraid to arouse the possible suspicion of arson. They knew from past experience how easily they would have been made the scapegoats under such circumstances. Eventually the fire subsided, but several homesteads had been overtaken and partly or totally destroyed. Slowly the peasants were drifting back.

Yojo called me to accompany him on an errand. Pulika's stallion was hitched to the two-wheeled flat cart on which had been piled a stack of empty burlap bags and several short but sturdy sticks. I could not guess the nature of the errand, but by that time I had become accustomed to the unpredictable ways of the Rom. Yojo was fair-skinned like Keja and he usually dressed in local peasant fashion. He wore the heavy, ungainly wooden clogs in local use. We drove back along the trail we had taken the day before. A few miles away from the camp Yojo took off the kerchief he wore knotted around his neck and suggested I take off mine too. Still no explanations were offered while we drove at a steady trot, but Yojo was never very talkative anyway and I made no effort to start a conversation but just let myself drift off. I was uneasy about going back, remembering the inhabitants' hostility toward the Gypsies. I had a premonition of trouble, and I realized belatedly why Yojo had invited me to accompany him: I was not a Gypsy nor did I look like one; for that matter, neither did he. Breaking his long silence, he cautioned me not to speak Romani in the presence of any outsiders and told me that if we should be asked if we were Gypsies I must deny it. I tried to speculate on the purpose of this senseless trip, and I was becoming more alarmed at our defenselessness when it occurred to me there were some heavy clubs near at hand hidden under the pile of empty bags.

We drove through the gloomy, muffled silence of the burned forest. There were no birds singing, no buzz of insects, no scurrying of small animals in the no-longer-existing underbrush: just gray and black oppressive silence mixed with the stifling stench of burning. Here and there stood mutilated trees stretching their atrophied limbs skyward in mute protest, like calcinated skeletons overtaken in the meaningless gesture of imploring an implacable victor. High above us a jubilant lark climbed dizzily into the sky, only to fall back to earth after exhausting its thrust, and then to start over again, soaring higher and higher.

Yojo slowed the horse with a deep-throated rumbling noise. He headed the recalcitrant stallion along the narrow driving path toward a deserted-looking farmhouse partly destroyed by the fire. We were met by several sullen, hard-faced farmhands who violently motioned to us not to come any closer. Strangers were not wanted, any strangers. Yojo did not insist. He maneuvered the cart and horse around, which was not easy because of the narrow approach, but he displayed no undue urgency. The farmhands did not even allow us to drive into the courtyard to facilitate the operation. Yojo let the reins hang loose and allowed the stallion to drift along at its own pace for a while. The desolation all around us was appalling. The creaking of the cart and the grinding of the wheels seemed to grow louder and to fill space; interlaced with it, in addition, was the persistent amorous whinnying of Pulika's stallion. We passed a number of places where shacks or other buildings had burned to the ground. Everything was blackened and eerie, as if we were treading forbidden ground. The sun was already high when, farther along, we saw a sprawling complex of buildings that the fire had partly spared because they stood in an open space. The roofs of what must have been the cowsheds had been destroyed; we could see the brick stalls and the twisted metal mangers. There were the remains of the hothouses; the glass panes had burst or melted. The chicken coops were burned to the ground and all around them were calcinated dots which might very well have been the chickens. Those parts of the buildings that had been spared were badly scorched and singed. Several farmhands were pulling farm equipment from under the half-collapsed roof of a hangar. They were sorting the twisted implements and trying to recover whatever was still usable. A dairymaid was pumping water in the paved courtyard. We asked for some water for the horse. It was given readily and Yojo and I took deep draughts of it before giving the bucket to the restless horse. Yojo pushed back his black hat, looked around and, sensing the Gaje watching him, shook his head in a slow movement of compassionate amazement. A short heavyset man detached himself from the others and ambled toward us. There was no hate in his eyes and no more reticence than would be shown other unknown visitors. Yojo said he was a horse dealer from across the border and was passing through on business. He said we had heard about the fire and asked what had happened to their livestock and horses. The farmer eyed our stallion appreciatively and we knew contact had been made. Some of their cows and one horse had been hurt in the panic, but the pigsty had burned to the ground, like the chicken coop, which was of less consequence. Yojo said little, but the inflection in his voice and the expression in his eyes were right. They talked as man as man, as equals. After shaking his head in sympathy, Yojo brought into the conversation a mythical brother-in-law who supposedly owned a kennel. For emphasis he pointed vaguely in the direction we had come from. Yojo spoke knowledgeably about hounds and greyhounds. As often happened, I was nonplussed at first; then, an hour or so later, to my amazement, Yojo's game suddenly came clearly into focus, for we had loaded several partly burned but nonetheless impressive pigs' carcasses onto our cart "to feed my brother-in-law's hounds." Of course, he offered to pay, but he had already started to thank our host for his generosity, saying how right it was that at least this meat would not simply be wasted. While talking dog races, pigeon racing and soccer, Yojo offhandedly had asked for a knife and proceeded to gut one of the pigs, without interrupting the conversation. He plunged the knife into the carcass and expertly slit open its belly. I retched violently and was surprised at the visceral reaction independent of my will or mind. Momentarily I felt my breath stick in my throat. The farmer smiled at me with a touch of pitying contempt. Yojo finished, quickly dumping the innards in an ugly gory pile. Wisely Yojo motioned me away and made me understand that I should tighten and buckle the belly strap of the harness and hitch the horse back into the traces. We soon disappeared into the oncoming dusk and turned back to the camp at full speed. But soon night overtook us and we were forced to slow down even though it was clear and visibility was good. The colorless landscape was monotonous and flat, and the unnatural silence added to the air of intangible menace, as if Death personified wandered abroad. We drove on, suddenly aware of how far we had gone earlier in the day when daylight and sunshine deceived us about the distance. Yojo was smoking silently, strangely remote, unaware of my uneasiness. In all the time we had not come across another human being, or even an animal. The horse was tired and persistently pulled to the left of the sandy road. Once it stopped altogether. Without moving, Yojo slowly surveyed the immediate surroundings. He whispered to me not to move. We strained our eyes and listened intently. He let the horse have its way, trying to discover what ill-defined presence had upset it. Its ears lay low and the skin of its neck and shoulders shivered briefly. There followed a short burst of defiant roar from the stallion, insolent, scornful, as if hurling a challenge. It reared its head and kicked its hind legs before lunging forward again. We rode away at full tilt and Yojo spoke to the horse in a deep, quiet voice to pacify it. We reached the borderline between the dead and the living, where fertile nature grew green, leaving behind the terrible destruction wrought by the fire. We drove a few more miles before turning off the road. The pigs' carcasses brusquely seemed to come to life. They changed position, rolled over and lurched to one side of the cart.

We pulled off some of the empty bags and wrapped ourselves in them, and I lay on the ground. The sacks reeked of scorched flesh, but I fell asleep anyway. Waking up with a start at intervals, I could see Yojo gutting the other pigs nearby. He crouched near the earth, hardly distinguishable from it, visible only by the glow of his cigarette. In my restless, uncomfortable sleep I had haunting half thoughts of the pigs accidentally killed by the fire and the collapsing sty. I was aware only of dead flesh at close range, and the essential distinction between animal and human somehow melted away.

At daybreak we drove on again. I was cold through and through, and we had not eaten since early the day before; we had only drunk some water. As compensation, however, we smoked heavily. The sounds of myriad insects made the air quiver, and roosters at distant farmhouses crowed in the new day. The first sunrays revealed green hedges and trees, cows out at pasture. Stray chickens busily scratched the soil for food. The sky was blue and pigeons cooed. Behind us lay the leaden landscape of nature carbonized, reduced to ash and frozen silence.

When we reached the wasteland where we had left the camp the day before, it had moved. We easily found the new location, but the Rom were still asleep with the exception of old Lyuba. The ancient one crouched by a small fire she had kindled, as it was her custom to do well before anybody else in the encampment rose. With her bare, dark, leathery fingers she held over the flame the battered lid of a tin can on which she slowly roasted a dozen or so green coffee beans. The aroma was enticing and sweetly nauseating at the same time. When they were roasted to her taste she ground them in a tall brass coffee grinder. After washing, Yojo went to crouch by the fire and share her early morning brew, while I took the horse to pasture. I still did not dare sit with Lyuba. She had always strongly disapproved of my presence among her people, telling them that a Gajo child could only bring them trouble. I was intimidated by her presence, and the very awareness of her venerable age, which she carried well and with quiet authority, made me ill at ease. She had outlived most of her contemporaries and she rarely spoke to the young ones directly, but she still was a power, stubbornly independent, always sleeping in the open whatever the temperature. In winter she slept under the wagon and her numerous descendants erected makeshift, protective enclosures around it, in lean-to fashion, of any material at hand: boards, horse blankets, tar paper. She barely tolerated this "fussing" over her, as she protestingly called it, her breath steaming against the cold. She loudly claimed she needed *balval,* wind, to live: not just air trapped within an enclosure but life-giving "flowing" wind. In this same sense the Rom attached much importance to the flow of water as the symbolic renewal of the substance itself.

I lay on my back among the grazing horses to brood on mortality. I had never been much exposed to death, and the awareness now obsessed me. The burlap bags we had wrapped ourselves in were shrouds of a sort and had smelled of death— an undefinable, sickly sweet smell. We had ridden a hearse and Yojo had performed a postmortem on the remains; and now the Rom would celebrate for days, if the meat did not go bad. Kore and Putzina came to join me in the meadow as soon as they found out we had returned. They looked well-rested and beamed in anticipation of the feast which would flow from such abundance of meat. They seemed unaware of my misery and for once I was grateful for it. At the camp the Rom skipped breakfast, content with drinking numerous cups of sticky black coffee, while everybody helped prepare a more abundant and worthy repast. Dinner was in the early afternoon and amply made up for the extended waiting. I sulked most of that day and refused to eat or participate in the feast. I could not liberate myself from my private nightmares.

The Rom ate beyond all measure, in a heroic feat of consumption, and all were in a joyous mood. At dusk I noticed that a number of Gypsy boys and also some girls were preparing to leave the camp. They had been washing themselves, combing and arranging their hair. Keja, Tshaya and several of their cousins had wet their hair with water, milky and viscous from the soap, and had made themselves one or more curls, which were held in place, stuck to their foreheads, with more soap. They said this was in the fashion of the Spanish Gitanos.

They were going to a dance at the local country fair. Two large tents had been erected on the village green. The boys first stopped in front of the smaller of the two, and we listened to a carnival barker praise the show, while the Gypsy girls dispersed. A man in a vaguely military uniform relentlessly beat a drum while a buxom, fair-skinned, red-haired woman, scantily clad, strutted up and down provocatively. The barker yelled through a megaphone and introduced, one by one, the "invincible" wrestlers of the house, to be challenged "in fair and equal combat." The wrestlers wore gaudy trunks and high laced black leather boots. They were a dissipated, arrogant lot with vacant stares. Some appeared punch-drunk. Several hard-faced farmhands who had been drinking accepted the challenge. With jaunty bravado each one picked an opponent from the lineup. A thin but mean-looking professional wrestler bared his teeth and was answered with jeers from the crowd. The drum beat more loudly and the red-haired woman continued to strut. The barker's words were lost in the din as the spectators paid for their tickets and jostled inside the tent. There was an air of cheap, artificially created hostility. One of the farmhands stripped to the waist, kicked off his wooden clogs and clumsily climbed to the ring, pulling himself up by the ropes, which sagged under his weight. He was heavyset, but appeared dazed by the harsh white light of the hissing acetylene gas reflector. His movements were unsteady and a little slow; he had been drinking. The crowd rooted for him, encouraging him to "kill" his opponent, the stranger. The professional, who was smaller and lighter than the farmland, manhandled him and made him grimace in pain. The next would-be wrestler jumped into the ring from the crowd to avenge his humiliated comrade, but hardly fared any better. The peasant boys had brute strength but lacked the training, stamina, agility and cunning of their seasoned opponents. With each fight the tension grew. The crowd of farmers, in a rage, verbally vented their hostility. The few female spectators had faces distorted by frenzy and lust and were screaming imprecations and obscenities. Violence begat violence. I felt the same repulsive surge of madness in me, but Putzina, Kore and Zurka, one of Tshukurka's sons, were laughing. To them this was a wonderful sight: Gaje at each other's throats. The show was brief and the crowd left angered, frustrated and cursing the outsiders: the *barakkenvolk,* as they disparagingly called them. This was the very name that Kore and I had only recently been called. By the time they reached the outsized round tent, where the dancing was, most of them had forgotten. Purged of their pent-up anger and frustration, they were ready for more action. A barrel organ provided the popular but mechanical music; the sawdust made patterns on the uneven wooden floor; it was dark inside. At the entrance each man was marked on the inside of the wrist with a rubber stamp as proof that he had paid the admission price. The women were graciously admitted free, since actually if unwittingly they provided the attraction to the place. We clung together, submerged and unnoticed by the fun-seeking Gaje. Surrounded by the boisterous crowd, I was seized without reason by my recurring sudden sadness. A few times we ran into the Gypsy girls. They were mostly dancing together, refusing the invitations of interested males. Many of the local girls also danced together. The men were content to watch, commenting aloud, jokingly or appreciatively. Accepting a dance with a stranger had definite implications, so most girls danced with each other, or with their cousins or their fiancés.

Some of us made gallant remarks intended for the chubby peasant girls. They giggled and coyly put their blond heads together and giggled some more. The local boys glowered back at us. In turn several of the Gypsy boys took offense at the comments from the Gajo boys. It was all in fun, but there was an undercurrent of resentment on both sides. At one point there occurred a disturbance at the opposite side of the tent, and hearing the derogatory term *barakkenvolk,* Kore and I pushed our way through the dense, sweaty crowd. Before we reached the spot a scuffle had started. The men standing around yelled "Kill them," as they had done earlier in the evening at the wrestlers. But more beer had been consumed since, and the presence of many women made the young men more aggressive and eager to show their virility. The place was also darker, and the Gypsies were badly outnumbered and therefore no match for them. Someone yelled in Romani to make for the exit and to stand and fight together outside. We pushed and pushed, but the peasants around us either hindered our progress or slyly kicked at us as we squeezed by.

Once the antagonists were outside, the fight really began. Small knots of young farmers clung separately to the more or less isolated Gypsy boys, pummeling and kicking at them when and wherever they could. The Gypsy girls had managed to leave quietly, and this gave us, temporarily unhampered by concern about their safety, greater freedom to look after ourselves.

The fighting grew meaner, and some peasant boys took out vicious-looking, curved-bladed pruning knives, the infamous *lierenaar*. Only then did Kore yell out to us to scatter. The Gypsy boys lunged forward, broke through and ran in all directions with more of the local men joining in full pursuit. I heard them cry for blood as they yelled "arsonists" after us. The accusation had finally surfaced, and it gave a purpose to the vague, unreasoned hostility. Two or three very young Gypsy boys were overtaken and beaten to the ground.

Laetshi and Kore ran ahead of Putzina and me, followed closely by Milosh. Several other young ones lagged behind us. Putzina and I almost simultaneously darted across a paved road. A rumbling noise isolated him from me, a split second ahead of a dark hulking mass. I was thrown to one side of the road, flat on my face, but in the flash of the truck's headlights I saw Putzina lying in the middle of the road. I had the premonition, the instant but absolute knowledge, of his death, which an instant later I was already trying to fight off. Brakes screamed. A man jumped out of the driver's cab, ran and knelt by the Gypsy boy.

Several soldiers in fatigue uniforms jumped from the back of the truck. They had been on their way to the disaster area of the forest fire. A rapidly growing number of peasants gathered to watch. Among them there must have been not a few of our erstwhile pursuers. They formed an impenetrable wall of curious indifference. Some were sullen; others visibly looked for sensation and were relieved it was not one of theirs who had come to an abrupt end. The women piously pretended commiseration and crossed themselves. Backing away from them, I went toward the knot of kneeling soldiers and the few civilians bending over Putzina's body. Even in his death he was a haven for me: somebody, something, to cling to. The soldier who had been driving the truck stood aside, distraught, swearing and cursing under his breath. He groped for the consensus of the Gaje bystanders. The knot of people opened when I stepped toward them. From some aspects of my appearance and my state of shock they recognized my being related to him. Against all reason and common sense the young, blue-eyed soldier lifted the body, and after only the slightest hesitation he carried it, following me. Kore and Zurka fell in step. A procession of curious onlookers marched with us part of the way and then dropped back. The Gypsy girls and some of our boys, who had remained hidden in the dark but had seen what had happened, ran ahead, and as they reached the camp they shrieked and wailed. From around the fires or hastily getting up from under their eiderdowns, men and women came running to meet us. The soldiers halted, startled, perhaps suddenly frightened. Unlike the local peasants, they had been considerate, almost brotherly, and had behaved as humans toward us. Putzina's name was repeated and spread, as the Rom howled, wailed, tore at their hair, ripped their clothes. Keja shrieked as if she were about to lose her mind. She gnashed her teeth and had a mad expression in her eyes. The violence of their grief shook me out of my own frozen stupor and I was afraid of them and of their unsuspected vehemence. The collective sound of the frenzied weeping rose and fell like an angry sea. More and more Gypsies gathered. They talked aloud to themselves, at times doleful and tender, at others with unusual bitterness. In their excessive display of grief the Rom were oblivious of me, and I felt strangely isolated in the awareness of the loss of what I suddenly saw was my only real link to them.

I was cold, sweaty, trembling in terror, and my teeth chattered. I became afraid they might hold me responsible for Putzina's death. Had not Lyuba often said I would bring them bad luck? But I could not leave. I did not know where else to go even in my fear of them.

I became aware that somebody was slowly pushing through the throng, coming toward me. I froze with a terrible sense of inevitability. It was Lyuba—she who always had denounced my presence among the Rom. It was Lyuba, and for some mysterious reason I felt it could only have been she. With slow motions she kept coming toward me. The expression on her face was inscrutable, and her old eyes were dry. I felt the touch of her parched fingers on the back of my neck and shivered. She pulled me away slowly and I allowed her to lead me like a lamb about to be slaughtered. Unexpectedly she sagged to the ground in a huddled crouch, pulling me down with her among a group of disconsolate figures rocking themselves back and forth. She bent my head forward and onto her knee and she comforted me with a tenderness I never suspected she could possess. Her stiff fingers played with my long hair. Up to that particular moment the intensity of the Rom's grief had sobered my own distress and had turned me into an almost detached observer, but now I could no longer contain my sorrow and I lost my inhibitions. In being able to surrender, I no longer felt cursed by life and rejected by Putzina's people. I was fully one of them and I mourned passionately, sharing with them what only shortly before had appeared to me a collective madness. The night was endless but no one slept. The mourning and wailing were hypnotic. Glasses of brandy were passed around and old Lyuba made me drink, on an empty stomach, as the others did, and it dulled my senses. Close to Lyuba I drank and wept all night, while she talked endlessly or softly sang to herself. At intervals when I paid attention to what she was saying, I had the impression that she somehow confused the dead boy, Putzina, with me. She addressed me as Putzina. When she forced to my lips the brandy that was intended for her, she called me by his name. She shared with me—she, the venerable one, who never shared with anybody. Only her short-stemmed brass pipe she kept to herself that night, and this was as well.

Shortly after daybreak two police constables on bicycles came to the camp to proceed with the inquest. They were joined soon afterward by the doctor from a nearby town, who had been summoned to issue and sign the death certificate, an indispensable formality required for burial. The red-cheeked Catholic priest of the nearby village came with some of the local elders and the part-time undertaker to help arrange for the funeral. That day there was no food, nor was there any the following day: only brandy and hot strong black coffee. Weeping was constant and above it rose the frightened, protesting wail of hungry infants. For the next three days nobody washed or combed his hair. Several times Pulika came to bring Lyuba some brandy. He looked haggad and uncouth but he was more restrained in his sorrow than most of the others. Rupa remained by the fire that had been built at the feet of her dead son. Keja and Tshaya were with her. Kore came and stayed with me, and he, too, unexpectedly addressed me as Putzina. The sobbing and moaning, instead of letting up, increased as if the Rom were intoxicating themselves as much with their grief as they were with the combination of not sleeping, fasting and consuming abundant quantities of alcohol. I lived through these few days totally benumbed, lost to the realities of the world around me, as in a time of paralysis. Like the Rom I was identifying with, I submerged myself in grieving for the dead with extravagant abandon. I fasted, drank and wept, while all around us the Gaje came and went and busied themselves with the numerous practical aspects of death and burial. There was the inquest concerning the accident. The soldiers had left, and none of the Rom had made a record of their names or army matriculation numbers, the unit they belonged to or the registration number of the military truck. From among the Gaje no witnesses came forward. Putzina was dead. This was a reality to the Rom, but they failed to see what a report about it would change. They pretended to listen to the officials, wondering about this strange, obsessive cult of the written word. The representatives of the law were in a quandary about how to report the circumstances of the accidental death of a young stranger passing through. They became impatient at what they probably misconstrued as the lack of consistency of the Gypsies, who wept and sobbed and wailed throughout the interrogation, appeared totally devoid of respect for the authority of the land, and failed to show the cowering restraint the agents were used to. The result was that the officials became suspicious of the Gypsies' strange behavior, and began to suspect them of actually having murdered one of their own. In this way rumors started and grew and were eagerly spread. An answer had miraculously been found to fill the blank in the police file. The suspect would never be discovered, the case never brought to court; but it would be remembered that the culprit had been a Gypsy.

The morning of the funeral the local brass band showed up at the camp, ahead of the arrival of the village priest and some curious police and civil dignitaries. The open coffin was carried away and the band incongruously played popular tunes of the period. Then came the priest in full vestment and the choirboys, followed by a horde of haggard Gypsies, unwashed, uncombed, with wrinkled clothes. As they left the camp the wailing increased. Some of the Gypsies walked in an unusual and special formation which they called "crosslike." One man walked ahead followed by another marching in single file. They were followed by one or two rows of four or five people walking abreast. After them again there followed a single file, which actually made the formation in which they proceeded look like a cross. They clung to one another, half supporting the others and in turn half supported by them. They stumbled and walked in a daze. All along the way stood entire farm families watching the—to them—strange spectacle of grief. I was carried along by the multitude and I was somewhat baffled myself by the whole procedure, which was the culmination of days of mourning utterly distinct from the Gypsies' behavior under any other circumstances I had witnessed before. They gave themselves totally to sorrow. They lived the moment, oblivious to all else, with a single-mindedness and intensity that disturbed the Western mind.

After the priest had said the prayers for the dead in Latin and a few brief words in Flemish, the Gypsies threw handfuls of money into the grave before it was closed and poured brandy and wine over it, to the surprise of the non-Gypsies present, who were shocked at seeing this pagan practice on Flemish Catholic holy ground.

The Rom dispersed in disorderly fashion. As they left they said, and made me say,"*Putzina, akana mukav tut le Devlesa*" (Putzina, I now leave you to God), and they walked away without ever looking back.

Much later Pulika elaborated on the habit the Rom had of pouring wine and brandy on their graves. He said he was aware that the Gaje derided this obviously pagan custom, scoffing at the Gypsies' supposed belief that this profited the dead in their journey onward. He said the liquor poured out to "honor" the dead, this offering of love made to them, was absorbed by the earth and left no trace, unlike the Gaje's more ostentatious custom of offering flowers, which in the final analysis gave as little pleasure to the departed.

The sedative effect of the alcohol diminished, and with it part of my identification with the Rom seemed to lessen. Back at the camp there was a meal prepared for those Rom who were not mourning Putzina as an immediate relative. We close ones ate bread and drank water. Early the following day the camp broke up and we scattered once again in all directions. Pulika decided to travel alone with Yojo's family for some time. The Rom observed very strict rules of mourning and he did not want to impose these on others because of our presence. Rupa, Keja and Tshaya did not comb their hair, nor did Pulika and Yojo shave for weeks. A young girl from another family moved in with us to cook and wash and clean up, as no woman from our family was allowed to do this. There was no drinking or singing, no rejoicing of any sort, no dressing up. Pulika's gold watch, a rare object in any Gypsy camp and one of which he was rightly proud, had been stopped at the very hour of death and remained stopped for a long time after. At the same time all vessels containing water had been poured out, and what pieces of mirror we had were covered with cloth.

Each time one of us thought of Putzina or was reminded of him by anything that he had particularly liked, we would say a silent prayer like *"Te avel angle tute"* (May this be before you) as we poured out some of the liquid we were drinking or let fall to the ground some of the food we were eating, as a form of offering to him. His few personal belongings had been burned. The Gypsies did not believe in keeping anything that had in any way been connected with a deceased person.

At the time the coffin had been ordered from the village carpenter, the Rom had taken the measure for it with a length of "Romany string." This was a narrow piece of cloth, roughly one to one and a half inches wide, ripped lengthwise from a piece of flowery cotton and left unhemmed. The Rom had insisted on taking the measure in their own traditional way, over the protest of the carpenter who had brought his own tape measure in centimeters. Afterward the long, homemade ribbon was cut into short pieces three to six inches long. Each was tied individually in a simple knot. These were possessed of great magical potency and were given to close relatives of the deceased. These bits of magical ribbon were called *mulengi dori,* or dead man's string. I was carefully instructed about their unique property and advised to carry mine on my person at all times, but to save it as a last resort, since it could be used only once. After having been used, it should be disposed of by being thrown into flowing water at the first possible occasion. It was only to be used against the Gaje. When in danger of being arrested by the police or seriously threatened in any other way, the Rom untied the knot of their *mulengi dori,* calling the name of the dead person it had belonged to, saying, "Sweet dead one, let the noose about to be tied around my neck be undone." If you could remember a specific situation from which the dead one addressed had successfully extricated himself, it was considered useful to remind him of the incident.

I learned from Laetshi that there also was another technique in which the *dori* could be used to outwit the Gaje, but it was less in favor among Putzina's people. It consisted on the contrary of *tying* the knot, at the critical moment, and saying, "Dear *mulo,* as I tie this knot, so let their big mouths be bound too." It was supposed to help avoid betrayal or recognition in a police lineup from which one culprit was to be singled out.

For a short period after these happenings the story about Putzina and me spread among the Rom. He was referred to as Putzina *o mulo* or "the dead one," whereas I was called Putzina *o juvindo,* "the live one," and it was understood that I had been adopted. Eventually the Rom became used to my newly acquired name, identity, presence and appearance, and for my status as Pulika's son no further formalities were required.

There never was a more specific initiation ceremony into the world of the Rom, and true to the essence of the Gypsies, no legal adoption was necessary. Pulika let it be known among all his people that from now on he claimed full responsibility for me.

The mystical mixing of blood from incisions made under propitious circumstances was to be left to the imaginations hungry for idle sensation and far removed from real life; for as a Romani saying reminds us, "There are lies more believable than truth" (*Si khohaimo may patshivalo sar o tshatshimo*).

PART TWO

CHAPTER FIVE

My first two stays with the Rom stand out clearly in my memory as definite entities, as times of wonder and discovery. I also distinctly remember my first homecoming, my anxious, guilty anticipations, the shock of relief. Thereafter the alternating periods with the Rom and at my parents' home seem to fuse together. I lived two separate but intertwined lives, true and intense in each but somehow unconnected. After each winter-long separation from them, it was not always easy to pick up the trail of my Gypsy family. One particular year my impatience to join them made me start out too early in the season, before they had actually taken to the roads, and I searched for them in vain for days. I turned for assistance to some circus people and fairground attendants, but they only tried to dissuade me from continuing my search for the Gypsies and encouraged me to join them instead, possibly hoping to gain cheap—or, better still, unpaid—labor.

As I grew older and more experienced in the ways of the Rom, I learned to make long-distance telephone calls to Pulika's various points of contact, at horse fairs, at inns and such, which I patiently spied out from him during my summer stay and wrote down stealthily, to be treasured in anticipation during the long winter of separation. It sometimes happened that Pulika and his *kumpania* left the country and crossed many borders, which made joining them again a spy hunt, involving illegal border crossings. Looking back, I wonder at my persistent luck. This aspect of my life with the Rom, more than any other, seems, even to me today, a chain of improbabilities. These were only a prelude to the years of war that were to follow, and in which many of the Gypsies I had known

85

played unsung but active parts, both as heroes and as victims, for they too had their calvaries at Maidanek, at Sobibor, at Chelmno, at Treblinka Belzec, at Bergen-Belsen, at Dachau, at Buchenwald, at Moravska Ostrava.

One year, for the first time, I stayed with the Rom throughout the winter. Lying half awake in the cold stillness of the long nights in Pulika's huge wagon, I heard the snapping noise of the nails in the boards as they creaked under the effect of the severe frost. The windows had been covered up with boards, old overcoats and army blankets, straw or pieces of tar paper, but the wind blasted through cracks too many to fill. The dogs whimpered all night. The drinking water froze in the buckets, and washing in the morning became an ordeal. Hands chapped, lips cracked and bled. The men ceased to shave. The small children cried bitterly when they were put outside and chased away from the wagons near which they had wanted to relieve themselves. Clothes could not be washed. The air inside the wagons was thick and unbreathable, mixed with the coal fumes from the red-hot stove, from which small children had to be kept away. During the winter months not enough dead wood could be gathered outside to keep the fires going all day and part of the night, so the Rom were forced to buy, beg or steal coal.

Often the Rom took off the lid covering a stove to check the too strong draft of the short stovepipe protruding from the roof. They also did this to light the wagon when candles ran out. I remember a makeshift contraption, not unlike an oil lamp in principle, made of a narrow piece of cotton torn from a woman's apron or overskirt, soaked in lard, burning in half a hollowed-out shriveled potato or sugar beet. The Rom had kerosene lamps, but because they considered these dangerous they were used only outside.

Then one day spring was in the air and its mysterious impact could be felt throughout the Gypsy encampment. The thirty-five wagons had been immobilized far too long on this loathsome spot. The wheels had sunk deep in the slimy mud, and the garbage, which was simply thrown out the side windows of the wagons and left unburied, had been frozen solid for months and was now smelling of putrescence. The men put their backs to the wagons and with strenuous efforts lifted them out of the mud. Ashes, stones and rubble were shoveled under the wheels to prevent their sinking back. The women aired the bedding, spreading it out in the open over the wooden fence at the far end of our campsite. The under-carriages were checked, axles greased, and the friction brakes relined by nailing pieces of tire against them. Huge tarpaulins were spread out on the ground to be patched and repaired. They were used in the summer to make lean-tos under which we slept when it rained, or to provide shade when we ate and drank. Some tarpaulins belonged to young newlyweds or to poorer Gypsies, who did not yet possess real Romany wagons and temporarily lived in open peasant vans covered by tarpaulins on a wooden superstructure. Inside of these there was barely space for bedding, sleeping room for two or possibly an additional few small children, and the pig-iron potbellied stove. There were no windows and only a many-colored rag curtain as a door.

After the cold spell the Rom removed all the material that had covered the windows. This was burned on the first open-air fire of the new season, to the joy and awe of the very small children, who did not clearly remember having witnessed such a scene before. Pulika and Tshukurka had been at the local tavern since early morning, making long-distance telephone calls to other groups on the verge of starting their spring wanderings. Up-to-date gossip was exchanged, information checked and passed on, warnings repeated, and good wishes for travel conveyed with earnest sincerity. Spring was in the air and we were excited. The Rom were leaving this garbage-littered place far behind. They would soon be on the road again where horizons changed from day to day, from hour to hour. They wondered aloud how they had ever been able to endure the dull monotony of sedentary existence.

For many months now the Rom had lived near the big city, where the women had told fortunes from door to door. The boys had roamed the taverns and mixed with the Gaje. They had often eaten outside the camp and the older people often wondered how they had been able to observe food rules and taboos in the circumstances. They had brought home strange stories, sayings and anecdotes from the Gajo world. Many had adopted distasteful mannerisms and Gaje superficialities.

Another winter I spent with the Rom, Pulika had managed to rent part of the courtyard of a rag and bones dealer on the outskirts of the city. Besides Pulika, Tshukurka, Yojo, old Bidshika and a few others, there were several covered wagons belonging to fairground people, who eagerly cultivated our friendship. Other Rom of our *kumpania* had rented enclosed camping space for their winter quarters. Huge double gates secluded our yard from the street. There was a water pump, which was usually frozen, and there was electricity available for a modest fee, of which no Rom ever availed himself. Down the street there was an inn kept by a man the Rom had befriended, where Pulika and the other men spent part of their day. There was a telephone, and contact could be maintained with the Rom stranded elsewhere.

Like the older Rom, I washed at the tavern and generally used the facilities as a convenient addition to our living quarters. Since the Gypsies were forced to live a stationary existence, which made them much easier to control, the police rarely came, unless specific complaints against them were received. I suspect that Pulika's mastery of the art of *baksheesh* may have played a role in the preferential treatment we received from the authorities. My fair skin and hair did not pass unnoticed by our immediate neighbors, but Pulika satisfied their initial curiosity by claiming I was his son, adding in a stage whisper that my mother was the most beautiful Swedish girl he had ever met.

Most of the Rom sold their horses during the winter, but Pulika insisted on holding on to his, not wanting to be stranded and dependent on the Gaje in case he urgently needed to depart, for whatever reason. Despite his genial, confident air and deliberate carelessness, to be on the alert was as instinctive to Pulika as breathing.

All trade activities of any sort were interrupted and the Rom were forced to live poorly on their very limited resources or to depend on the charity of others. They ate sauerkraut with rice and bacon, fried potatoes with bacon, red cabbage with apples and bacon. Rupa would bake *bokoli*, thick pan-cakes with small pieces of meat inside. Some very poor Gyp-sies went as far as eating eggs. This was a time when the Rom pawned part of their hoard of gold pieces, hopeful of being able to redeem them when the weather turned fair again and they could resume traveling and horse dealing.

It would be good to feel the wind blowing again, health-giving and purifying. It would be good to see varied land-scapes, trees, mountains, fields and meadows passing by and meet groups of relatives and friends at the crossroads or the wayside stopping places. The Rom would meet and rejoice and part again before having exhausted friendship's resources, before having satisfied their curiosity, as full of joy and exuberance as on the day they met, and they knew as they parted that they would meet again, for in Romani it was said that "mountains do not meet but men do."

The sun was stinging and the mud-covered earth was drying up into a dullish gray, dusty surface with manifold cracks. What had been our winter quarters was now a deserted wasteland, deeply scarred by wheel tracks, with ugly heaps of refuse and ashes from the winter fires. It was all that was left to tell of the Rom's sojourn. The wide-open road was ahead of us. The Rom dreamed again of fresh green pastures and clover fields for their horses, and barley and oats. They longed for cool clear water at mountain sources and the smell of burning wood that added savor to the roast meats and a new gusto to wine. Physical exercise, the sound of horses' hoofs, the rattling of wagon wheels, the jingling of the trace chains, and sun and air would obliterate the weariness and inactivity of winter. For a few days they took pleasure in traveling long distances for the sheer joy of rolling along and feeling the wagon sway. They were drunk with travel, wind and air.

The men talked little these days. The women and unmar-ried girls were silent too, exhausted by the various camp chores newly found. They had grown lazy and fat during the idle winter months and were unused to hard work. The very old people found renewed vitality. They sat erect in the corners of their wagons, watching the road ahead with intense eyes. The children shrieked with excitement.

On the third day, toward noon, we met a large group of wagons at a junction in the dirt track we were following. Without stopping we merged into a single line, forcing the horses into a trot to bypass the wagon of the group ahead of us, in a loud and joking mood. When night fell there were over fifty fires burning at the overnight encampment. Smoke mingled with the smell of roasting meat. We wandered about the camp, testing the newcomers' hospitality, and we made it a point of honor to find out and remember the names of the Rom at whose fires we ate and drank and with whose dependents we talked. It was a night of rejoicing and festivities on a lavish scale.

These ceremonial celebrations, with lavish food and libations, followed by dances and songs to "honor" special guests, were called *patshiva*, and most Gypsies throughout the world lived from *patshiv* to *patshiv*. These occurred at irregular intervals and were impossible to predict, as they depended solely on the favorable opportunities of casual encounters at perpetual but providential crossroads; in this sense the *patshiv* is the true Romany celebration. Besides these there were a limited number of feasts with a set date, which included Christmas, Easter and All Souls or Halloween, the true meaning of which totally escaped the Rom. They observed these partly in conformity with local custom and partly because these feasts conveniently coincided with midwinter and with spring—the one the beginning of the season of travel, the other a day as good as any to consecrate to the dead of the tribe. In areas where the Gajo religion was Russian Orthodox the Gypsies often celebrated St. George's Day, or *Slava*.

On the present occasion Tshukurka was giving a *patshiv* in honor of three brothers, sons of Troka of Old, with whom we were sharing the same campsite, and with whom—from the way things looked—we might be traveling for a while. The Trokeshti, as they were called after their father, were distant relatives of Tshukurka's wife, white-haired Mimi, who was a very "important" woman. "Important" was the euphemism used in Romani to describe a beloved person's corpulence.

Around the fires the men talked and the drinking was in true Gypsy tradition, joyous, gracious and unrestricted as the night wore on. Suddenly, or so it seemed to me at that time, one of Tshukurka's sons, Zurka, started singing a song to toast the Trokeshti men. His voice was strong and full and he sang with deep emotion. Tshukurka listened, tears in his half-closed eyes, nodding his head in silent approval; then he too, softly at first, joined in the singing. It was an ancient song which Troka himself had composed and sung long ago in honor of Tshukurka in his youth. Now they were singing it back to Troka's sons and descendants to show them how much alive he had remained in Tshukurka's memory during the years of separation and of travel and, through the medium of song, in the memory of his children and grandchildren alike, but it also served to underline how close their ties had been.

Tshukurka opened his eyes just long enough to single out one of his young daughters in the surrounding crowd and beckon her to come to him. She was dark-skinned and very young. She joined him in singing, in accompaniment, in a high metallic voice, which although shrill was deeply moving. She seemed remote as she sang; her eyes were closed and she looked as if in a trance. When the song ended after many couplets, Tshukurka sank back leaning heavily on his sons, as if exhausted by the emotion of the evocation, shaking his head slowly in a gesture full of meaning but impossible to translate. The Trokeshti men crowded near him, thanking him with almost exaggerated humbleness for the resuscitation of the memory of their long-deceased, much-respected sire. Everybody was hushed and for a lingering moment still under the impact of the *patshivaki djili* or *patshiv* song, as if time had stood still. Then the Rom hastened to regain the normal rhythm. Zurka's brother stepped inside the open circle, slightly away from where his father stood in the middle of a knot of older men, and with a slightly forced gait he started humming a Gypsy dance tune. The joyful melody gradually grew in vigor, and as the singing sounded more self-assured other young men joined in the hand clapping and in the singing. They beat out the rhythm with their feet until one of them grew more restless than the others, leaped into the small open space and started dancing. He beat the ground with angry-sounding steps, preserving a strangely contradictory and nonchalant facial expresssion, with a touch of mocking irony in the eyes. His arms and torso moved in slow undulating gestures. The improvised words of the song were full of mirth and humor. The stamping of the feet grew louder and gradually more vigorous. A second dancer joined the first in frenzied motion. The onlookers were in a happy mood. They encouraged the dancers with rhythmic hand clapping, shouts and staccato bursts of whistling. A young man of the Trokeshti group joined the dance circle. The other Trokeshti still stood around Tshukurka, old Mimi and Zurka. Here the reminiscent mood of the ancient song lingered on. The dance song had changed cadence and several young men had replaced the previous dancers. Women and children had gathered and stood in a close throng to watch the merrymaking. The young unmarried men led the singing and the dancing, eagerly taking turns at what they pretended was an earnest personal challenge. The older Rom eventually joined the circle, gently pushing their way through the crowd, beaming with good humor and joy. The happy radiance on their faces softened the impression of their intense, powerful personalities.

Presently the words of the songs reverted to themes of old times. The young men left the dance floor and approached the older Rom with merry faces and made a request, put humbly but jestingly and with emphasized politeness. The older men shook their heads and refused the extended invitation to demonstrate some old-time steps, intricate but full of vigor and zest. The boys insisted.

Kalia, with mock reluctance, was the first Rom to step forward. He executed an unenthusiastic performance which was received with wild applause, laughter and derisive yells. His older brother Luluvo, a grandfather himself, then took up the singing of the next few dance stanzas. Kalia responded to it with another solo dance, the energy of which put to shame all our young men. He slapped his knees, clicking the toes and heels of his riding boots in succession on the ground. Another singer took over and hand clapping increased and kept up a wild tempo until Kalia stopped, swinging his arms in a wide crosslike attitude as he ended his dance. Several men closed in around him to thank and congratulate him, while a few paces away the dancing was resumed. Several young girls were dancing now, and when they tired the newlywed brides replaced them. The dance circle grew in diameter until it lost its shape, becoming oblong, and one part broke off and formed another and independent unit. And so it went for hours.

Older women showed their granddaughters what they too were still capable of, with laughs and jokes and merriment. The Rom sat by Mimi's fire, where chunks of roast beef, chicken and suckling pig were served. Nearby stood a huge barrel of foaming beer, with a bicycle pump attachment to maintain the pressure. From every fireside, all over the camp, women sent specific dishes to Mimi and old Tshukurka's tent, where by now all married men of any importance had assembled. Mimi's many daughters-in-law were busy cooking, serving and sending out dishes with food to the women and children remaining by their own fireside, wagons or tents. Nobody should feel forgotten, neglected or left out on a day like this. A *patshiv* must convey good will to one and all, without exception; the most humble on such occasions would be treated as kings.

Hours passed, hours full of food and drink and joy, until every man, woman and child was satiated with food and tired of the wild merriment and dissipation of the day. The small children were sleepy and huddled close to their mothers as the women relaxed after their cooking and roasting; the men were telling stories about Romany life, its many joys and mishaps, its adventures and rewards. They told of the Rom they had met, eaten and drunk with, Rom who were fabulously wealthy, righteous and daring, and from whom they had parted one day at a fork in the road. They told of wondrous times, of *patshiva* and the singers of ancient epics, and they told also of new epics.

The older brother and spokesman of the Trokeshti begged permission for one of his young men to sing for us one such new song. With a loud-spoken "May God bless him, give him wisdom, vitality and courage," Pulika and Tshukurka and the other Rom showed their appreciation. The young man was called Betshi, son of Yoska, grandson of Yiswan and descendant of Troka. I knew him. Earlier in the day we and many others had matched our strength during challenging bouts between the boys and young men of both groups, which to us was an essential part of festivities of a joyous kind.

Betshi sang the "new song" or *djili nevi,* after having humbly acknowledged the good wishes of the elders of the Yojeshti group, by answering, "May the blessings of wisdom, vitality and courage you wished for me and mine be shared by us with you all, and may God be with us." The new song was powerfully beautiful. It told of the proud deeds of the Trokeshti's travels through seven nations. It sang of their way of life in its fullness, intensity and dignity. More good wishes and blessings followed the climactic end of the song when young Betshi added in a low, solemn voice, *"Patshiv tumenge Romale"* (This song was offered as a gift to worthy men). Pulika embraced him and offered him a silver beaker full of brandy. It was considered a signal honor for an unmarried youth to be invited to eat or drink by the older men. After a few more mock-solemn pleasantries, Tshukurka asked the Trokeshti present, addressing their chief, if this youngster had a wife and children of his own, though he knew all the time this was not the case. The negative answer gave him the opportunity to remark, half jokingly, half reprimandingly, that among Tshukurka's own people it would be the custom to start looking for a suitable bride for him. The Trokeshti answered diplomatically, but with that witty humility all well-bred and self-respecting Rom liked to display, that perhaps he was still too young. Pulika replied that to him he looked a man, worthy of the Trokeshti. And so it went, in mock-dignified exchange of praise on one side, and exaggerated display of humility on the other—which hardly disguised the natural pride in the honor and attention this young man was attracting. Pulika offered to help find him a worthy bride, and with this the "official" part of the evening ended. Around some fires the celebrations went on until early morning. Individual parties broke up and whole groups of guests wandered off to pay social calls on the father-in-law, or the brother, or the business partner of their host. The night was full of singing and music, and the later the hour the more earnest the moods of the Gypsies grew, and the more profound and significant the words of their songs.

I woke up very early the following morning. The moon was still high and full. In the distance a few fires were still burning and the chill night air carried the smell of burning wood. At the farthermost boundaries of the encampment an impressive troop of horses stood sleeping. Several hundred men, women and children were asleep in the open all around us. The hour before daybreak, with its diffuse mysterious light, had for me an ever-new enchantment. When the day finally dawned dozens of dogs began to bark and howl. The horses shifted their places and became restless and even panicky. Harsh voices shouted and swore at them. A dog yelped in pain while the others gave tongue even more wildly. A shot was fired in the air and a dozen mounted policemen stood outside the camp. It was very early, and for a while nobody seemed to react. Then a very old woman hurried forward, chasing the barking dogs away from the policemen with a stick and throwing stones at them. She spoke in a high-pitched voice and tried to appease the accursed *shangle*. They only shouted louder, but the vicious-looking dogs stood guard, barking dementedly, and this prevented the police, at least for the time being, from entering the camp or coming near the many reclining Gypsies, who naturally pretended not to notice anything at all and did not move. For a long time the shouting went on. The old woman understood very little of the local language, or at any rate pretended not to. I could hear her shouting back at them in Russian, in broken German, in Hungarian, in Greek, interspersed with Romani curses and insulting remarks. The dogs went on barking. Unable to gain access to the camp, the police eventually went away. Hours later when the men were awake and up, they came back. This time they were met by a group of husky Rom, headed by Pulika and Tshukurka, followed by growling wolfhounds. Pulika greeted them and, after having identified himself as "the King of the Gypsies," asked for a special interview with the commander of the nearest police station in order to obtain temporary permission to retain camp in this place. He did not allow himself to be interrupted by anyone. "This is the eve of a great religious feast among my people," he said, "the feast of the patron saint of all Gypsies," having recourse to typical but effective Romany mystification. Putting his hand in his pocket, he took out a handful of gold coins. With clever showmanship, he said that his people were wealthy, peaceful and honest, that all they wanted was permission to fulfill their religious obligation in peace. "We are not like some of those Gypsy bands who are dirty and steal and quarrel and fight and make a general nuisance of themselves. We are good and decent people," he declared, "and we are prepared to leave as many gold pieces —as security to prove our good will—as the honorable head of the police force may indicate." Other Rom displayed several more handfuls of gold coins, and a middle-aged man of the Trokeshti showed off a thick bundle of bank notes. The mounted police officers were almost convinced. They relaxed a little, talked about the weather and, with a touch of envy, asked about the distant countries we had visited in recent months, about the economic conditions we had found there and about the rumors of war. They admired our horses and made an effort to show us their understanding of horsemanship, creating an unexpected and sudden bond between us. When the mounted police departed, the entire camp suddenly became full of activity. Several dozen fires were lit in no time, and thin corkscrews of transparent, bluish smoke rose into the clear morning air.

Right after breakfast Pulika harnessed his stallion to our *taliga*, the two-wheeled light cart, and took several Rom to "his" nearby coffeehouse. Wherever Pulika and Tshukurka went, they left a trail of inns, taverns, teahouses and coffeehouses whose owners they had befriended and where they were forever after welcome. They spent lavishly, and they always brought along an entire band of followers. When Pulika took over a place in this fashion it was under his "protection," and no Gypsy woman or girl would dare bother a customer with fortune-telling, begging, or tricks. Whatever was broken or damaged was paid for in full by Pulika, without questions or protest.

Later in the day the Trokeshti joined us. They did not have light *taligas* as we did, and therefore their men all traveled together in one single heavy covered wagon, put at the disposal of the group by its owner, a younger man, and his wife and children were allowed to come along for the ride though they were expected to remain in the background. Pulika bought beer by the barrel and had his people serve it. The owner of the place sat at his table and was served as a guest of the Rom. Afterward Rupa and Keja and some more girls joined us. They had walked from the camp to the nearest telephone, from which they called the local taxicab to take them to the inn in style. Gallantly one of the Rom offered Rupa a glass of brandy from the main table, but the young girls remained outside. After a few words with Pulika, Rupa left again by taxi to buy the necessary food for a festive Romany meal to be prepared by them at the inn. The Gajo owner knew Pulika's idiosyncrasy about food, and let him assume the management of the kitchen, for which he knew he would be rewarded in kingly fashion.

Our light *taliga* shuttled to and fro between the camp and the inn, fetching more guests, taking others back, and carrying food and drinks to those who had stayed at home. To the old people, the novelty of eating away from camp and in a place of the Gaje was highly unorthodox, despite the fact that the food was prepared by our women in strict observance of Rom traditions.

Meanwhile two police inspectors had come to the camp to see the Chief of the Gypsies. They found only women and children there. Several little boys volunteered to take them to Pulika and the other men. They were emboldened by the joyous mood about them, and only too happy to find a pretext for joining the feasting men. The representatives of the law were received kindly and offered food and drink, which, because they were on duty, they could not accept. As a perfect host Pulika nonetheless persuaded them to drink to his health. A crowd formed in the street and eagerly watched the Gypsies in this rare genial mood. The police informed us that we were being allowed to remain in this locality for a period of ten days, on condition that no complaints were received from any of the permanent inhabitants. The welcome news about the "ten-day truce" with the police spread rapidly to the camp, and soon women in twos and threes, carrying their half-naked children sideways on their broad haunches, invaded the nearby villages and market town in an orgy of peaceful shopping. The suspicion of the Gaje was soon allayed, and they too rejoiced in this unexpected but welcome increase in business. The women and girls bought dress material, dozens of yards at a time. They bought cooking pots, tallow candles, carpets. Some even bought chairs, besides quantities of spices and groceries. The Rom went so far as to make arrangements with nearby farmers for pasturing the horses, and *purchased* firewood. Under the conditions of the truce, the Rom gladly paid in ready cash for many a thing which at any other time they would have acquired by the "license of the road."

Days went by, days spent in endless *patshiva* and merry-making, in friendly intercourse with Gaje, including the police. The Gypsies behaved like "gentlemen." The full and multicolored long skirts, the bare feet and the jet-black hair of the Gypsy women, covered with gold coins, were becoming part of the everyday life of the place, and some people—inn-keepers, butchers and general storekeepers—were saddened at the thought that these freely spending nomadic guests would break camp and depart. Every night groups of boys and girls would come to the big camp on bicycles to stand at a distance, watching the activities around the fires, wondering about the strange people we Gypsies were. They dreamed, no doubt, restless dreams about our free and expansive way of life, which only too frequently they mistook for the sordid license that some of them might have longed for.

Soon the ten-day truce reached its end. The Chief of Police came to the camp to see Pulika and Tshukurka. They were by now on almost friendly terms. He had had a lifetime of more or less unpleasant experiences with nomadic bands of Gypsies, but seldom had he come across a Gypsy chief who either kept his word when making a pact or had sufficient authority to force the families under his leadership to adhere to its conditions. Once or twice the superior officer had come to visit at nighttime, in a private capacity, and had sat by the fire of either Tshukurka or Pulika and watched the dancing, singing and feasting, full of wonder and half-revealed sympathy.

Proudly Pulika heard the police officer praise the disciplined behavior of his tribe, their cleanliness and their honesty. He admired their horsemanship and their physical prowess. He wished he could speak as many languages as they did and adapt himself as easily to ever-changing circumstances. He said he envied them their extensive and adventurous travels and their unique gift of enjoying life to the full. In a gracious show of playful courtesy, Pulika replied that all he envied was the commandant's official status and the privileges attached to it, and that, if his wishes could be realized, he, Pulika, would grant all Gypsies freedom, peace and an abundance of the fruits of the earth.

Many hours later Pulika still sat by his fire, alone, silent, enjoying the good news he had not yet shared with anyone. Tomorrow we would move a dozen miles or so toward the big town, set up camp for a few days alongside the stream, then return here for another ten-day truce. Pulika smiled; he was satisfied with the present, he had trust in the unknown, and he had no anxiety for the future.

Early the following morning the camp was cleared, as one by one the heavy wagons were led away, dragged by our well-rested horses. The first wagons were settled down on the new site, beside the flowing river, before the last ones had left the old encampment. Spread out over the whole twelve-mile length of the winding road, heavy vans were traveling in single file. Our wagons and those of the Trokeshti traveled in random order, since we formed one happy homogeneous group, without rivalry or tension.

Toward the middle of the night bad weather set in. Jumping out of bed, we made sure that all fires were extinguished. All loose tarpaulins were fastened and solidly pegged to the ground, and we fetched the horses from their grazing by the river to the camp, where their individual owners tethered them at the backs of their wagons. A sudden sharp gust of wind frightened an old gray mare. She gave us much trouble before we managed to subdue her again. We braced the swaying wagons with long poles against the upcoming gale. The women hurriedly put inside the vans all small utensils usually left in the open, such as cooking pots, pails and basins, that might be carried away by the wind. We crawled back into bed under the big, soft, silk-covered eiderdowns, which the women had moved inside the wagons. It was crowded in our wagon, and all the doors and windows had been protectively closed, but through the short chimney, protruding from the roof, the wind was keening. The wagons shook and rocked as the horses pulled wildly at their halters tied at the rear of the vans, and through the thin wooden wall of his *vurdon* one man was shouting short rhythmic sentences to quiet his frightened animal and alternately cursing at it. In the distance sudden loud cries were heard, but soon the wind drowned all other sounds. The windows, doors and stovepipes rattled continuously. A tarpaulin which had torn loose flapped in rapid erratic cadence. Old newspapers and pieces of clothing, left outside or forgotten, were noisily carried away by the wind and occasionally thudded against a tent or wagon wheel. Dogs moaned and dashed about seeking better protection. At last the wind dropped and a sudden invasion of empty silence contrasted with the noises of the storm. The hushed lull seemed more disquieting than the blasts of the gale. For a few moments I could hear the excited chatter and babble of the river and a distant peal of church bells telling the time of night. A baby was crying not far away when once again everything was blotted out by the deafening drumming of a cloudburst on the wagon roof, not more than a few feet from where we lay in bed listening and wondering. I lay on my back and gradually felt the tension leave the nerves, sinews and muscles of my body as I finally yielded to the hypnotic rhythm of the streaming rains outside. The next morning we lit a fire in the stove instead of out in the open, for the whole campsite was mud-covered and swampy. Most Rom slept late and little enthusiasm was displayed for the new day.

The storm had markedly cooled the temperature. We washed ourselves on the wide footboard at the front of the wagon without even climbing down and dashed back inside to enjoy the comfort of strong, black and very sweet coffee. Several boys from another family came running through the mud. They climbed into our wagon, and after politely greeting the older people they accepted the hot coffee offered them. They brought news about other people in the camp and the damage done during the night. We accompanied them and went to take care of the horses. We rubbed and brushed them vigorously and raced them for a while, to warm them up after the cold wet night in the open. The earth was soggy and smelled strongly. Soon the ground fog lifted and the sun came through and the sky cleared. Some women left the camp, going far down the river to wash clothes, while in one corner of the camp young children were challenging one another to a dancing contest.

Several days passed peacefully in active preparation for the forthcoming annual horse fair in the district capital. Everybody refrained from doing whatever mischief might, in other circumstances, have forced the *kumpania* to take hasty flight. The horses had to have plenty of rest. They had been given a dose of salt to heighten their hunger and their thirst. The grazing was good where we were, and they were currycombed and groomed with more vigor than usual; their hoofs were polished and a few were reshod for the occasion. The Rom spent all day in the pastures, discussing their horses with one another, estimating the prices they could obtain for them. They instructed the young boys, showing them how to bring out the horses' good points, and how to make their defects less apparent. If a horse was to be bought by the Rom from a Gajo, the boys were shown how to minimize his otherwise obvious good qualities by running him however slightly out of step, by holding his head a trifle too low for comfort, and by many other tricks of the horse trade. Only the better horses were taken to the yearly fair, for the Rom often returned year after year, and had reputations to maintain among friendly traders.

Pulika possessed a team of powerful so-called "Belgian" plow horses, which were harnessed to pull the wagon, and one frisky gray thoroughbred stallion, which was attached to the back of the wagon and gave us much trouble. As we roamed the countryside, Pulika had traded our good horses for lesser ones. The difference in value was paid in cash by the buyer. Pulika was willing at all times to barter our animals for others, as if indulging in a taste for gambling. In this manner we successively acquired a collection of horses representing an encyclopedia of equine defects. Some horses were simply refractory and considered incorrigible by their previous owners, who were only too happy to get rid of them. Others had been ill-treated and abused; some were poorly trained and skittish; some had festering sores from wearing badly adjusted harnesses; a few were short-breathed, but all were incapable of heavy farm work when Pulika bought them. Mostly they needed only prolonged rest, adequate feeding and understanding treatment. Not infrequently Pulika invested in five or six such horses. He would spend entire days in the pastures, talking to them in a low, hypnotic, grave voice. He moved slowly so as not to frighten them and they observed him with curious eyes. He bled his horses or forced purgatives down their throats, performed worming operations. He never failed to rejuvenate them.

In due time these horses were sold again in locations far enough from their places of origin so that their case histories were unknown. Pulika's knowledge of horses was equal to his understanding of men.

The day of the horse fair we young ones got up before dawn. We braided the horses' shiny manes and tails, tied them with flame-red ribbons and set out before breakfast to take the herd to town. I went with Kore and Nanosh and Zurka, the son of Tshukurka, and Yayal, and several other boys, riding bareback, surrounded by fast-trotting, nervous, rearing, kicking horses, enveloped by a cloud of dust. For hours while the sun was climbing the skies we rode like this toward the city, drowned in the sounds of the pounding hoofs and the quick short crack of whips, the whinnying of the horses and the high-pitched yells of the boys urging them on. The sweat of the horses smelled strong and the sun grew hot. The wild ride and the continuous noise and the feel of the broad muscular flanks yielding to the nervous pressure of my knees and heels gave me an intoxicating feeling of power. The older men and the few women who would follow us later to the fair would catch up with us by taxicab. We made good speed and it was still early as we reached the fairgrounds, which looked like a peaceful sea of slightly moving tethered horses, tied to long ropes, fastened between sturdy metal poles. The official state veterinarians in their long white coats smelled of strong disinfectant. They inspected all arriving horses, and marked the approved ones on the rump with a white stamp.

The Rom, as a rule, met at one specific inn, which—strangely enough—was kept by a retired police officer. His inn had become a meeting place, to which Gypsies had their mail sent from all over Europe. In free moments he always volunteered to read these letters for them. For the price of a few glasses of beer he was willing to write the replies, since most nomadic Gypsies were illiterate. At the time of the horse fair many long-distance telephone calls were made for the Rom at this inn. It was Bidshika who ordered the first round of the day. It was before ten A.M. and there were already twenty-five to thirty Rom standing around. They held their long horsewhips in one hand, and heavy walking sticks with curved crooks hung from their left elbows. Thirty bottles of heavy dark beer were opened. To start his day well Kalia ordered another thirty without waiting for the first ones to be emptied. At the horse fair the three brothers—Luluvo, Bidshika and Kalia—were important people; they were the sons of old man Putzi the Dead One.

Business was brisk, with vehement arguments about prices and quality, clever sales talk and loud bidding, emphasized by noisily slapping the upturned palm of the hand, extended by the opposite party, who in turn slapped the hand of the bidder in the same fashion, giving him his counter bid. Boys and young men fetched the horses under consideration, and trotted them up and down to show off their points. The bidding was done at the inn or on its doorstep. When a deal was concluded the boy who had lent his services was given a commission. A very old Gajo wandered round carrying an enormous bunch of whips which he tried to sell. A man and a gray-haired rough-looking woman sat in a cart, offering for sale secondhand harness, bridles and saddles, as well as currycombs and special horse blankets.

By the time I drifted back to our inn headquarters, more than one hundred Rom had gathered there. They had come from all over the country to keep this date. There were a great

many Gypsies who had recently come from Italy to seek out
their relatives. They hardly spoke the local language, which
handicapped them in their business; and their horses looked
tired and badly kept.

The men from our *kumpania* sat with their Gaje horse-
trader guests around long tables, next to the large window
overlooking the stone-paved plaza where the horses stood.
Each new round of drinks added a green bottle of dark beer to
the already impressive number of empty ones, which, according to tradition, were left on the table next to each guest. This
was a much appreciated gesture of courtesy extended by the
owner of the inn toward the entire membership of Pulika's and
Tshukurka's groups, since such a large number of empty
bottles could become dangerous weapons in case of a brawl.
This mark of trust in the Rom's responsible behavior has never
once been broken.

Toward two o'clock in the afternoon trading slowed down.
The women of our *kumpania* brought food which they heaped
up on the clean-scrubbed wooden tables. There were cold
broiled chickens, pork chops, various cheeses, slices of raw
onion, hot peppers, fresh young cucumbers and stacks of
bread. The house provided salt, pepper, vinegar and quantities
of paper napkins. Before we left, Pulika made sure all bills
had been paid or credits approved. The newly bought horses
and the unsold ones were taken back to the camp, but I
managed to stay on with Pulika, Rupa and Keja, while another boy took my place for the long ride back.

At the horse fair the Rom were in their element and most of
them were known and respected by the other traders. In the
city, however, they moved about in compact, noisy groups. It
was still early in the afternoon, but they had been drinking
abundantly and were now in an expansive and festive mood.
For most of them horse trading had been profitable, but in any
case it was an important annual event, which could only end
in loud celebrations.

Moving with brisk self-assurance among the city dwellers,
the wild-eyed and long-haired Rom stood out strangely. The
Gaje would stand still to look at them with perplexed expressions. These were the kind of Gaje Pulika characterized as

"lying all their lives on one side." For a short moment I saw the Gypsies again through Gajo eyes: the women in deep-colored dresses, hung with a profusion of gold pieces, their big expressive eyes and strong white teeth standing out against their dark skin, the blue-black hair in long braids, the full, ankle-length skirts and the bare feet. The men were sturdy, a trifle heavyset, their eyes eager and alert. Some wore riding boots, some wore shoes, without socks, a few were barefoot, carrying their shoes in their hands. They spoke too loudly and, to the outsider at least, always appeared angry and intense. Without apparent warning the entire group would veer to one side of the wide, tree-shaded avenue to take over an entire sidewalk cafe terrace, before any of the waiters or the patrons had had a chance to object to their patronage. Once seated in large numbers, they were impossible to eject without creating a major disturbance. After the first flurry of apprehension everything settled down again. If they were treated correctly there were no incidents; and if not, pandemonium broke loose and the Gypsies were certainly not the ones to be most sorry about it—they saw to that.

Pulika, Rupa, Tshukurka, Luluvo and a few others remained at the terrace, consuming endless *café-filtre,* while we visited the big, elegant shops and roamed more or less aimlessly through the business district. Keja and the other young women bought dress materials in quantities that bewildered the salesgirls, as well as printed silks to cover eiderdowns, while the men stood outside philosophizing.

Yayal, Kore, Zurka and I trailed off to look for an old Jewish tailor we had heard about from the other Rom, whose dark, narrow store we finally located somewhere between the red-light district and the railroad station. We found him sitting cross-legged, on top of the counter of his shop. His beard was an unlikely reddish blond, his wizened eyes had a patient, pained expression, his face was pale. A yellow tape measure hung over his stooped, narrow shoulders, reminiscent of a prayer shawl. He wore a black yarmulke, and wisps of curly hair extended from behind his ears where he had pushed back his sidelocks. A glass of steaming tea stood among the shears, pincushion, various cuttings and basted garments. The place smelled of new suiting material, with an aftertaste of naphthalene. Busying himself without even lifting his eyes, he let us look at piles of samples by ourselves, as the skilled angler plays out line. When he did look up it was as the knowing arbiter of fashion and taste. And I have to admit that the choice he made for us at the time was in fair accord with our wild appearance.

Zurka acted as our spokesman, and as such he insisted on extra-wide trousers, flaring out slightly at the bottom. He wanted the wide vent in the back of the jacket that gives one more freedom in making extravagant gestures, and which ended in some form of ornamental stitching at the height of the shoulder blades, after the latest fashion of the Balkans. I thought I detected an amused glint in the melancholy eyes of our demure but quietly authoritative tailor. We were asked to leave so substantial a deposit that I was sure it amounted to very nearly the total price. The money earned at the fair burned holes in our pockets, and the man knew we would come back to fetch the suits with none left. He could not easily have disposed of our rather special suits, and he knew he would have to let us have them, even if we refused to pay the balance of the price. All this was sound reasoning, stemming from long human experience. We paid without a murmur and departed elated. If the Rom remained in the neighborhood of the city we were to return within the next few days to see our tailor. Luckily for us the Rom of our *kumpania* moved little in the next few days; instead of moving away from the city they circled around it, roughly within the same radius. This permitted us, against all our expectations, to make a short sally into town.

The four of us came strutting back to the encampment like young fighting cocks, restless, aggressive and boastful, because we felt uncomfortable and did not really know what reaction to expect. Kore and I had battered shoes, though Kore's had no laces; the others went barefoot. It was only now, when we were wearing our new suits, that we realized, with some dismay, that our shirts were old, torn and dirty. I was bareheaded, as usual, contrary to the accepted Gypsy custom. Nanosh was the only other one, besides myself, to dispense with hat or cap of any sort, even on the coldest winter day. The Rom, like the Orthodox Jews or the Moslems, wore hats at all times, even inside a tent, wagon or house. The Rom took their hats off only when they were very sick and even then nobody knew exactly why. They never tried to force Nanosh or me to change our habit.

At first nobody paid much attention to our new clothes, with the possible exception of a few very young girls, who had not yet reached puberty and perhaps wanted attention. We walked over to Pulika's fire, still tense, to receive a reception out of all proportion to our hopes. Pulika and Tshukurka jumped up; several other visiting Rom followed suit. We suddenly felt shy, our pride unexpectedly deflated. Everybody expressed admiration for our looks, for our choice of color and the quality of the material; they asked us the price we had paid and they praised the elegance and the cut. Slowly, we regained our vanity and pride, insensitive to the undertone of mockery. Pulika stood close to me, admiringly fingering the wide lapel of my new jacket with his right hand, his left hand holding on to Zurka's. In a flash he tore off my lapel and part of Zurka's collar, without apparent reason. It had not been done in anger. I stood thunderstruck. As if far, far away I heard him say, "May your clothes rip and wear out, but may you live on in good health and in fulfillment" (*Te khalion tai te shingerdjon tshe gada, hai tu te trais sastimasa tai voyasa*). As unexpected as had been their stormy demonstrations of admiration, as suddenly did their mood subside. The men returned to the fireside without any further hooting, taunting or mocking. The incident was never mentioned again, and it might never have happened, except for my torn lapel, which I proudly wore as a badge of my Rom-ness. Needless to say, the lapel was never sewn back on again.

When a Rom acquired a new suit he wore it every day, in all weather, under all circumstances, for work around the horses, for leisure and for the most festive occasions, until it fell to pieces or was replaced by a new one. The old one was passed on or simply thrown away. No Rom in his right mind would have cared to own an additional suit. The Rom had no conception of distinctive wear for special occasions.

CHAPTER SIX

Anumber of weeks had passed without a sign of life from Yokka, the son of Tshukurka, who was a member of our *kumpania*. We had not come across his wagon at roadside or wasteland camping grounds. We had not heard from him. Nobody mentioned his name, and it seemed I was the only one to worry about him, until it dawned on me that his young wife Vadoma had been great with child and that the time of birth might be near. In this case, they would travel away from the main group, because by Gypsy custom Vadoma would be *marhime,* or impure, during this period. Later I found out that they had closely followed our caravan but remained out of our sight, while the women of our group unobtrusively kept in touch with them, helping Vadoma with her daily chores, cooking for her and for her husband and, when the time came, assisting her in giving birth. In our camp not a word was ever said about this until one humid dusk we arrived at a camping ground to find Yokka's wagon already there waiting for us. It was a small stump-filled clearing at the edge of the forest, and countless crickets sang out. The greetings were mock-demonstrative and very loud but solemn all the same. The young girls ran to the wagon and silently disappeared inside. Yokka poured drinks for the men of the *kumpania* he was openly joining again. They remained standing and waited their turn as only a single goblet was available. Yokka explained that the drinks were offered by *O Rom O Nevo,* the "New Man," his son. This was the first time the baby had been mentioned, and to his health they drank. Boisterously they all toasted his admission into the horde, as if they were welcoming a newly arrived adult guest. The Lowara drank most of the night huddled around the fire as each Rom in turn offered a toast, wishing "to become better acquainted with our new kinsman." It was a night of light-hearted banter mingled with mock-ceremonious homage. It started drizzling, and throughout the rest of that night trains whistled frantically in the distance.

The police did not bother us and we stayed for a while at the clearing. A few days later as we passed through the nearby village, the long line of wagons slowed to a halt, after what seemed like some hesitation and stalling. I followed Pulika to the office of the Registrar of Births. It took some time before he could be located, as the job was obviously a part-time one, in view of the size of the locality. Pulika and I were joined by Big Sidi, Luluvo's wife, by our Keja and by another woman called Putsha. A bunch of uninvolved young Gypsies trailed behind us like a kite's tail, as always. The date of the newborn baby's birth was officially registered as the day before. How many days old he was by now seemed immaterial to the Rom. Pulika declared the mother to be Putsha, who was present, while the registrar stared in disbelief: Putsha looked well past childbearing age. To my knowledge she was in no way, even distantly, related to the child. Pulika sensed my surprise and grunted to me in a stage whisper in Romani, "Of course we are only fooling the Gaje"—which he considered a perfectly satisfactory explanation. There was nothing else the official could do but register the birth as declared, in the absence of other witnesses, accepting on paper what appeared improbable even to him. Had my sense of suspicion been better developed, and had I been more critically aware of cultural differences, I should have realized that Vadoma's motherhood would have made her a juvenile delinquent by the standards of the Gaje—she must have been twelve or thirteen. It would have caused a scandal, possibly a trial leading to years of "corrective" treatment in a reformatory for wayward girls. Because the mother of the baby was a minor and because the Rom married only in accordance with Gypsy law, no civil marriage contract was recorded; the child would be considered illegitimate by the authorities, and risked being taken away from the Gypsies to be brought up as a ward of the state.

One year or so later Vadoma most probably would become a mother again. The child could still not be registered as hers, because of her age. It was therefore not unusual among the Lowara that the first two, three or even four children of a young married couple were officially recorded as born to other parents. When, because of chance circumstances of the road, it happened that the young couple was not traveling with the same family who had volunteered to "adopt" their first child, another couple of legal age would perform the same service and register the child as theirs. The result was that not only were the first few children of most "normal" Lowara marriages not acknowledged as theirs legally, but each single one might be listed as belonging to a different family and carry a different surname. Only they themselves knew they were brothers and sisters. In this way and quite unwittingly the Rom made lies of the written records of Gajo society.

I remember one case which turned out badly. A Gypsy woman had been arrested for stealing chickens, and investigation into her record seemed to prove that the man she was living with was her brother. The charge of incest, made more serious by the fact that the couple had several children, caused quite a stir in the European press. In actual fact there was no basis for it. Their respective families had, at different times, registered them both as children of the same couple, to whom neither of them was even related. Incest was as much against the moral and religious code of the Rom as against that of the Gaje. Sometimes, because of complications in trying to arrange the immigration status of a young bride joining her husband's group, it was found more expedient to let her assume the identity of the groom's sister.

Many of the Rom I have known were considered stateless and possessed temporary identification papers. Theoretically they were allowed transit passage through a country only on their way to the next one. In each country they passed through, different arrangements had to be made in connection with their immigration status. In France there was the much hated and oppressive institution of the *Carnet Anthropométrique,* one of the most discriminatory permits of residence, requiring registration every twenty-four hours at the local police headquarters. Some Gypsies of the Kalderasha tribe traveled under so-called Nansen passports, which were issued to the White Russian emigrants after World War I. Others I have known managed to be "repatriated" from Turkey, supposedly as Greek nationals. Others claimed to have fled into France, *become* Spanish Republicans, and, after some delays, these were helped to adjust their legal status accordingly. After the Allied invasion of North Africa, some Gypsies applied for temporary French citizens' papers, as replacements for those presumably lost in wartime circumstances. Because France was at that time cut off from Algeria, Tunisia and Morocco, they claimed it was difficult for them to obtain duplicates of their birth certificates, but it was equally impossible for the authorities to investigate their declarations.

One group of Gypsies, known as the Baba Tshurkeshti, who lived in the Netherlands during World War II, somehow managed to obtain Guatemalan passports, which had been made available to Jewish refugees from Eastern Europe. This also was the time of "Good Samaritan" passports and visas from Brazil, Nicaragua and the Dominican Republic. In 1943–44 in Spain I met several families who, as Polish refugees, tried to go to England; or who went to Egypt as Yugoslavian subjects, with the help of consular agents. Others, claiming to be Greek refugees, landed at a camp at El Shatt in Palestine. For all of them, this was just another halting place on the road. There are Gypsy families who long ago, presumably more or less legally, emigrated to the United States. After a fairly prolonged stay, roaming their new homeland, they returned to Turkey and the Middle East. A whole new generation had legitimately become American-born United States citizens, only to return to the old country. Among the Gypsies they are still referred to as "Turki."

During and after World War II their freedom of movement increased as they joyfully joined the ranks of displaced persons and political refugees. It opened many new horizons for them. In the late 1950's several large bands went from Poland to East Germany, which fairly willingly let them "escape" into West Germany. There also appears to be a steady trickle of similar escapees through Yugoslavia into Italy. Others more recently came from the Far East as non-Asiatic political refugees. There are of course infinite variations on this theme, but I leave these as a challenge to the Gaje's imagination.

On the surface they changed and adapted as readily as their environments and circumstances changed. They did this spontaneously, but it helped them preserve their inner core unchanged. The Lowara always remained themselves, seemingly untouched, even at times when they were not consistent with the Gaje's image of them. The covered wagon the world associates with them as a matter of course was only used by them in some parts of Germany, the Low Countries, Scandinavia, the north of Italy and France. In all these places numerous non-Gypsies also lived in similar wagons. An interesting fact was that these "typical" Gypsy wagons were built by Gaje manufacturers for the Gypsies, down to the sculptured wood decoration that adorned them and the occasional choice of gaudy color. Various types of tents were used from the Transylvanian plains at the foot of the Carpathian Mountains to the Porte de Clignancourt and the Zone section of Paris. In many parts of the Balkans and Turkey the Gypsies traveled in peasant vans or in wagons with a tentlike superstructure as shelter. These were more adapted to the local road conditions or more practical in mountain country, and also less obvious along the roads in territory unfriendly to the Rom.

In their role of refugees, they abandoned or sold their wagons, and simply dragged along bulky parcels of feather beds, some pots, and the well-hidden hoard of gold pieces sewn into some dirty petticoats. Today in most parts of Western Europe and the United States they travel in large private cars, with a marked preference for the Mercedes Benz, the Opel and, on the American continent, the Cadillac.

The Rom were forever on the move. They often had no alternative but to cross borders by sheer stealth and cunning, in flagrant defiance of the Gaje's laws. When available, they bought the professional services of smugglers; when not, they used discreetly but skillfully dispensed bribes. In Romani this was called "to sweeten the man"; they also said, "Gold does not rust." Once the border was crossed, they quietly followed trails laid for them and joined a local group of Gypsies with whom they merged. These "fronted" for them and warned them of the dangers and peculiarities of the new host country. The local group had usually developed an understanding with the authorities, and was often in a position to help the newly arrived with so-called "open" identification papers, which the newcomers could fill in. An older Rom with grown sons and daughters had the privilege of keeping for himself the identification papers of those of his family who temporarily left the group or who had provided themselves with other and possibly better papers. In some rare instances, an influential go-between might obtain a special dispensation from "those in power," solving the need of the moment, temporarily "legalizing" an irregular situation. The most critical period was the time between the actual crossing and the first clash with the local police authorities. If they were prematurely discovered in a border zone they were promptly expelled, often to find their way back barred by immigration officers of the country they had left, so that they were helpless between neighboring countries. This happened to a large band of Tshurara in 1938, who came from Norway and were caught between France and Spain. They were forced to remain in no-man's-land for many weeks, at the price of inhuman hardships. I never found out how this case was finally resolved and only regret my ignorance. The difficulty inherent in an extradition was the understandable lack of cooperation of the Rom. They claimed, with the unself-conscious inconsequence that Gypsies resort to in emergency, not to know where they had come from. Suddenly they would lose the use of coherent speech, though still going through the motions of extreme cooperation. They babbled away endlessly, wearying the most enduring of investigators with their display of good will and their feigned stupidity.

Sometimes one Rom would volunteer to mediate. He was the "King." Pityingly, he "explained" everything, avoiding the contradictions in their declarations, dismissing any information detrimental to them as misrepresentation or misunderstanding. The "King" in such cases was always someone familiar with the country, whose status was above doubt, willing to play his game by ear, willing to risk all. With an air of injured innocence the King offered his services to help enforce the laws of the land upon his subjects, giving the impression that he was definitely on the side of the authorities. Quite frequently the authorities accepted this self-imposed office, though with many reservations on their part. In Romani it was said that "the marketplace knows no anger."

The representatives of the Gajo power structure were called *Ray Baro*, or Great Lords, the same term applied to judges. Depending on the particular country, these were delegated either by the Department of the Interior or of Justice, the *Sécurité Publique,* the *Deuxième Bureau des Nomades,* the Ministry for Minorities or some other special agency. If a Gypsy King was caught in flagrant lies—for example, when Gypsies who he claimed were permanent residents of the country and had always been his subjects were proved to have recently and illegally arrived from abroad—he changed his tactics, appealing to the authorities as one diplomat to another, expecting to be helped out of an embarrassing position. He would flatter and excite their sense of personal importance. If the *Ray Baro* proved implacable, the King was pushed aside by "rebellious" elements within his tribe, who thus eased him out of his dilemma. The Rom would then revert to "playing hedgehog," settling back to wait for whatever calamity was to come. Having exhausted all their tricks, they knew that only fatalism could help them through another crisis. It was not without intimate knowledge that they said, "Some shade is good for everyone."

There was a third category of leadership, namely that of the Gypsy Kings of hearsay. I advisedly use the word Kings in the plural, since among the Rom there were many Kings. The King was only an impressive figurehead with no real authority of any kind. His function, if any, was to act as a liaison between the local Gendarmerie and the *Kapo,* who was the real chief and actual technical adviser of the community. His position was not elective but rather self-chosen, inspired by petty motives of personal vanity and conceit contrary to the spirit of the Rom. To clarify what he meant Pulika asked me whether I had ever noticed, in the capitals of Europe, tall, hefty, imposing men strutting about in red, blue or bright green uniforms with gold braid, looking and behaving like army generals, who in fact were merely doormen at expensive hotels or cabarets. In our own *kumpania* there was a man called Yojo la Mimako Jamutro. As his name in Romani indicated, he was identified, strangely enough, as Mimi's son-in-law. It was customary to designate a young men, one who had not yet left a definite mark of his own, as the son of so-and so; otherwise the name of one's wife was added for identification. The Yojo under discussion had married into his bride's family instead, which was unusual if not actually considered somewhat of a dishonor. In view of this one would expect him to have been tagged with the name of his father-in-law, who was an important man, Tshukurka, Pulika's brother. Instead he was derisively identified as the son-in-law of the latter's wife, Mimi. This Yojo, namesake of Putzina's older brother, was tall, clean, good-looking, always wore shoes and was dressed with care and taste. He was considered as a pleasant nobody by the other Rom. Often I had heard Gypsies, when talking to the Gaje, refer to him as "the King of the Gypsies." At first I had dismissed this designation as just a nickname, later to discover that he was the King, as far as the outside world was concerned—or at least one of them, since at a later date I was to meet several more.

There was one such self-styled King who had a flair for publicity in the world of the Gaje, but otherwise had few followers. He liked to be known as Nicolas de Vaugirard, *Roi de Paris*. To us he was just plain Stevo la Gulumbako. Luluvo la Sidako was another King. He was kind, considerate, and a dreamer. In his youth he had spent many years in captivity, where he learned to read printed characters but never to write. Eventually he returned to his people a changed man. Consequently nobody held his need for importance in the eyes of the Gaje against him; at worst they pitied him for what jail and isolation from his people had done to him. I never was able to find out for what crime he had been imprisoned or in what country. Luluvo chose to be known as Josef XIII. Who the previous twelve Josefs were supposed to have been was never clear to me. He died in Bergen-Belsen concentration camp.

The Kalderasha roaming in Poland at one time also had a

famous King of their own, one Janus Kwieck I. For reasons unknown to me but by a stroke of audacity, his protocol-wise manager succeeded in having him "officially" crowned by Marshal Pilsudski in 1937. The title of King was only a symbolic one: he had no power, and what was worse for him, levied no taxes and received no contributions from his supposed subjects. In fact the King was prevailed upon by his followers, as often as was feasible, to entertain them lavishly in order to prove his ephemeral royalty. The unfortunate man and his family had to work hard to pay for this mock tribute to his vanity. With a smile hidden in his fierce mustache Pulika added that in the old days in Russia and in the Balkans, whenever the representatives of authority wanted to interfere with Gypsy affairs, the first step was to capture and incarcerate their King, in the belief this would destroy the Gypsies' social organization, being convinced that the King was the fierce autocrat they were led to believe him to be—whereas in fact life went on much as before with the exception of the foolish and fooled King.

CHAPTER SEVEN

I clearly remember stealthy long marches into unknown countries, by night. On one such march the horses' hoofs were padded with straw and bound with strips of colored dress material. Rain fell steadily. For days Gypsy wagons had been massing near the border. They had traveled mostly at dusk and camped overnight in well-hidden spots far away from the Gaje's world, avoiding contact with them as far as possible. One night they all converged and fell in with the long line of other moving wagons, to punch through the border en masse. Leaving the roads, we traveled cross-country through rugged terrain which only Gypsy wagons with their silly-looking high wheels could tackle. The caravan plodded on through the flailing rain. At times it slowed down to a crawl and we waded ankle-deep in the slippery mud, pushing, shoving, urging the horses on with low clicking sounds. At other times the wagons would suddenly hurtle forward, pitching and swaying. Without even catching their breath, the young men raced back through the downpour to help stragglers left behind or bogged down. Unrelentingly the Rom pushed onward, leaving behind a trail of deep mud mashed by numerous horses, wagon wheels and people on foot. A low, repeated whistle came from the direction of the lead wagon and slowly passed down the staggered line of wagons. The sound was deep and low and strangely reassuring, in contrast to the unrelenting howling of the wind, the splash and suck of horses and men wading through the mud and the occasional wail of an infant quickly hushed. Suddenly the startling sound of loudly pounding hoofs told that we had reached a paved road. The padding had long since worn off and been lost in the mud behind us. The oncoming wind smelled of smoke from wood fires. We had finally caught up with other Gypsies camping nearby, probably waiting for us at this spot. We were met with subdued but joyous greetings. Because of the rain, fires had been lit in the stoves inside the wagons. We tethered the horses at the backs of the vans, rubbed them briskly and covered them with blankets, tarpaulins or pieces of carpet; we watered them and hung bags of oats from their heads. Every effort possible was made to remain unobtrusive. The wind whipped the many-layered skirts of the women.

That night we visited several other wagons, drinking numerous Turkish coffees, silent with exhaustion. Stripping off our mud-caked pants, Kore and I slept in our wet shirts, as none of us—in true Gypsy style—possessed a change of clothes. Throughout the night trucks and cars roared by along the highway. The glare of their headlights somehow seemed incongruous to me after the mad scramble through the muddy fields across the border, and by its familiarity accentuated the strangeness and tension of our present situation. I was not aware at what precise moment we had passed the ill-defined borderline and I doubt if anybody else had taken notice. The strain and discomfort of our reckless assault, groping through the double darkness of the blindingly rainy night had absorbed all our concentration and our strength.

Hidden by the storm we had come through without skirmishes and without a single mishap. We woke at daybreak the following morning, harnessed the horses, and, dispensing with the customary early morning coffee, we followed the other wagons as they swung onto the main highway leading away from the border. A thick mist turned everything a luminous, milky white. The wagons and horses ahead of us and those behind us, when we saw them at a wide bend in the road, were edged with sunlight. We were listless with fatigue and everything about us was caked with ugly, dried mud.

The long line of fast-moving wagons meandered through the landscape like a trail of laboring ants. The Rom were moving very quickly away from the telltale trail of mud left by us newcomers, which led straight to the border and could not fail to be noticed. For, as the Rom claimed, "even flies would not alight on a boiling pot."

Several young men from the *kumpania* we had joined came over to us and took over the driving of the wagon. They would answer for us in case we were stopped by police and in general would be responsible for our security. At a fork in the road several wagons swerved to the right and left of us. At each crossroad ahead small groups of wagons peeled off and by rather casual prearrangement went their separate ways, to disappear in the mist. At sunup, when the mist lifted, the sky appeared a clear, luminous blue. We had driven for a long time when a man jumped down from the lead wagon we were following. He waited by the side of the road till our wagon came to where he stood and he joined us. With a supple movement he put one foot onto a spoke of the revolving wheel, using it as a foothold to step up and inside the *vurdon*. The Rom exchanged greetings with a certain display of formality but without constraint. His name was Dodo la Kejako. Dodo was a Lowari and, I gathered, a first cousin to Pulika. His face was round and full, his eyes were humorous but very shrewd, and he had a good round belly that told of his joy in living. He smoked a meerschaum pipe with a well-chewed cherrywood stem. Like all the Lowara he wore a mustache, but his was more closely trimmed than I was accustomed to seeing among the Rom. He wore a sportsman's cap of loud checkered woolen material, reminiscent of racetracks. Pulika and Dodo drank black coffee together, smoked, and talked of fine horses. We traveled along narrow, winding back roads, lined on both sides by tall shady trees, the trunks of which had been whitewashed, until we arrived at a well-hidden campsite through which a brook ran. It lay at the end of a long, rarely used dirt track, overgrown by tall weeds. Nearby were spongy but lushly green meadows. Butterflies by the hundreds fluttered over the pasture, and as we approached they rose and drifted away in a cloud of bright color. Soon several fires were kindled, drinking and cooking water was drawn and we busied ourselves with the horses. At the water's edge we washed off the dried mud that covered their legs and bellies. They snorted and their nostrils flared. Pulika's jittery "red" stallion sidled, stepping high, and splattered the other boys who were wading knee-deep nearby. We rubbed and cleaned the horses until they shone with renewed luster and all the traces of the previous night's adventure had vanished.

Dusk fell, and, leaning against the warm flanks of the horses, we watched the waters darken. We heaved ourselves onto their broad backs, and guiding them by the pressure of our thighs, we slowly rode back toward the encampment and the grazing patch beyond it. The usual clang and clatter of the Gypsy camp was damped down or absorbed by the dense overgrowth surrounding it. We could hear the steady babble of the brook and the faint purr of the wind playing in the telephone or high-tension wires overhead, punctuated by the irregular cadence of twanging sounds and the steady hum of various insects. The Rom were gathered around the glowing fires and happily drinking to friendship. Night fell and the smell of food pervaded the camp. I remember noticing Dodo's appetite; it was the kind that makes others envious. Kore and I went from fire to fire to visit the boys we had spent the day with at the edge of the water and at the pasture. At each fire Gypsy women gave us tidbits to nibble, which we refused, in proper Lowari fashion, and accepted only after much insisting and coaxing on their part. We ended the night by Dodo's fire. The entire family seemed as jolly and full-faced as Dodo himself. They had three older sons and two nubile daughters as well as a whole bunch of little ones. The two girls, Ludu and Djidjo, had a stunning combination of innocence and sensuousness. I was also struck by their long black braided hair, their dusky skin and the grace of youth not yet fully awakened to womanhood. Kore had to remind me of Lowari propriety before I could take my eyes off them.

We remained at this camp for several blissful days; time enough for the horses and for us to recuperate leisurely, but we stayed also to let time diminish the immediacy of the searches by the police that were to be expected. Once again the Rom must have proved elusive quarry.

After the midday heat, one day, we moved on again, well rested and relaxed. We soon ran into roadblocks and were submitted to tedious searches. Dodo good-humoredly joked with the police officers, and, disclaiming any knowledge of their reasons for the inquiry, he made them tell how a band of "foreign" Gypsies had surreptitiously invaded the country. Dodo feigned horror and with a broad grin on his face pleaded for police protection "at least until those horrible criminals have been caught." He invited the police patrol to spend the night in his wagon and extended full Gypsy hospitality to them. Needless to say, that put the police at ease, and they left without bothering to check anybody's papers. It seemed a good omen and gave us confidence in Dodo's abilities, but we wondered how the other members of Pulika's old *kumpania* were faring with their various mentors in the new land. When Pulika had decided to cross the border and "seek out new lands," as this is called in Romani, many other families had chosen to stay behind. One family had no choice because one of their members was in the hospital and another was in jail; and neither could be deserted.

The *kumpania* of Pulika, like any other *kumpania* for that matter, was at best but a loose, temporary association, forever kept fluid, scattering and regrouping as new patterns of interests developed, alliances shifted and old relationships waned. Like the flowing of water, the *kumpania* adapted itself to all circumstances, without in any way changing its own nature, endlessly remolding itself but forever remaining true to its own essence.

The chief of the *kumpania* was sometimes referred to as *Rom Baro,* the "Big Man," or as the *Kapo,* before World War II and the concentration camps gave this particular title an unwholesome connotation. The position of *Kapo* carried no material advantage aside from the satisfaction of the extra challenge and the heightened self-confidence derived from responsibility. The Rom proudly said that the measure of a man is only equal to the responsibility he is willing to shoulder. At the same time it was not unusual, when a *kumpania* crossed a border into a foreign country, for its members to join forces temporarily with another *kumpania,* and let the *Kapo* of the new group assume responsibility for them. The newcomers contributed part of their earnings, in fair exchange, to the benefit of the community.

Specific districts, provinces or countries were divided into "hunting territories" or reserved areas "belonging" to a specific *kumpania*. Whenever another group, or even a single wagon, passed through an area not its own, it was the accepted custom to compensate the present Gypsy "owners." In exchange, they helped the new arrivals in their dealings with the authorities, vouched for them or, if this was mandatory, arranged to post caution or bond, usually in the form of gold pieces. The "native" Gypsies taught the "foreign" ones as much of the language, trades, laws and customs of the country as was essential for them to survive. The Rom were aware that in rendering these services to other Gypsies they were building up good will and that in return they could hope for repayment in days of need. A large part of the system of jurisprudence of the Rom, the *Kris* (this same term can designate the trial by judges), is concerned with contractual law. There are a number of possible forms of relationships, or alliances, governed by specific and complex legal ties, despite the superficial impression the Gaje have of Romany life as completely free.

The Rom protected their "hunting reserves" against depletion or erosion; they did not exceed the limit of endurance of the local population, and strictly limited their pilfering in proportion to their requirements. They often limited their radius of action and remained "peacefully" within a certain region, at times for periods of many years, even willingly paying a yearly head tax. By agreement, other Rom stayed out of their territory, and in case of infringement the original Gypsies were not always reluctant to appeal to the Gaje authorities, cooperating with them to have the newcomers extradited, thus protecting their fief. With the proper authorization duly obtained from the Rom, however, other parties were helped to cross the territory or would even "sublease" parts of it from them. Many of the older Rom remembered the days they had been the victims of organized manhunts, when they had lived on acorns, hiding in the heart of the forest, and suffered untold atrocities under oppressive governments. They were wise enough to counsel moderation. They were the ones who knew that justice was only what the rulers made it, and they said that the angry and the weak were their own worst enemies. To them, as Pulika often repeated, communism and capitalism alike were merely reflections of the foolish Gaje's fixation on the accumulation of things, which in time enslaved men. But the young men grew foolhardy with extended periods of peace, and danger increased with success.

Each *kumpania* was autonomous and their interrelations were based only on the awareness of eventual reciprocation. There existed no formal or central superstructure of power. The Rom who fell on hard days through illness, death or accident, or who became impoverished through Gajo harassment, were always welcome to join bands of more or less distant relatives in other lands. They could work off whatever credits were extended to them by a kind of voluntary and limited bondage. This was called *montshimo,* and during the entire period of servitude their creditor was held responsible for them in every way by the law of the Gypsies.

Not all migrations were prompted by the desire to prospect for future brides for the sons of the group. The Rom migrated for the sake of sheer adventure in search of new territories to exploit, or because the old ones had become "depleted"; or because of local wars, revolutions and persecutions. They fled before outbreaks of epidemics, and they fled the ever-recurring night of the long knives.

The atrocities committed against them lessened in direct ratio to the progress of their westward trek. Cruelty and harassment, instead of being a national policy, became the more or less exceptional behavior of isolated individuals. The main defense of the Rom was their mobility and their feigned poverty, their freedom of movement, their indifference to form or ritual. But above all it was their mobility which spared them. They did not fight back; they simply moved away. In their minds the distinction and the division between the Rom and the Gaje were never forgotten. They did not expect anything from a world which was not theirs, and in logical consequence they never surrendered to the temptation of hope. Nomads, they felt life should always be seen as a horizon: "The road leading to a goal does not separate you from the destination; it is essentially a part of it." The Lowara did not believe in accumulating "things," nor did they see power in possessions. To them the enjoyment of possessions was only in the spending of them. Many years ago I met a Rom of the

Tshurara tribe whose name was Pitti la Kaliako. He was dressed in awful rags and had the most dismal of expressions. Everybody referred to him as "the millionaire." At that time I dismissed it as a joke, until Keja explained to me that "he was a millionaire because he spent a million." I forget in what specific currency it was supposed to have been, nor would I vouch for the accuracy of the figure. The point is that he was rich not because he was in possession of a fortune but because he had spent one.

CHAPTER EIGHT

The wheat was about to be harvested. For several weeks Pulika's *kumpania* had been traveling through prosperous farm country. In the courtyards of the sprawling farms with their gray roofs and thick stone walls, plump cats drank milk from deep dishes; in the meadows the hay had been cut and stacked high; everything indicated well-being and affluence, yet the country people were more hostile toward the Gypsies than even we expected them to be. The peasants barricaded themselves in their farmhouses and cottages. They refused to sell milk, bread or meat. They refused the Gypsies access to the wells and communal waterpumps. Gypsy women carrying babies were chased away with brandished brooms and ugly threats; the men found no opportunity to trade their horses. We lived on meager fare. Clothes went unwashed. We had the unpleasant feeling of being under constant organized watch, and not just from the usual onlookers or curious scoffers we had grown accustomed to. The police officers meticulously inspected all identity papers, insisting on an actual lineup and counting of heads. Wagons were searched arbitrarily. After nightfall when the young boys tried to let the horses loose in the neighboring grasslands, they were confronted by vigilantes carrying shotguns. We ate nettles picked along the road and stewed in flour browned in goose fat, with some salt and lots of pepper, together with potatoes stolen by night, baked in the embers of a meager fire of twigs. We ate gruel made from fresh wheat or oat kernels gleaned casually, pocketful by pocketful, and which took hours to cook to an edible consistency. Because the village shops refused to sell us even sugar, we had to eat this too with salt and pepper—so long as we had them. The children made bold raids on cucumber and melon patches, and every day we hoped tomorrow might be better, but it was not. Eventually Pulika's *kumpania* broke up into smaller units of not more than three or four wagons each in order to be less noticeable. Under the present circumstances, however, they avoided traveling alone in order to be able to protect themselves against Gajo brutality or actual attack.

The group was on edge and preparing for real trouble to strike. Pulika warned me to be even more alert than usual. He explained that in case they were chased away and had to break camp under police surveillance they might be forced to leave me behind. In this case I should wait a few hours before taking to the road after them, to keep from arousing the Gaje's suspicion and drawing their attention to myself. The Rom would leave a trail for me to follow and he proceeded to explain of what this *vurma*, as he called it in his language, consisted. Pulika said the Rom at all times left a variety of messages along the roads they traveled, in case I had not become aware of this yet. I had not, but I was proud to be let into one more secret of the Rom. Shreds of material from an old dress or bits of colored thread torn from it were left hanging in seemingly haphazard fashion in the branches of a tree among broken twigs pointing in the direction the caravan had traveled. The signs were left at the height of a man standing on the driving board of a Gypsy wagon or slightly above the habitual line of vision of a passerby not consciously looking for them. When there were no trees bordering the road, the signs often consisted of the dark spots left by a small fire made of twigs, with next to it a small heap of stones, pinecones, chicken bones, broken glass or crockery, or whatever other objects were available that did not seem too out of place and therefore obvious.

We heard that other members of our *kumpania* traveling in the same direction, roughly parallel to us, had been in a fight with local peasants and had been badly beaten. Both Kalia and Zurka had broken ribs and Yayal a painfully sprained shoulder, but according to the story repeated around the camp-fires, a number of Gaje had suffered worse. The rumors had it that the fight had started because our boys objected to what they felt was the insulting behavior of some local men toward Gypsy girls. Later we heard that quite possibly it had been the other way around: young farmers resenting the attention paid by the Gypsy boys to some nubile wenches of their village. The various groups of wagons, which had split up recently, joined forces again and the mood of the Rom grew mean. As the caravan grew in number and in strength, their ways became insolent and provocative. Passing a clover field, they would descend upon it en masse in bright daylight and take as much as they felt they needed for the numerous horses. Wherever geese or chickens strayed across their path, the women pounced upon them without restraint or precaution, not caring who saw them. Abundant wood was "requisitioned," as they called it mockingly, rightly to make up for the fires they had lately been deprived of. Access to water was haughtily demanded and general license to plunder was decreed, supposedly in retaliation for the ungenerous reception the Gaje had given them in the first place. The Gaje no doubt explained their own attitude as due to the Gypsies' general misbehavior, which by now verged on terrorism. The outnumbered police officers hardly inspected the fast-moving, rowdy wagon camp, probably waiting impatiently for reinforcements to come to their aid from the district capital. Some of the hamlets we passed through appeared deserted, their houses' shutters tightly closed; the only evidence of life was the watchdogs, which barked as if demented. We knew hostile, scared eyes watched us everywhere. Somehow only worse could be ahead, and the wholesale senseless ransacking went on without restraint and well beyond pure necessity. Running amok, the *kumpania* covered extensive territory in forced marches with only hasty overnight halts, to avoid being easily located and caught up with. The horses grew thin and skittish, the men irritable, the women quarrelsome; but now we had to keep on the move, not knowing how to alter the unhappy sequence of events.

One evening at dusk, trotting by the wagon side, I was stopped in my tracks by the sight of a big, black, dead crow nailed to a barn door with its wings spread wide. It struck me as a symbol of sacrificial death. When we reached the next available overnight halting place, we found a large number of Gypsy wagons already assembled there. The waters of the lake beyond the camp were ashimmer in the last pale light of sundown. Numberless tiny fires of lake reeds flickered restlessly. Shrill voices rose into the sky. Rupa curtly told me not to stray away from our wagon, not to mix with the Rom whose camp space we were sharing for that night. She had never done this before. I had always been allowed full freedom of the camp wherever we were. Rupa emphasized that these people were Tshurara. I had never heard the name before. I knew that *tshuri* meant "knife" and tried to guess a possible pejorative derivation from it. Could it mean something like knifer or murderer? Pulika sat by the fire silent and only half listening.

The horses of the other Gypsies looked neglected and in bad condition. Their wagons, which were smaller than ours, were battered, most of their windows broken. The children looked impudent, wild and hungry; naked babies sat playing by themselves in the dust near the fire, without supervision, crawling far too near the grazing horses. A few of the younger women were primitively seductive, some of the men fiercely handsome. Nearly all of them were tall, lean and tough. Most of the older adults had teeth missing, in contrast with the people of our own *kumpania,* many of whom had gold teeth. Our people were heavier in build, more dignified in appearance. The Tshurara, as Rupa had called them, had long drooping mustaches, and wide-brimmed black felt hats not unlike those of our own people. Noticing several young men with close-cropped hair, giving them a very un-Romany look, I learned they had only recently rejoined their families after spending time in jail for various kinds of mischief. Few of the women wore any gold pieces as jewelry.

As soon as the evening meal in our section of the camp was prepared, the Tshurara children crowded around us like a swarm of fresh, greedy little sparrows, with an unappeasable hunger. They seemed to eat mostly because opportunity offered.

The headman of the group was called Gunari, and with him were his two brothers, one Nanosh, the other Pani. They had come from Norway recently and were on their way to Spain. There was Pani's oldest son, Tshurkina, with his wild wife Liza, and the three sons of Nanosh with their families. One other wagon belonged to Tshurkina's son-in-law, who less than a year ago had married the now twelve-year-old and ravishingly beautiful wild-eyed Shofranka. The groom had been forced by Tshurkina to join his wife's group instead of the other way around, which was the accepted custom.

Later that night we noticed their section of the camp was deserted and quiet. All the men and most of the women had sneaked away without telling anyone, leaving behind only the old people and the small children. They were drinking wildly among themselves at a nearby inn. They drank without eating and without inviting others to share. They drank in a hurry without joy or graciousness. The women drank like men, while they nursed their infants. At dawn they were back at the camp arguing loudly. Children started crying, and on the grazing patch the horses neighed restlessly.

Early the following morning we were washing ourselves and I was rubbing my teeth with coarse cooking salt on my index finger in Gypsy fashion. On the other side of the encampment everybody was sleeping late, when I saw two young Tshurara girls, bare to the waist, washing themselves, splashing and shivering. They had well-rounded, slender bodies and firm, high, full breasts with purple-black nipples. Their dark smooth skin was wet and glistening. They had large feet and hands, which gave them a sweet awkwardness. They wet their long, raven-black hair with soapy water to braid it more tightly and each smoothed a small lock of hair into a curl, which she stuck to her temple with more soap. Kore was scandalized. Had these Tshurara no shame? How dared they comb their hair in full view of young men who were not even their kin? And they wore red skirts to boot. And if they were not defiant they were sulking. Who wanted a wife like that? In answer to what must have been my look of surprise, Kore rudely warned me to stay away from "those people." These so-called Tshurara were obviously much disliked.

As far as I could judge, they spoke the same language we did, and at first I attributed our people's dislike for them only to family differences, possibly jealousy. The Tshurara themselves did not show in any way that they were aware of this dislike or for that matter were in the least concerned about it.

We spent the day caring for the horses, watering them at the slippery edge of the lake, inspecting the horses belonging to "the others." The women as usual went on their errands to gather food, while the unmarried girls fetched water, cared for the fires and watched the numerous small fry. It was good to remain in one spot, undisturbed, and to be able to rest the horses, gather our strength, reorganize and let the women launder. Harnesses needed repair, wheels and axles had to be greased. In appearance and in mood the encampment remained a fortress preparing for siege. Because of the large number of wagons they were parked very close to one another, with their backs turned to the wind, and I knew that all approaches to the camp were being scanned at all times. A rumbling noise told us that one of the wagons was leaving. It was a light peasant van belonging to the Tshurara, and several of their men rode in it. They returned only toward dusk. The horses were winded and overheated, indicating they must have covered a fair distance. They brought back impressive quantities of new fence pickets as firewood, and sacks of onions and potatoes. In a boisterous mood they finally unloaded two full-grown live pigs, trussed up solidly, and a huge barrel of beer. Roaring, they admitted that only this last item had actually been paid for. As the only reply to Pulika's annoyed inquiries, Vedel, the son of Pani, opened wide his hands, with fingers spread out, in a gesture of both denial and mock despair, as if to say "What else did you expect from us awful Tshurara?" This had been their raiding party, their *paguba,* and we were to be their guests. Several young men of our group helped the Tshurara slaughter the grunting, squealing pigs, and clean them at the far end of the camp. Keja kept me from joining them. Large fires were built from the hardwood pickets, over which the whole pigs were roasted on spits. The viscera were thrown at the yelping dogs, who ran away with them fighting each other, growling and yapping, tearing and stretching the pigs' guts and bladders. The boys chased them away from the immediate vicinity by throwing stones at them. Men from both groups crouched by the blazing fire and took turns at turning the spits, pouring ladlefuls of lard over the roasting pigs and keeping the fires stoked with pickets. They guzzled moonshine liquor from a massive stoneware crock: Each man would sling it over his right shoulder, his right arm bent around it, his head and mouth twisting toward it. One held his left hand, open and palm outward, just above the small of his back; another held his left hand against the back of his neck in a gesture of bravado. While they gulped and gulped, laughing and trying to catch their breath, the liquor ran down their chins and throats, staining their shirts, which were unbuttoned to the waist. The women squatted by their own fires, preparing various side dishes and large portions of salad. A flock of ravens fled silently through the coming darkness.

Before the night was over nothing that could be eaten was left. The bones were thrown in the lake to dispose of incriminating evidence. The children's faces gleamed with grease from the meal, and their eyes expressed complete physical contentment. Life had been good to them. The blazing fire highlighted the relaxed, monumental attitudes of the reclining Rom and their women. Small children sprawled over their elders, sleeping peacefully and replete. The drinking had been unusually moderate, due to limited supplies, except for the young cooks, who were sound asleep. A few of them had abandoned the roasting pigs before they had finished their tasks. This was not held against them, as long as they remembered their position in the group and behaved with respectful restraint in the presence of the older members. They had been drinking steadily and had not eaten. For a while we could hear their boisterous singing and whooping at the far end of the camp near the pastures, where they had gone in search of semiprivacy. Then only a few unsteady, dissonant voices were left to roar before the whispering silence of the nearby forest took over once again.

The following morning all the Rom slept late or at least lingered in their feather beds longer than was the custom. When I woke, only very few fires had been lit throughout the sleeping encampment, which looked like a battlefield in an Eisenstein film. Old Lyuba was crouched by a smallish fire of flickering twigs, smoking her short-stemmed brass pipe, holding her Turkish coffee maker over the restless flames. A few feet away Pulika stirred, then leaned on his left elbow, facing the large spread-out feather bed which I shared with Kore, who lay with his head in the opposite direction from me. Pulika's tanned face was lit by the direct sunlight; his long black hair and drooping mustache stood out against the faded crimson silk of the eiderdown cover with its gay overall flower pattern. I rarely saw Pulika without his hat. He looked through the pockets of the colored shirt he wore in bed—we slept in the same shirts we wore in the daytime—and fished out a cigarette butt, which he lit with an old-fashioned tinder lighter with several feet of yellow wick hanging from it. As he had not yet washed, I refrained from greeting him.

Without addressing me by my name, but obviously for my benefit, Pulika said, "And we are *Lowara,*" as if completing a previous unspoken train of thought. A longish silence followed this cryptic statement, until it dawned on me that what he was telling me was that they, the others, were Rom and, as I knew, therefore distinct from the Gaje, but that as Rom we were Lowara. Remembering various disparaging remarks made by Rupa, Kore and others, I added for myself "and not Tshurara." I heard myself ask what distinguished a Lowari from a Tshurari. Without looking at me directly, Pulika half smiled and let the question sink in and grow in me. When he finally spoke, and I remember it with the quality of dreams, he said that there were many different kinds of Rom; not all of them necessarily traveled—some not only lived in houses but had lived in one specific location for many generations, like the Cale or Gitanos of Spain, who speak a language all their own, much influenced by corrupt Spanish. He named sedentary groups in Serbia, in Macedonia, in Turkey and in particular the Rudari of Romania and Transylvania, who speak only Romanian and have lost all ties with their Gypsy past, which many of them even try to deny. Then, he said, there are the true nomadic Rom, all of whom speak a basically common language.

Pulika reminded me that there were many other roving bands living off the land, who traveled in covered wagons, and they also were loosely called Gypsies by the population of the countries in which they lived, although in fact they were of local extraction and had "gone wild," as Pulika put it disapprovingly. Distinct from the true Gypsies, they limited their wanderings to restricted geographic areas. They spoke no other language besides the local one, sometimes developing a slang of their own in addition, such as the *argot des voyageurs et des chineurs* in France, the *Gaunersprache* or *Rotwelsch* of the Yenishe of Germany. Or yet they spoke the survival of an older tongue as in the case of the Shelta of the tinkers of Ireland, the Bargoensch of the Kramersvolk of Flanders and the Tatars of Scandinavia. Their loyalty, with the fierce pride of the insecure, usually centers around a small family core. Another similar group consists of fairground attendants, circus performers and other transient entertainers, associated more by a common trade than any deeper bonds, and these also are often and wrongly classified as Gypsies. The term Gypsy is often and as inaccurately used to connote romantic dreams of unfettered, unrealizable freedom, adolescent yearnings for a passionate way of life, contempt for the menial, or to specify any good-for-nothing vagrant of questionable honesty. Besides the groups of nomads who are unrelated to the Rom, there is one which is related yet very distinct from them. They call themselves Sinti or Manush, which in Romani means "person or human being" as differentiated from the aristocratic designation Rom which means "Man." They are mostly musicians and makers of stringed instruments, who at times even indulge their fancy for constructing lovingly weathered fakes of antique violins. They are of smaller stature than the Rom, often dark-skinned, and are easily angered. Unlike the Rom, the Sinti women are always clad in black. Marriage is only by elopement, and their tribal organization is matriarchal. The Sinti dialect, practically unintelligible to the other Gypsies, has preserved the purest and most ancient forms of words and pronunciations, but they have lost most of the original inflections and, to a considerable extent, have substituted faulty German grammatical structure for their own. Like Romani, which is spoken by all the Rom, their dialect is a derivative and distant relative of Sanskrit and has certain similarities to the Aryan languages of India today, like Gujarati, Kurbat, Hindi.

The Rom, properly speaking, are themselves divided into four main tribes—the Lowara, the Tshurara, the Kalderasha and the Matchvaya, all of whom wander extensively and to the four corners of the earth. They differ distinctly in physical makeup and in temperament, language, occupations and in their way of life in general. The Lowara and the Tshurara are mostly horse dealers, and because of this occupation they live in wagons. The Kalderasha, by far the most numerous group, are mostly coppersmiths and more often live in tents. At one time in Czarist Russia the members of a Kalderash subtribe were also entertainers.

Spurred on by a particular question, in which I referred to the Kalderash he had just spoken about as "Russian" Gypsies, Pulika wearily told me how misleading it was to single out Gypsies by a national identity, in view of their constant, wide-flung traveling. He said I at least should know they were "a race of strangers." He went on to tell me how his own family, at various times called Hungarians or Germans, had lived and traveled extensively in Russia, which should have made them Russian Gypsies too, or would it? They had lived in Turkey, throughout the Balkans, in France and Spain. In every one of these places they had relatives who had either stayed behind, traveled ahead or left them at a fork in the dirt road to go right or to go left, and whom they would someday meet again at another crossroads of the world. They were Rom; they were not Turkish, Bulgarian, Greek, Spanish or French Gypsies. It was, however, none of the Gaje's business to know what they were or who or where they came from, and as to where they were going, even the Gypsies did not know.

Members of the four tribes often lived side by side in any part of the world. In Russia there were both Kalderash and Tshurara as well as Lowara, just as these same groups could be found almost anywhere in the Americas. The Rom called these tribes the different "races" of Gypsies, and as far as possible they married only within their own tribes.

Each "race" was divided into what the Lowara called
tzerha, the word for tent, and the other tribes called *witsa*.
These smaller units were descendants of one grandfather or
great-grandfather, who was or had been a great man and
whose name they used generically. If descendants of one
Duntshi, they were Duntsheshtshi. The sons and grandsons of
Yojo became Yojoshtshi, but they did not necessarily live or
travel together. The other subdivision was into actual traveling units or caravans, of a more arbitrary nature, and was
called the *kumpania*. This was a temporary alliance between
various families not necessarily related by kinship and was
restricted primarily to economic pursuits. They were bound by
one of a variety of contracts of reciprocity which ruled the
division of both spoils and obligations. A *kumpania* could be
dissolved at any time by mutual consent. It often consisted of
several brothers, cousins or in-laws, but it was not necessarily
limited to members of the same tribe or "race."

For several more days Pulika and his *kumpania* shared a
common campsite with the Tshurara, who seemed to quarrel
constantly among themselves. All day and part of each night
had been spent in talking and eating but mostly drinking.
Leisure had been too plentiful and old jealousies had been
revived. Early one morning, after we had drunk, standing up,
just one pre-breakfast cup of sweet, black coffee, Pulika
proceeded to break camp without any explanation or account-
ing to anyone. The Lowara followed his example one by one
as if prearranged by conspiracy. The fires were put out. We
departed silently, leaving the sleeping Tshurara behind us.
The campsite we deserted was strewn with ugly rubbish. The
period of rest had been necessary, even welcome, but the open
road drew us like a beacon. Yapping excitedly, the dogs ran
up ahead, waiting for the wagons to catch up with them, and
then they would dash off again. Urging the well-rested horses
into a sharp trot, we traveled at a brisk pace. The other
wagons of the *kumpania* were scattered along the road like a
broken necklace. The excitement that gradually permeated all
of us proved how bored everyone had become by remaining
stationary even for those few days: Keja said it had been

almost like winter. Back on the roads even the very small children seemed to cry less. Swift swallows were plunging close to the earth—in prediction of coming rain, according to folk tradition. Pulika sat on the driver's board all day, either intoxicated by movement or trying to put a long stretch of road between the Tshurara and ourselves. I knew he did not relish their company even though the special courtesy of the open road imposed a certain amount of protocol if not tolerance. Traveling in too large a number of wagons, and under divided authority, was bound to create a number of problems and conflicts, especially in a mixed group of Lowara and Tshurara, among whom even a minimum of discipline was unenforceable. The intoxication, however short-lived, of being an unruly majority led to inexcusable excesses for which the Rom were bound to suffer later.

Before arriving at our last camp we had been forced to live almost as Tshurara, treated badly by the peasants of all the villages through which we passed. We had been hungry and in order to survive had reverted to near savagery, "like Tshurara," who knew peace only as a dream. It occurred to me that the unreasonably hostile behavior of the Gaje toward us during the preceding period might have been due to our having followed the same trail the Tshurara had traveled a short time before us. As it was, the life of the Rom was one endless improvisation, requiring endless resourcefulness and cunning, without its being further complicated by the reputation of the shiftless and destructive Tshurara. Their hordes were forever dissolving without leaving a trace, always hunted, always evading punitive squads sent after them. They traveled in small groups of two and three wagons, covering large distances in forced spurts, not sparing horses or people, terrorizing the lone farmers and the inhabitants of isolated hamlets on their way. They had no concept of group loyalty, no permanent formation like our *kumpanias*. They continually shifted their allegiances, forming new associations almost daily as old groups split. There was an awesome disparity between the "races." The Lowara sought to ease their lot as undesirables in the eyes of officialdom by observing some form of self-imposed discipline, making a living at horse trading rather than exclusively at malicious pilfering. The Lowara liked to live in large groups and they frequently posted "peace bonds" with those village authorities they knew they could trust; these "peace bonds" consisted of gold pieces or sometimes cash, to be forfeited if the Rom violated their "peace contract." Occasionally bribes to the police were offered and accepted. I remember how Pulika always carried several small gold pieces, I believe English sovereigns, jangling, loose in the pockets of the vest from which his heavy gold watch chain dangled. "For emergencies," he would say quietly, knowing my fear of the gendarmes. I admired his imperturbability. He had the sense to keep quiet at the right time in contrast to the younger, lesser men, who lacked his capacity to listen and often talked too loudly with exuberant defiance. He had an intuitive gift for the immediate understanding of a situation.

I climbed into our wagon to escape the scalding midday sun, leaving the other boys running alongside the horses. Gently rocked by the constant swaying, I overheard Keja and some of her unmarried cousins talk about the Tshurara girls. For a while I could not make out if the jesting gossip was actually disapproving or just a little envious, since in the final analysis the Gajo was the dupe anyway. Darkly beautiful, wild little Luludja, the youngest daughter of Tshukurka, with her primitively seductive brown eyes that seemed to melt, told how she had joined several of the Tshurara girls on some errands. Full of fun, they had surged into the shop of a butcher in an otherwise unremembered small village. They swarmed all over the place, handling goods. At first the Gajo had been amused by the implicit mischief, the eye-winking and provocative giggling of this jostling crowd of gay young things in their exotic dresses. When his wife joined him they both suddenly panicked, realizing belatedly that these Gypsies were capable of anything. One of the girls, Jofranka, the daughter of Tshurkina la Lizako, had ordered so many pounds of this and so many pounds of that. She put two large, tin, lidded kettles on the counter. As the butcher busied himself, his wife kept a sharp and suspicious eye open. The other girls bought sausages, lard and pork ears. When time came to pay the fairly high bill for the choice cuts of meat in the casseroles, Jofranka claimed to have lost her money. With eager eyes she pleaded to be allowed to take the kettles home; her entire family was starving to death, she told them, and could not wait a moment longer. She swore she would return with the money right away. The butcher's wife was not fooled that easily; she remained deaf to Jofranka's pleas. Jofranka was forced to leave the two heavy containers on the counter, and she hurried away "to fetch money from my mother." Proud of herself, the Gaji looked at her husband, winking knowingly, and they relaxed. The Gypsy girls never returned. At nighttime the butcher gave up waiting and decided to put the meat in the cellar; then he found that the bottoms of both lidded pots had been cleverly cut away before being put down on his counter. All the meat had slipped through and into the hidden pockets under the aprons of the little Tshurara. No Gypsy would ever again be welcomed in this shop or in this village.

Thus behaved our Tshurara companions of the road. Listening to this tale, I thought that our own Lowara girls were not so innocent themselves either. I remembered how they invaded village stores on our road: Before anybody had the presence of mind to stop them, they would scratch themselves with vigor, then lovingly caress hams or sausages with dirty little brown hands. Quite often they were chased away, but only after having been given the soiled articles at a low price, or for nothing. Once the desired goods were acquired, the demonstrative scratching usually stopped, and they walked away quickly before the merchants had time to change their minds.

Toward dusk one day we saw seven wagons far ahead of us moving in close formation, crawling like snails. Standing upright on the driving board of our lead wagon, Yojo snapped his whip and forced the tired horses to a faster pace. Soon we overtook the caravan ahead of us with gleeful yells and with loud, shrill staccato bursts of whistling from the older men. This was the *kumpania* of old Bidshika, to whom Pulika was closely related, and the meeting was especially joyful. We pulled off the road at a deserted spot. The members of the two *kumpanias* had, by common accord, chosen to set up camp according to their sympathies for each other, rather than strictly following their more formal allegiances. This gave the camp the aspect of deliberate carelessness. In the merry confusion that ensued several young unmarried men from each group stealthily left the camp after dark. They were restless and better-groomed than usual. One or two were chewing on cucumbers. Their silent departure, though not unnoticed, was tacitly ignored. They were going to a village dance in a nearby rural community, intent on wenching.

The night was hot and a heavy full moon hung low. The eiderdowns had been spread and covered the entire campsite with a colorful overall pattern. There were a number of them around the glowing embers of each of the numerous, almost burned-out fires studding the camp. Several of us had gathered at old Bidshika's fire, and we had coaxed him into a story-telling mood. His wife and his two daughters, Fifika and Bisnu, had retired to bed a few feet away in the shade of their covered wagon. One of the young boys had volunteered to keep the fire going in order not to interrupt the stories or distract our uncle. The coffeepot was kept simmering throughout the night. After each long-drawn-out story he told, the old man lit his short-stemmed brass pipe once more; to tease us, he pretended to be sleepy. We sensed his satisfaction in telling story after story to so eager an audience. Some of the children were half asleep, but even so could not bear to interrupt the magic. Six-year-old little Papin, one of the daughters of young Koloro, slept curled up against my knees. So did Tshilaba, the son of Gunada.

Old Bidshika told us about his own youth in the faraway Russian lands and how the Rom of old, his grandfather, uncles and brothers, had traveled and lived. The stories filled us with wonder. He told us how in the icy winter nights the Rom tied their horses together circling one single pole or tree, with rumps facing outward to keep the prowling wolf packs away. He told us how at the time of the wild torrential Russian spring at night the "black wind" howled and the *detlene* took hold of the long wooden shaft of the wagons and violently rocked them and rocked them. Then his own mother, braving all her fears, would open the door and howl back into the black night. She loudly shouted names of boys and girls. As long as the black wind howled and as long as the *detlene* rocked the wagon, she shouted names and more names, until the wind died down and one by one the *detlene* went away. She herself had lost her voice and crouched down, exhausted by burning fever, happy and proud at having saved the young children of her family. She never fully recovered the use of her voice, as everybody well knew.

We had all heard, but only half believed, that the *detlene* were little souls of stillborn or aborted human creatures searching mother love, who could only be pacified by being given individual names, each and every one of them. They could also be the souls of infants who had not lived long enough to be kept in mind by their relatives.

Old Bidshika paused a moment, took a few deep breaths and continued: "The story I am about to tell you I did not witness personally, but it was told to me by Yanko o Melalo himself and therefore let all credit for it go to him. He was a wealthy, much loved and respected old Lowari, who at one time possessed many a property in and around Berlin, Germany, and it is there that he died. May the road ahead of him be as good as the one he traveled on this earth. Our tribespeople had newly arrived in Hungary—or was it Transylvania?—with horses and wagons, all the way from the Russian lands. We had many weeks of steady travel behind us. It had been a difficult and tiring journey, but however this may have been, here we had arrived. Now, in Hungary there were many wandering tribes at this point, and it was 'with God,' as the Romany saying goes, that we found some of them living in large tents at the edge of the forest. They greeted us in friendly enough fashion, welcomed us and gave us *patshiva* days on end. Food and drink and joy and song I will not describe to you, as this might well take up all that is left of the night to tell about. These particular Rom belonged to a tribe we called the Khorakha and they had traveled extensively in the Near East and whatever may lie beyond it. Among them was one wise old Rom, whose name I have long forgotten—may the dead one forgive me for this neglect. It is about him, in a way, that I want to tell you a story now. This Rom had come into the possession of a most powerful magical *draba*. It was said, and boasted about, that with this magic of his he could at will make himself invisible to human eyes. You may hesitate to believe this but it is literally the way old Yanko o Melalo, long ago, confided it to me. The two of them got drunk together one day, giving each other *patshiva* the old-fashioned Gypsy way, with songs and dances, and thus it happened that the other Rom of the Khorakha tribe, in a moment of prideful, drunken boastfulness, gave away his *draba* charm. In his old age it was Yanko himself who told me his secret. But then again, who among us Lowara would have the insolent defiance to fulfill the necessary conditions to obtain the use of this *draba?* May God keep away from us the evil thought of it. The way to do it is to catch a young male frog on a Friday night when the moon is full, to imprison him in a red pottery vessel, such as the local peasants use as flowerpots, and into which three hundred and ninety small holes have been carefully drilled beforehand. Not one more and definitely not one less. Then the one bold enough to seek magical powers such as these must deposit the contraption in an ant heap, which in turn must happen to be in a burial ground (the thought of it alone!), and he must run away faster than lightning in order not to hear the cry of anguish of the frog. After nine days he must fetch the flowerpot back. All there will be left are numerous white, brittle little frog bones. Placing himself before a mirror, he must then put these in his mouth, one by one. When he doesn't see himself any longer in the mirror, he will know which one of the bones has the magical property. It was said that the great-uncle of the Khorakha Rom I am telling you about had tried the same procedure long before him, but not having correctly observed all the rules such as running away faster than lightning, he heard the frog cry and remained deaf ever after. The old man who told our Yanko o Melalo about all this took full advantage of his power of invisibility, playing tricks on the unaware Gaje, getting fresher and fresher every day until some village hunters shot him through the head, from one ear to the other. Because he was totally invisible to the human eye, he got so carried away by his mischief that he overlooked the fact that he did leave clear footprints in the virgin snow."

The weird mating call of a tomcat, not far away, startled us back into everyday reality. It broke the spell, and it was without further protest that we let old Bidshika get up. He spat into the fire, smoothed his long fierce mustache, and walked away. We walked back through the camp looking for the location of our *vurdon*. Bats dipped in the air and through the gaps between the wagons, swiftly and without sound. An infant wailed throughout the night. At daybreak the following morning a group of three wagons of the Tshurara drove into our sleeping encampment with unnecessarily loud cries of mock joy mixed with more than a touch of defiance, as if saying, "We will show you it is not that easy to shake us off." I went back to sleep with the unpleasant knowledge that the Tshurara were back with us again.

During the clear summer nights at the perennial crossroads of the world the Gypsies enriched their leisure by listening to the great storytellers of their people. The oral tradition of the Rom was expanded and renewed, depending on the extent of their travels and on the chance meetings with older Rom who had lived, seen and heard, and could tell about it to others, for the Gypsies had no written records to go back to and relied only on the memories of the old to keep the tradition alive and to pass it on. To the young the Rom said that you learned nothing when you did all the talking yourself. The rambling stories which formed the chronicle of the Rom were called *Swato*, or in the plural form, which was more often used, *Swatura*. In these, fact and fancy blended in a sophisticated way, and the interpretation and evaluation of these tales depended essentially on the critical faculties of the listeners. For the Rom, the fantasy elements were easy enough to isolate but added wonder to the narrative. The didactic elements accurately portrayed the character, customs and weaknesses of the Gaje in many lands, their superstitions, their attitudes toward the Rom. Sometimes these stories included rudimentary lessons in linguistics and the proper pronunciation of key words connected with trade, or, if women were involved, of

fortune-telling. I knew young girls who were able to tell
fortunes, after a fashion, in seven or eight languages without
otherwise possessing a speaking knowledge of any of them.
Through graphic descriptions of the successful handling of
specific emergencies the *Swatura* helped perpetuate Romany
lore. There were *Swatura* dealing with magic, superstition
and the supernatural phenomena. They were called *Darane
Swatura* and were told just for fun. It was through the *Swatura*
that I became familiar with the Balkans long before I ever
went there, and it was like a returning when eventually and
for the first time I saw the vineyards and the plum orchards of
Serbia; the mining villages with their terrible poverty; the
isolated sawmills in the wooded foothills; the imposing
Romanesque or Byzantine monasteries with their dependen-
cies and their silent monks simultaneously haughty and
humble; the swarming marketplaces; the carelessly kept Mos-
lem cemeteries; the rural East European Jewry and their
excessive intimacy with God; the patches of sunflowers that
crackled and rustled as they ever so slowly turned to face the
sun; the patient, suffering oxen with their tender but unseeing
eyes; the mournful and suspicious Gorale mountain people in
their bleak villages clinging to the sides of craggy, wind-swept
granite heights; the stretches of road overhanging precipices
without outside retaining walls; the rich cultivated valleys
below; the sullen black water buffaloes that reminded one of
Southeast Asia; the persistent traces of centuries of Turkish
occupation; and, as we moved south, the transition in modes
of transportation from truck to horse to ox to donkey to
camel.

The *Swatura* reflected all this plus the entire fluctuating
world of the Rom. The whole body of it could never be known
by any one single person and it was forever being added to. It
was a truly living chronicle, possibly too rambling and at times
too formless to the Western mind, but it had an inner coher-
ence of its own nonetheless, "flowing like a widening stream
and with the profusion of a flood."

The Rom used the same vague approximative designations
they used to indicate the time of day, the months or even the
passing years, to single out cities, provinces, districts or even

countries. They spoke of "horse-market towns," of "the city where the Lowara became wealthy" or "where one of the Kalderash took over" or "where So-and-so was jailed" or "where So-and-so died," or they spoke derogatorily of "Tshurara country" or of *anda l thema,* "the lands beyond."

Specific local currencies such as dinars, leva, pengö, lei, liras or drachmas were casually translated as equivalent to the price of a bride, the price of a horse, or "enough to feed guests."

It was only much later, when revisiting the Balkans extensively, that I realized the extent and the intensity of my involvement with the Rom: the depth of my identification with them and my nearly total acceptance of all things Romany, while I lived with them. I seem to remember the Romany aspects of life more clearly than those of the countries we visited.

The Rom never tired of spending nights listening to the *Swatura,* and each meeting with a new *kumpania* promised renewed delights. The *Swatura* were always told in the first person and they ranged from drama to comedy and sometimes mystery thriller; or they might unfold like a horror tale out of Edgar Allan Poe. Although on occasions the tone was heroic, a touch of humorous self-knowledge was never totally absent. Each raconteur had his own style, which was, of course, colored by his and his family's experiences and the countries they had lived in. Nonoka of old, who died in Austria long ago, like our own Butsulo, was usually aloof, but once he had thrown himself into a *Swato* he grew extravagantly tender, and his remembrance of pre-Revolutionary Russia filled us with wonder and longing for the expansive dignity and splendor he evoked. Old Lyuba would pick up a glowing ember with her bare leathery hand and light her short-stemmed brass pipe. Her unblinking eyes roamed through the rapt audience with a detached look, and in a monotonous voice she would intone a monologue about the years of unrelieved calamity that had forced the Lowara to leave Russia and go back to the Hungary they had once come from. Nonoka would smile undisturbed, implying that maybe Lyuba misremembered, or remembered only what she cared to. After a few sentences she would fall silent again. Anyway she was no bard and her interjections as a moralist were soon dismissed as the old man again shared expansively his love for the Russian land, his eyes shiny and moist.

Just as I became acquainted with Russia and the Balkans long before ever having lived in the latter, I became familiar with many a legendary Rom roaming the world today whom as yet I have not caught up with. There was one Loiza la Vakako, always one jump, or rather a few months, away from wherever we went. The last time we crossed his trail in the early 1940's in Paris and in Madrid, he had left for Brazil only shortly before. He was reputed to be one of the richest and wisest and most generous among the Lowara, and the descriptions of his wealth and his entertaining were fabulous. In Spain lived three famous old Rom, the brothers Notarka, Mutshoro and Pali. They had many sons and lived as kings. They had abandoned the *vurdon* and dwelt in spacious cool whitewashed houses or, during parts of the summer, in temporary but elaborately built arborlike constructions which in Spanish were called *tiendas de campaña*. They did not deal in horses as we did but had developed special skills related to the tempering of steels and thrived on this. From their base in Spain they ranged all over Morocco and North Africa and were respected by Rom and Gaje alike.

There were the many stories about Stevo o Africano, who was also jokingly called Diamond Jim. He and his *kumpania* had gone to South Africa and found some rather mysterious but lucrative occupation dealing in diamonds, as his nickname implied. Every few years he and his followers would come alternately one year to France or Spain, to Yugoslavia, to Italy, and shortly before his death to the United States. They would come "on holiday" and spend the fortunes they had amassed for the purpose.

There were tales of wise and generous Rom, others of unreliable or even treacherous ones. The *Swatura* told wondrous sagas of the Lowara's prolonged stays both in Hungary and in pre-Nazi Germany. Pulika and his brothers Tshukurka and Milosh owned property in and around Berlin, at the time Yanko o Melalo held sway there. Old Bakro and Yishwan and

Mitsho, Yanoro, Boboko and Honko and so many others lived there on a heroic scale, while already the clouds of wrath gathered around them. But even as blood flowed, life went on, and even from this period of Nazi genocide there emerged a particular brand of *Swatura,* told by the scattered survivors. In 1961 I spent nights in Zagreb listening to the *Swatura* of a great Lowari, Mitsho la Marako. He had known the stupor of grief and the hopeless passivity of concentration-camp life, but he had retained a life-accepting sense of humor and the wisdom to leave bitterness and hate to those not strong enough to love. He sang of the perpetuation of life. Mitsho la Marako was a powerful teller of tales and like all Lowara he had a tendency to idealize virility. The August night was peaceful and the white wine of Croatia flowed profusely—a fortune's worth in dinars—in consecration of friendship, in memory of the murdered dead, and as an inspiration to the younger generation.

Next to the living, flowing tradition of the *Swatura,* or tales of experience, the Rom had a more formalized kind of story, the *Paramitsha,* or fairy tales. These were mostly told during the winter months, that otherwise dreaded period of enforced immobility. On these occasions Keja would bake wagon-wheel pies filled with poppy seeds and honey, and with the pie we usually had tea in glasses. The *Paramitsha* were in no way didactic or even directly related to Gypsy lore. Their value lay purely in the artistry of the storyteller, and many of them may very well have been borrowed and adapted from the various populations among whom the Rom had lived. These tales were usually told and retold in almost the exact same word sequence, which everybody knew, but they could only be told by and were considered the exclusive property of the particular storyteller. Only after his death could the *Paramitsha* eventually be repeated by another, sometimes after not having been heard for many years, but full credit had to be given to the original teller. On cold winter nights, we might be squatting or lying on our big soft eiderdowns, enjoying the comforting warmth of the potbellied stove in our winter quarters, while outside the strong wind would be blowing and making our wagons rock on their high wheels; then a man might say,

"This is the *Paramitsha* of the Tzintzari as I learned it from Nonoka many, many years ago, and as he entertained us by telling it, so I will try to entertain you. . . ."

Unlike the respected men of substance and experience who told the *Swatura*, the tellers of fairy tales, though much appreciated in their own place, were considered slightly odd and their interest in repeating *Paramitsha* not very dignified, for these tales were pure entertainment and nothing else. In the same way, the Rom did not play music just for the entertainment: songs had a precise meaning and a function. The poetry and the meaning of the words of the songs were considered more important than the delivery or the singing ability. The songs were accompanied only by hand-clapping. Musical instruments were reserved for entertaining the Gaje. There were the *patshivaki djilia*, friendship songs or songs to honor important guests. These were mostly epic. There were the *brigaki djilia*, or sorrow songs, that told of hardship. There was the important body of *mulengi djilia*, or dirges, and there were fun and dance songs. The actual variety of melodies was fairly limited and they were called *glasso*—the Slavic root for "voice"—or *mode*, to which new words were forever being improvised.

Among themselves the men spoke mostly of horses or about legal matters, recounting and analyzing judgments by the *Kris*, the law court of the Rom. These cases or legal precedents were called *bayura*, the plural of *bayo*, and formed the oral and only record of their jurisdictional system.

CHAPTER NINE

Sharing a common campsite with the Tshurara always had led to friction. Their unrestrained raiding parties intensified the peasants' hostility toward all Gypsies, and mere survival became an all-consuming preoccupation. The Tshurara apparently enjoyed stirring the pond for the pleasure of muddying the water. Lowara and Tshurara alike were Rom and therefore our prime loyalty was to our own people, even though we could often sympathize with the peasants' grievances. Whenever the Tshurara were in the vicinity our relations with the Gaje deteriorated steadily, but our sense of cohesion grew in response to outside pressure. The Tshurara creed seemed to be "Survive who can," ignoring the Lowara saying, "Some shade is good for everyone." They were given to violence and had an irresistible urge to plague the countryside. This was an invitation to further retaliations by the Gaje. Because they constantly had to break camp in haste, the Tshurara lived in filth and squalor and there was a general air of decay about their appearance, in sharp contrast to their almost brutal healthiness and insolence. There were times when, wherever Pulika and his *kumpania* traveled, they were unable to shake off the Tshurara, but an open rupture would have been against all concepts of basic hospitality of the Rom. The opportunities for horse trading dwindled as anti-Gypsy sentiment mounted. Fortune-telling along the roads was virtually impossible.

One night we were camped at the edge of a muddy river, far away from "civilization," where we were unexpectedly joined by a large number of wagons from our own *kumpania*, which until now had been scattered. The campsite was farther removed fom village or farmhouse than we would have cared for under ordinary circumstances, but presently it seemed ideally suited for the purpose. At daybreak the next morning we were once again joined by two wagons of the Tshurara group. One of the wagons belonged to Tshurkina and his wife Liza and their numerous brood; the other was that of Tshurkina's widowed father, Pani. With him lived his two trouble-making, no-good sons, Vedel and Merikano, both of whom were several years older than Kore and myself, and their much younger little sisters. The oldest, nine-year-old Simza, cooked and washed for the entire family. Several of Tshurkina and Liza's small children were sick, and Rupa grumbled something under her breath about the minimum courtesy of the road and the unwritten tradition of the Rom that prevented families whose members were sick with possibly contagious ailments from joining others until the nature of the disease was known. But since most of the Lowara were still asleep, and few of us had washed, Rupa turned aside and tactfully refrained from expressing her opinion to others in the camp. The Tshurara unhitched their horses and hastily set up camp, spreading out the feather beds on the ground even though the sun was already rising. We noticed that all the windows of their wagons were broken.

Liza, Tshurkina's wife, came to our fire, unconcerned with accepted formalities at this early hour; and without an apology or a hint of explanation—out of sheer laziness—she asked to borrow some fire, a thing that was never done. Keja abruptly offered her the pot of freshly brewed coffee to take along instead, which she did, insensitive to the intended slight.

Kore and I squabbled teasingly for the privilege of pouring water for Pulika, Tshukurka and Dodo's morning ablutions. We let water pour out over the Rom's hands from the spout of an old brass coffeepot that was reserved for this particular use, as a makeshift but expedient Romany equivalent of running water. We handed them the soap and held the towel ready for them. Here man and child met on an equal footing, free of restrictions of convention or respect. It also allowed one to follow the men around for part of the day and to share their breakfast and cigarettes. We went from one family fire to the next, greeting the Rom with a loud *"Droboy tume Romale,"* the traditional greeting, to which they answered *"Nais tuke"* (thank you). At each stop there would be more coffee, some choice tidbits of food and plentiful gossip.

Suddenly, from the distant river edge Tshaya's voice was heard scolding on and on. Several women hastened to the spot to find her and Pani's nine-year-old daughter Simza quarreling violently, even though it hardly seemed Simza could match Tshaya. It appeared that Tshaya had surprised the little Tshurara girl drawing water from the river without properly observing the rules of *ujo* and *marhime,* and to the Lowara this was a serious offense. Along the riverbank five points were roughly designated for drawing water. Water for drinking and cooking was to be taken farthest upstream; next came the water for washing dishes and bathing. Farther downstream, in order, was the water for the horses, for the washing of clothes, and last for the clothes of pregnant or menstruating women. Separate buckets were supposed to be used to fetch water for each particular use. This concept of clean and unclean was a constant concern to Gypsy families. A Rom should never touch anything *marhime.* The same term also applied to someone banished from the tribe by the *Kris* for serious misconduct. Banishment was the most severe punishment the *Kris* could mete out. A woman was considered *marhime* from the waist down and she must avoid letting the bottom of her skirts touch a man not her own, or anything he used. If her skirts should brush against plates, cups or drinking glasses, these were immediately destroyed, so as not to "soil" the next male user. For this same reason it was deemed good form to share the same plate with an important guest to show that the dishes were "untainted." It was difficult for me, at that time, to accept or encompass this concept of the "uncleanliness" of women, but after living with the Rom for a prolonged period I learned not only to accept but to appreciate the beneficial effects this restraining injunction could exert in a closed society, living in every other sense under conditions of promiscuity. The custom assured Gypsy women an absolute sense both of privacy and of protection among their own kind anywhere at large. Far from being derogatory, the notion of *marhime* gave a woman added dignity and a heightened awareness of the mystery of her femininity. On certain specific occasions it even offered a woman a form of power over a man. There was once a fight between a young man from the Trokeshti group, who with his wife was visiting the powerful, numerous and mean Voyatesha, who at that time "owned" and "ruled" the greatest part of the industrial north of France. It was an inconsequential drunken brawl, but several of the Voyatesha banding together senselessly brutalized the outsider. The young wife was helpless and her alternate pleading and cursing were to no avail until, after having duly warned them, still without effect, she ripped off one of her manifold skirts and symbolically flailed them all with it. The fight stopped instantly as they realized they had become *marhime* and no Rom, not even their closest male relatives, would have anything to do with them until the case was brought before the *Kris* and the burdensome onus of the *marhime* lifted.

Shortly after the incident between Tshaya and little Simza and the subsequent flaring of tempers among the women of both "races," a group of small children came running excitedly, bringing the news that the river was filled with floating dead fish. Without a moment's hesitation the Rom agreed to disband. They left this spot only after having overturned every bucket and pail containing river water. Kettles of food and soup were poured out, coffee was spilled. The fires were scattered and the embers were stamped out or covered by loose dirt and ashes. We would not be marked among the Rom by the stigma of doubt concerning our ritual cleanliness and would bear no onus because of it, but it proved once again that the Tshurara must be watched closely. Keja took it upon herself to remind the Tshurara women and girls again about the observance of all restrictions imposed by their womanhood. A woman, for example, should never pass in front of a man or between two men, but behind them; and if this was not possible, she should ask the men to turn away, saying, "Bolde tut, kako" (Please turn away). She should also at all times avoid passing in front of horses hitched onto a wagon, and let the wagon pass and then cross behind it.

Hours after leaving the site we regrouped at another Godforsaken spot. The Tshurara were still with us and, as was to be expected, insensitive to our disapproval. Repeated incidents like that of the dead fish had earned them the reputation of "defilers of the rivers." Later that same night we were joined by several more wagons. Again Tshurara. Among them were Pani's brothers, Gunari and old Nanosh, who was married to Pita, and a large number of their married sons and their families. They invaded the camping ground with wild yells to encourage the tired and thirsty horses to pull more strongly on the uneven ground. The heavy wheels screamed on their dry axles. As usual they drove in a savage hurry and at every rough hump or furrow in the ground, crockery, glassware and cooking pans crashed loudly inside the swaying wagons and slid from side to side as on a ship on a rough sea. The men laughed but some women yelled in anger and swore. We stayed round our fires and pretended to continue our conversations undisturbed. In their part of the camp the usual disorder prevailed. All night long they argued violently among themselves, drinking wildly on empty stomachs and failing to invite others to share.

Contrary to my expectations, we did not break up camp the following day. The men squatted or sprawled leisurely in small groups near the fires or at the edge of the pastures. We were too far away from the nearest hamlet for the women to go shopping or fortune-telling. The sun was hot and the country-side around us was alive with the sounds of buzzing insects, cooing wood pigeons and the crunching noises of grazing horses. Nearby several dogs panted drowsily, daydreaming of action. Merikano showed us his newly acquired brass knuckle-duster, while his pockmarked older brother, Vedel, strutted about ostentatiously sucking a lump of sugar on which he had sprinkled a few drops of liquid from a small bottle he kept in his trouser pocket. It smelled repulsively of medicine and turned our stomachs. It was ether and he had acquired the habit in jail. Several of Gunari's sons joined us in games of challenge. They started innocently enough with stone throwing and wrestling and progressed to bareback horse-racing contests between two and three horses. A small crowd of children and young girls gathered by the chestnut trees to watch us. Yokka, Gunari's youngest son, was an accomplished rider but he lost to Kore riding a superior horse. The game, which had started in friendly enough fashion, turned increasingly competitive and the onlookers' comments and encouragements became unduly partisan, taunting, and even insolent. The atmosphere suddenly seemed electrified beyond reason, but we realized too late that we could not pull out of the contest graciously or—as the Tshurara said tauntingly, sensing our momentary hesitation, "without being forced to eat dirt." It was not the realization of their large number or their ugly mood that made us want to disengage ourselves but rather the knowledge that the outcome, whatever it would be, could only worsen the tension between our elders. Instinctively the boys regrouped themselves according to their allegiances, into two confronting, hostile camps, as the mood grew meaner. A young Tshurara—Inga, the son of Nanosh— had been holding a horsewhip, and he suddenly hit out. There was a slight whistling whisper followed by a sharp whipcrack. Suddenly and unexpectedly one of our boys brought his hand to his face and instinctively bit the spot on his hand that had just been grazed. Kore, who also was holding a horsewhip, snapped back, but Inga jumped away and he missed. Now they circled each other cautiously, alert but with calculating patience. The group rapidly spread out and left a wide-open space for the contestants because snapping whips reached far. Never before had I seen Kore angry. I was impressed, and I felt a tinge of Lowari pride. Warily each anticipated his rival's move. Their faces were impassive; only their eyes showed anger and their lips turned pale in tense preparedness. Inga hit out a few tentative whip snaps, probing, as if rehearsing. Emboldened by Kore's unruffled stoicism, Inga became restless, too sure of his superiority, and impatient to savor the humiliation of Kore's whipping. He was flushed, and slowly an insolent smirk spread over his face. Carried away, Inga pranced and swaggered shamelessly, accompanied by the derisive catcalls of the other Tshurara youths. Then he spat at Kore in scorn, only to double up silently with a thin red whip mark across his gaping mouth. With a well-aimed quick flick of the wrist Kore had answered Inga. The expression on his face remained unchanged; only his eyes had narrowed slightly in expectation. The pause that followed seemed endless, as if time had frozen. A split second later, however, the Tshurara were throwing stones at us. Kore replied by chastising Inga with a few more accurate lashes before taking cover behind the trunk of one of the chestnut trees. Attracted by the commotion and the yells and screams of the young children, Pulika and several other Rom came to the meadows to investigate, and their arrival dispersed the combative youths. Several of the Tshurara men were with him. Inga was led away by his cousin Vosho to hide his shame. Pulika took the horsewhip from Kore without any show of anger or even annoyance and flung it away. The other Rom shrugged their shoulders and gently reprimanded everyone within earshot, without singling out any one person. Pulika warned us all against starting any further trouble. He forbade us to have contact with the Tshurara youth, but it was hard to calm ourselves and not easy to surrender our grudges.

As we walked back to the camp, the Tshurara children hooted from a distance and made various other sounds that were meant to be insulting. All the Tshurara women, girls and children, who at all other times gathered by our fires, were sent away unceremoniously. The camp was clearly divided. Before going to sleep several of us went, as was our custom, "to look at the horses," to use the Romany euphemism. We met Nanosh's boys, who must have been waiting for us, and there followed some silent but angry scuffling in the dark. Some punches were exchanged, easing our frayed tempers, and we all went back to camp and to bed. The next morning the Rom acted as if nothing had happened but the young ones exchanged hateful stares, tensing closed fists. The women were on edge, and it was time we separated before more serious trouble erupted. Besides, the Tshurara were constantly on the rampage, looting and destroying property and, whereas all Rom shared a sublime scorn for the Gaje, the Tshurara were unaware of and rejected the dignity of rest, the lyrical ecstasy the Lowara sought in the joy of being alive. Tshurkurka said the Tshurara had a mentality that defied fulfillment; they ran to digest, drank only to get drunk and were like wolves on the Russian steppes, which, pursued by horsemen, kept running, even when decapitated, so great was their urge to run. For his immediate dependents and for his *kumpania* Pulika refused to live at the expense of losing the reason for living. The Rom anyway were considered as "undesirables" and the only way to salvage their dignity was by contributing something, after a fashion, to Gaje society: exoticism, romance, nostalgia, the awakening of dreams, questions, longings, to distract the Gaje from their routine. Half in jest the Rom claimed that by the same token the Gaje needed someone to tell them "what time it was." The Rom commented on the Tshurara's way of life by saying that even misery and grief must appear good to those who have become used to it.

For several more days we crisscrossed the countryside and kept coming upon the trail of the Tshurara, weaving in and out of their wake, as it were, and reaping the corrosive bitterness left by their sting. They seemed to have been before us wherever we went, as if omnipresent, leaving the entire territory sullen and inhospitable toward us. Continued police harassment threatened to shatter Pulika's *kumpania*. We were forced to travel only at dusk and with great stealth, camping overnight in desolate locations. Even to obtain enough water for the families' needs and for the horses became an ordeal, as we were vilified and ill-treated and often failed to obtain the minimal requirements for bare survival. Doors were slammed in our faces. We were rebuffed, abused and threatened, and our pleading protests that we were not "like that" fell on deaf ears. Pulika sent out very young children to supplicate the coldhearted peasants for water and bread or potatoes, in the hope that the innocence of their tender age might soften the farmers' resolve. But they too were chased away with uncalled-for brutality. The Gaje remained implacable, hoping to get rid of the Gypsies by making them suffer. A certain bitterness contaminated the very young, while the older people comforted themselves with the comparison of degree, intensity and duration of similar past experiences they had survived. Pulika cautioned us to remain in sight and within earshot at all times and to be ready to break camp at the spur of the moment. He advised us to have endless patience and, for the time being, to avoid anger. He also implied that a day of reckoning before the *Kris* was coming for the Tshurara, who were doing us the disservice of spreading panic among the Gaje and in this way were responsible for our present hardship.

At sunset of an autumn day Kore, Zurka, Nanosh, myself and a few other boys were raiding an apple orchard to still our gnawing hunger. We lay under the gnarled trees savoring some half-ripe apples, soaking in the pungent mustiness of the shady place, when a sharp, stinging sensation in my lower back made me leap up. Kore jerked upright at the same moment with a shriek. Simultaneously a burst of gunfire reverberated through the still dusk. We scattered, Kore and I limping but obviously more scared than hurt. An old farmer loomed out of his concealment behind a woodpile, like a malevolent apparition. We ran back to the camp, instinctively making a wide curve so as not to betray the location of it in case he wanted to pursue us, hoping to lose him in the oncoming night. By the firelight I saw the blood smudging Kore's shirt and trousers, and suddenly realized we had both been hit by shotgun pellets, which we insisted on calling bullets. An excited crowd of yelling women and children briefly surrounded us upon our arrival at the encampment. When they realized we had been hurt in certain parts below the belt, however, the women left to give us a sense of privacy and returned to their fires. Keja spread out the feather beds for us on the ground. Three very young boys crouched a few feet away from us in silent watch. We painfully slid into the bed and undressed awkwardly. After a while Pulika came to probe our wounds. He slit a small crosslike incision around the entry holes made by the pellets. Kore gnashed his teeth and grunted in pain, while I silently awaited my turn. Pulika failed to extract any lead pellets and he came to the conclusion, somewhat belatedly for Kore's sake, that we had been hit with rock salt instead of lead and it now burned deep in our flesh as it dissolved, but at least it would not need extracting. He spread a thick paste of mashed cucumber on our wounds and gave us some more brandy and a whole cigarette each. I worried about the possibility of infection, suddenly aware again of the relative degree of cleanliness of the Rom. The dissolving salt must have adequately substituted for other disinfectants since nothing of what I feared happened.

As our consternation ebbed away and the sensation of imminent danger lessened, a bitter resentment grew in me, along with a blinding compulsion to seek revenge. I couldn't sleep all night from the pain. I tossed about and my grudge swelled from resentment into choking hate, like the throbbing of a spreading infection. Repeatedly I woke Kore from his somnolent resignation. I was annoyed by what I could only construe as plain fatalistic equanimity and surrender on his part. I was equally annoyed by what I felt was Pulika's indifference to our fate. I hated the Gaje and I resented, was stunned by, the Rom's unconcern. Until dawn I lay awake, upset by seething anxieties and at the same time half aware of the exaggeration of my ranting and my slow self-intoxication with anger. I knew this was due to the overconfidence, and dependence, of a protected childhood and the desperate awakening to the realization of my vulnerability.

The Rom broke camp before being chased away after the initial twenty-four-hour period of grace and traveled a few short miles. I slept intermittently most of that day and carefully nursed my unhappiness into full bloom. Kore slept and recovered while I brooded on. It was Keja who first became aware of my condition: the result of prolonged pressure from the Gaje world, the constant slights and aggravations, and also of my confusion about the Rom's distinctions among themselves, which I had not expected. Because of my own age I had oversimplified life, overlooking its endless but essential shades. Keja tried, as much as she could, to temper my distress, but strict observation of the division between men and women and between boys and girls limited her expressions of sympathy to occasional conspiratorial winks or half-masked reassuring waves of the hand. Pulika was imperturbable, but somehow I knew him well enough to realize he was anticipating my next move. Toward dusk I could no longer contain my distress and I told Pulika of my resolve to return to "that" village to put their haystacks to fire and avenge our degradation. Pulika listened gravely to my heated propositions. He let me speak out fully, allowing me to partly exhaust my bitterness. The futility of my urge became apparent without his ever replying to me. Pulika then said a few words to Keja, and she and Rupa got up and after a short preparation left the encampment. Because I expected a direct reply to the formulation of my own dilemma, the meaning of what he had suggested to them escaped me at first. The two of them were going back to the location of our last camp to put a curse on the farm and the orchard of the man who shot Kore and me. Having experienced the farmer's ruthlessness, I was shocked at the thought of the two unprotected women going back to taunt him on my behalf, as I guessed rightly, only to right my inordinate humiliation and to soothe me. I was amazed at the casual way in which Pulika had asked them to do this and the equally undramatic way in which they just went. Night was falling fast. I felt ashamed, bitter and miserable. To the Rom the night was a protective cover that shielded them from the outside world and dramatized the separation between them even more as the Rom stayed with the Rom and the Gaje with the Gaje, whereas by daylight they mixed to a limited extent. The shuttered windows of the Gaje protected them against the darkness that was descending around us, protecting the Rom.

The insistent barking of the Gypsies' dogs told us of Rupa's and Keja's safe return. They had gone straight to the farm, purposefully walking at a rapid stride as the lonely Gajo walker still on the road at this hour unconsciously averted his gaze, sensing a certain uncanniness about them out alone so late. The women knew that the effectiveness of their action was based solely on the underlying assumptions on the part of the Gaje. They knew that they were being watched and that every detail of their behavior would become magnified and laden with mysterious meaning. They felt fairly confident that no one would dare do them violence and that no one really would be surprised that they had come or bear them malice for wanting to settle accounts with the farmer for his uncalled-for brutality against one of theirs. They made deliberately slow, sweeping, crosslike gestures, putting a spell on the entire estate. Other Gaje would stay away from this place for a while to avoid the possible risk of exposing themselves to the bad luck that would be associated with it from now on. The women must have been relieved, as they approached the camp on their return, to hear the familiar barking chorus of our dogs in contrast to the lonely, maddening howls of the solitary watchdogs of isolated farms they had passed.

Not another word was said about the women's expedition. The Rom sat around the dying embers of the fires and went to sleep early. The following morning we left at dawn and traveled out of the district as if fleeing some looming disaster. After a few days the multiple but tiny wounds were healing well and the stinging sensation left. Kore and I had practically forgotten the incident except in its potential as a dramatized story to be told, but only now did Pulika allude to it in that fashion so typical of him, indirectly but very much to the point. He started his rambling monologue by quoting what he said was an old Lowara saying "not to eat the food as hot as it is while being cooked," and I remember wondering for an instant if he was paraphrasing the French saying, *La vengeance est un plat qui se mange à froid*. He went on to say that "you must greatly love him who manages to make you cry or angers you." He said I was still "straddling two horsebacks with a single behind," and that I must abandon my attachment to the Gaje, for that was the reason I still resented them and expected good things from them. To the Rom life was an endless flow, like a torrent without form or goal, beyond good or evil, and man's place in it was like a process of self-definition, forbidding the all too human cowardice of weariness and doubt. With a driving urge to seek out what was elemental in life, man was free to react in his own way to its challenges, be what he could make of himself. *This* was his freedom.

Dusk came early and I thought I read new meaning into it as I watched the fireflies squander their lights.

Occasionally my bitterness would suddenly flare up again, and it was from Keja that I learned to bend my head when I was unable otherwise to hide the hatred I could not transpose.

CHAPTER TEN

One day as we were tending the horses, Pulika asked me abruptly, "Which is greater, the oak or the dandelion?" I was weary of such questions, knowing him well and sensing a trap; I grinned and tried to gain time but he pressed me to answer. The too obvious reply would have been "the oak" because it was bigger and more useful. Instead I slyly replied "the dandelion," realizing that this was bound to be wrong. The correct Romany solution was "whichever one of the two achieves fulfillment." A matured dandelion would be greater than a stunted oak, irrespective of its size or usefulness. The ultimate measure, the fulfillment of one's potentialities, was the valuation: the truthfulness to one's own seed and nature.

Another day Pulika asked me if I knew that all Gypsies, and possibly all humans, had two successive lives. He said that since I had almost become one of theirs it was time for me to be informed about some of the facts of life. His expression was inscrutable. Pulika expanded on the subject and told me that because God was just and loved us He gave us a first chance to live the way we wanted, making all the possible mistakes we cared to make, and afterward the second life was meant to correct and avoid the errors of the first one. It sounded like an improbable, rather wild theory, but then on the other hand it seemed to offer some appealing possibilities; and since Pulika appeared to put a certain emphasis on proposing it, I felt it my definite and pleasant obligation to try to fulfill these conditions of my first life. Pulika pushed back his dark, wide-brimmed hat with his thumb and leaned over toward me. He clearly guessed the thought he had deliberately called up. With a broad grin that turned into a deep belly laugh he added that, unfortunately for me, this happened to be my second life, in which I was supposed to correct the errors I had committed in my first one.

Overhead a falcon slowly circled in an ever-narrowing orbit, abruptly to fall from the sky.

There followed an unending string of undistinguished overnight camps and hasty departures, of hostile receptions in village after village. The days were hot and drinking water was in short supply and often had to be begged for. A few times we ran into a single wagon of the Tshurara horde. Our horses started looking badly fed, neglected and overworked, and we ourselves almost had the appearance of Tshurara. The Lowara children, unused to the extent of this harassment, were reacting by being on the wild side and overly aggressive whenever they could afford to do so. To themselves they justified this un-Lowara-like behavior as retribution to the Gaje, who in turn felt theirs was only a reaction to the Gypsies' misbehaving.

Toward nightfall one day, I saw old Bidshika, absorbed in thought, squatting by some pools left by the previous day's rain. With his heavy walking stick, ornamented with inlaid silver bands, he traced a narrow gully from one small pool to the other. When he looked up after a while and saw me stare in amused puzzlement, he simply said, "What divides is evil, and what joins, relates, flows, is good. Life is a flow, a dialogue, and death is an isolation, a dividing, leading to chaos and subsequently to disintegration." Bidshika was as unself-conscious as he said this as if he had remarked that the day had been hot. It was in no way meant to be wise, didactic or superior.

The same afternoon, uncomprehending, I had watched Pulika playing with one of his small grandsons, Palko, the son of our Yojo. Pulika sat half crouching on an upturned bucket by the log fire. Little Palko stood between his knees, leaning with his elbows on Pulika's sturdy thighs. Occasionally the child pulled up his legs and swung nonchalantly or gravely observed his grandfather smoking. Pulika leaned over and loudly whispered in his ear, pointing at Tshaya who crouched nearby cleaning some vegetables. Half reluctantly, the child fairly shouted in baby talk something which to him was a bad or naughty word. Tshaya pretended at first to ignore him but Pulika encouraged the child to persist in teasing her. These words—like *kula* or *pulpa*—had no particular meaning except as a symbolic release of pent-up displeasure or of mockery, but when repeatedly directed at one person they were considered to be provocative. Tshaya looked up and threateningly shook her open hand in a chopping motion. Still prodded by Pulika, little Palko repeated his words and Tshaya pretended increasing anger, till she took the trouble to get up and come over to hit the child and the grandfather both. The child turned to Pulika for protection, which he gave with mock exaggeration. The insult was repeated endlessly and as the child displayed less fear, Tshaya gradually became more violent. The boy received more of the mock slaps and thus, in playfulness, lost his fear of them. There were bouts of angry, protesting cries as Tshaya hit him harder than expected, but the "lesson" was repeated until the child was able to continue insulting independently of his reasonable fear of immediate consequences. This entire mock battle was controlled by tacit understanding between the grown-ups and was never allowed to get out of control. The purpose of this game was to teach the child not to do or refrain from doing anything because of fear of physical pain, and to prevent him from developing a cowardly disposition. The only form of discipline the Lowara recognized ultimately was self-discipline based on understanding, or in other words a discipline of responsibility. To the Lowara, fear was the symbolic attribute of *Beng*, or Evil, because it destroyed man's soul.

Then one day again, quite unexpectedly, there was a growing concentration of Gypsy wagons, including many of the Tshurara, and, despite their misgivings, the Lowara rejoiced at the prospect of extensive communal festivities that such occasions lead them to expect. The site was ideally situated near flowing water, with abundant pastures and, being at the edge of a forest, within easy access to plentiful firewood. The next few hours were spent in active preparations. The cooking fires roared and the women busied themselves, while some of the men drove away on the two-wheeled flat carts to fetch adequate supplies of brandy and beer at the nearest inn, some miles away. Once again the Lowara prepared to indulge in their unrivaled tradition of hospitality and erase the tart memory of recent hardships.

By their fires the Rom and their families ate to satiety and drank happily the rest of the night. Young girls were asked to perform dances to honor their fathers' guests. Old songs were remembered and some new ones made up under the happy inspiration of the moment. The trees were swaying in the wind, and the rustling of the leaves was one of the reassurng sounds of the night in the background. The Prussian-blue sky was occasionally scratched by a succession of flashes of summer lightning. Slowly the exuberant merrymaking gave way to a more serious mood as the young ones grew tircd of dancing and the abundant roast meats and liquor slowed down the gusto of the enchanted night. The young men of the group waited on the Rom with ease and gracefulness, and only now could the very old and respected Rom be prevailed upon to remember and sing the songs of their youth and young manhood, epic and sorrow songs, until they were drunk with words such as alcohol could not have induced, and time vanished. Most of the small children were asleep, sprawled all over their mothers and their older sisters and brothers, who by way of tender, intimate caresses, scratched their little necks and scalps, and lovingly searched their long hair for imagined or real lice. I listened until dawn, when it carried me to sleep.

The following morning the euphoria was partly undone by two successive incidents involving the Tshurara. The priest of a local Catholic church some miles off came, accompanied by a number of indignant parishioners, to complain angrily about the little Gypsy girls who had stolen candles from his sanctuary the night before. When the first Rom they cornered shrugged his shoulders noncommittally, and lamely denied that it could have been children from this particular camp, the priest stated that he personally had surprised them in the act, and with a mounting hysterical undercurrent in his voice he accused the little girls of devilishly having attempted to put a spell of sorts on him by lifting their little skirts indecently high before scrambling off and before he recovered from the shock and could catch them. His indignation was understandable.

Half the previous night the wagon of Shandor and his wife Pesha had been lit up by candles, which in summer was most unusual among the Gypsies since everybody sat in the open by the fires rather than inside their wagons, and also to avoid the waste and the unwanted heat of burning candles. Pesha's swarthy, wild-eyed little girls had giggled among themselves for hours, distracting the grown-ups until Shandor, their father, rudely made them be quiet, lest some of the other guests misinterpret the giggling as being at their expense.

Even after having been chastened they had difficulty smothering their merriment. They remained unusually excited, even for Tshurara children. Now, unexpectedly, the reason for it became clear even if it appeared a great deal less amusing. As the priest continued his exhortation and endlessly repeated his accusations against these pagans, these servants of the Evil One, more and more of the Rom gathered to find out what the commotion was about. Deeply shamed before the Rom by their daughters' indiscreet behavior, Pesha and Shandor soundly thrashed them in public, until they had to be restrained from injuring them permanently, heightening the embarrassment of the moment. The entire camp was astir, excitedly discussing the impudent Tshurara brats. What upset the Rom was not so much the Tshurara girls' offense, or even the consequences of the village priest's anger, but rather the fact of having to face and discuss actions with however slight sexual connotation of the girls' exposure, before the Rom.

Even before the Gaje had left the camp, Shandor had harnessed his horses, hitched them to the wagon and departed stealthily. In part it was to atone for the shame his children had brought him in the presence of the Rom, but also he fled to escape whatever retribution the priest and his parishioners might have in store for them and by the same token to distract the anger of the villagers from the Gypsies who stayed behind them. The men went back to the pasturelands and the women went their way. It was a hot day and the fires were allowed to die out or were just kept as smoldering embers easily to be fanned to flames. Only the very young children remained in the camp under the supervision of older sisters and a few old people too dignified or too tired to wander far by themselves in search of adventure. Some Tshurara men had crept into the underbrush at the outer edge of the campsite and slept in the shade, not to emerge before dusk. In the privacy of the enclosed space of the wagons and unseen by the men, women and girls, naked to the waist, washed their long, black hair.

At sundown a large group of gaily chattering Tshurara women and children returned to the camp with quantities of ripe strawberries they had gathered at some cultivated patches. Before any of the men had tasted any, an ominous question arose as to their possibly being *marhime*. At first it only created puzzlement. Some thought it was a joke, except that one did not joke about *marhime*. Then old Tsura, the shrewd one, asked the Tshurara women a few innocent questions: did strawberries grow close to the ground? How numerous and how close were the rows in which they grew? In what sequence had the women walked while picking the fruit and had any of them at any time walked ahead or behind the others? Slowly the pattern of her suspicion of *marhime* grew in our minds. The Tshurara women walking ahead of the others must have stepped over the plants from which those who followed were bound to have gathered fruits. A Gypsy woman's having stepped over them made the strawberries *marhime* beyond a doubt. The "soiled" fruit was promptly, if regretfully, discarded. These Tshurara were almost as bad as Gaje in this respect and a great deal less careful. They must be watched closely. I was given to know that from now I must not, under any circumstances, eat of their food by their fires.

Most of us had noticed and worried about the fact that many Tshurara lustily and persistently scratched themselves well beyond the minimum restraint of Romany modesty. They did this even in the presence of older and respected members of our group and we felt ashamed at their lack of decorum.

It was not the open suggestion or the obvious implication of vermin that bothered us, since to some extent this was unavoidable under the conditions in which the Rom lived, but rather the admission that they did not care enough to keep them reasonably under control. I was advised to avoid unnecessarily close physical contact with Tshurara. Then one day it came to Kore's critical attention that Vedel, Vosho, Mericano and many of the other Tshurara youths not only scratched themselves continually and inordinately but that they itched in unlikely places like wrists, ankles and between their fingers, which displayed open sores. Kore passed on this observation to Yojo, who, after talking it over with his wife, repeated it to Rupa, who in turn drew Pulika's attention to it. Tshukurka was made aware of it and after some casual but huddled discussions about this among the Lowara, Pulika called all the men from the camp together, both Tshurara and Lowara. The men sat themselves casually in a wide circle, crouched or sprawled, with the members of both groups freely intermingled. After the usual rather elaborate and courteous preliminaries, Pulika abruptly came to the point by saying that certain members of the present *kumpania* had transgressed against the law of the Rom. If this had been done unwittingly and they were willing to make amends, he would ask the council of the elders to consider this, but in any case, for the present, he demanded at least temporary exclusion from the group. If the charges were found correct—and would he, Pulika, go so far as accusing certain elements unless he felt he had sufficient proof?—he swore a dire oath he would have no truck with them for six weeks, whatever happened. As Pulika slowly poured part of the contents of his beer glass on the ground, he said, "May my brains flow out the way this beer flows out if—" (*Te shordjol muri godji sar shordjol kadi bera*—). There followed a stunned silence, as the Rom were not used to Pulika's acting emotionally and he was visibly angry. Tshukurka took over and said that there were people in the camp who had scabies, that troublesome skin disease, and had chosen not to report this or for that matter had not tried in any way to treat and get rid of it, nor taken any measures to prevent contagion. By their irresponsible and disloyal attitude they threatened all the camp followers. Eventually everybody was staring at everybody else's hands. Several Tshurara walked away. Tshukurka and Yojo reached out and inspected some hands, as others offered theirs for inspection and proof of their innocence. Before supper most of the wagons belonging to the Tshurara had departed, but an uneasy mood remained as most people became aware of the possibility and danger of infection. We had lived close to the Tshurara for a long time and in many cases had unwittingly used the same tools, plates or drinking cups that they had. At sunup the following morning we broke camp. For days we traveled at forced speed in order to leapfrog, as it were, the present Tshurara area in the hope of finding territory as yet not overtaken by them and the formless mob that coalesced around them.

Pulika claimed to have no ill will toward the Tshurara as such; he would not seek to avoid them if only they would behave more responsibly. God bless them, he said, may they travel safely, may they prosper and multiply, but let them stay at a distance at all times; let us live again as Lowara, to roam the land freely without ever-present harassment from the authorities, aware, but without resentment, that we are only strangers on sufferance, undesirable aliens and by implication expendable, forever eligible for deportation. We should tread more softly. By ending our uneasy alliance with the Tshurara and their competitive rivalry at cross purposes with ours we stood only to lose what at best was only their token allegiance to our *kumpania*. Old Bidshika disapprovingly scolded them for being anarchistic, *Narodnaya Volya,* followers of Nechayev, who in prerevolutionary Russia advocated "terrible, total, merciless destruction." But among the Rom nobody paid much attention to his "Gaje gibberish" anyway.

One day the caravan halted at the outskirts of a small town, and Pulika and his brother visited the local hospital in search of a cure for scabies or preventive treatment. Reluctantly we were all made to use the prescribed greenish-yellow ointment with the sharp, unpleasant smell of sulphur.

We traveled without leaving the usual *vurma*, or trail of roadmarks, which under other circumstances all Rom were expected to do as a matter of course and the neglect of which was an offense punishable by Gypsy law. Pulika, the pragmatist, said that "in the village without dogs the farmers walked without sticks" (*ando gav bi juklesko jal o pavori bi destesko*), which no doubt would be a pleasant change from the harassment of the last few months. The new land "be-

longed" to one Finans, who could hardly afford to turn down
Pulika's courteous request for asylum, but his small *kumpania*
was soon crowded out by our migration. Eventually he decided to move on.

At first I had been amazed and also a little puzzled by the
simplicity and the total effectiveness of Pulika's curse or
armaya, to impose his will on the ubiquitous Tshurara, especially since at no other time had various expressions of disapproval, irritation or anger been of any use.

Soon after I joined the Lowara the boys had instructed me
in the basic facts of life among the Rom, such as the *armaya.*
At first they expressed total disbelief when I informed them
that most Gaje did not currently resort to the use of curses to
solve practical matters but that at best, or at worst, this was
frowned upon only as a release of pent-up anger and nothing
more. The Rom called all forms of curses *armaya,* and I
learned there were many different kinds. For example, when a
Gypsy openly cursed a Gajo to his face, or at least in such a
way that he would readily learn about it from others, the Rom
believed that this had no real power except that of frightening
him, which in such a case sufficed as far as they were concerned. As in the case of the fortune-telling the women practiced, they knew that the effectiveness of their actions was
based solely on the underlying assumptions on the part of the
Gaje. When used among themselves, however, the Rom firmly
believed in the actual potency of the *armaya* and often resorted to it, but they were always careful to use it only in the
conditional sense, like "May you die a violent death if—"
Among Pulika's people the *armaya* had developed into an
accepted, even a polite, form of social pressure, and this was
currently used in everyday life, but in this case the hurtful
intent of the curse was turned against the person uttering it to
make the other party accept a favor or an invitation to eat or
drink. The original refusal that led to this form of insistence
was often only proper Gypsy restraint, humility and good
manners, and the seemingly dramatic resorting to the *armaya*
was only intended to convince someone to withdraw his refusal. The invitation was then promptly accepted to avoid the
various disasters the host would have called down upon him-

self, his immediate kin or his property, had his offer been declined. Yielding to this specific form of social pressure among the Lowara, one loudly answered *Bater,* may it be so (if I refuse), or an equivalent of sorts of Amen. Laetshi told me that one should hasten to wish that no evil should ever happen under any circumstances to the person who cursed himself, or for that matter to anybody present on the occasion. It was further a point of *savoir-faire* and of courtesy to bless one's host or wish him well in accepting his invitation. This also was done instead of saying "Thank you," which the Gypsies said only once upon leaving and was meant to cover an entire period of hospitality rather than each individual act or part of it. The Lowara were always careful to use this form of *armaya* with their own kin and with people they knew or hoped had no reason to bear them a hidden grudge.

At first I learned, and learned to use, fairly simple, straightforward *armaya* like: "May I die if" (*Te merav*), "May my father, mother or brothers die if" (*Te merel muro dad, muri dei*); "May our favorite stallion die if" (*Te merel amaro kuro o lasho*), according to the requirements of the occasion. Each Rom of a certain standing or repute had his own personal and particular *armaya,* almost like a signature and by which he was known to everybody. Pulika, in calling a curse upon himself in case the Tshurara did not stay clear of us for a period of at least six weeks, had said while pouring out part of the beer he happened to be drinking at the time, "May my brains flow out the way this beer flows out if—" (*Te shordjol muri godji sar shordjol kadi bera—*); Tshukurka used the variant "May my blood spill" (*Te shordjol muro rat*), etc., or he used "May you burn candles for me" (*Te pabaren mange memelia*), in obvious reference to funeral ritual. Such expressions were used by all members of a particular family or yet one might semiconsciously identify with a much admired person who had died by saying, "May I buried next to X if—" (*Te prakhon man pasha o X—*). When the *armaya* was used to emphasize a negation or a denial, a specification of time was often added for effect, such as "before I even have my next meal" (*may sigo sar te may khav*), or "before this fire burns out" (*may angle sar te merel kadi yag*).

CHAPTER ELEVEN

When it finally stopped raining, after weeks of intermittently bad weather, it was unseasonably cold. A leaden sky pressed down. The air turned misty and the Rom huddled close by the blazing fires. At night we slept in our damp shirts; the women took off one or more of their soaked overskirts from the manifold thickness of their petticoats, but the small children were privileged to strip, and slept naked. Smells became more pungent, and, combined with humidity and the smoke of the wood fires, they were almost nauseating. The meadows turned to mud. Shifting camps day by day, we steadily plodded along, a few miles at a time. At night we camped in sprawling bivouacs. More and more wagons joined our traveling unit, which grew perceptibly. Everywhere along the roads were signs left by other Rom traveling ahead of us. Instead of veering off their trail, which from my past experiences of life among the Gypsies would have seemed to be the accepted pattern, our group continued its slow, regular march onward in the same general direction. When I asked Kore about this, he appeared mystified by my unawareness. Had I not seen the recurring signs? And our caravan kept growing. At crossroads other wagons simply took their place in the long line. We passed small roadside camps of two or three wagons. Small children ran excitedly to watch us drive by. Some hours later the same group would overtake us and fall in with us in a single column, which by now extended over several miles. The weather grew warmer and the mood of the Rom more exuberant.

Speaking to local horse traders, shopkeepers or the owners of taverns, the Gypsies consistently spread rumors that they were heading toward a "convention of all Gypsies of the

170

world" in order to "elect the new King." Others spoke of the "religious aspects" of this gathering of the tribes, but all attempted to reassure the local population that the Rom were not up to their usual mischief. And they saw to it that this promise was kept. The small children were discouraged from begging, and the more aggressive fortune-tellers among the women were warned. The Lowara boys ran ahead of the wagon train to chase away the livestock in the road, and though they openly flirted with the peasant girls, nobody paid them any heed. The Gypsies kept bargaining to a minimum and paid cash for all the necessities they acquired, even though the old women and a few young girls found it almost impossible to comply with the new order.

Numerous *kumpanias* were gathering. Many of these consisted of old friends and relatives. Dodo la Kejako was there; so were Luluvo and his brothers. There was old Bakro's *kumpania*, which we had not come across for several years, with a whole new crop of young children. There were Rom with whom we had had earlier encounters over the years at unremembered crossroads, but these previous meetings had been too brief to produce trust or lasting affection. There were also numerous Tshurara: Merikano, Vedel, and Vosho, the son of Tshurkina, all of whom sported the most unlikely, wildly colored shirts with what they claimed was the latest style—collars eight or ten inches long, with a useless button dangling at each tip. A number of small camps were scattered over a large area. The Rom continually shuttled back and forth in their *taligas* as they visited from settlement to temporary settlement. The young men volunteered to gather large enough quantities of firewood to last for days.

To judge from the preparations, I knew the Rom were readying themselves for a protracted stay. At twilight Zurka, Laetshi and several other of the young unmarried men came back from errands, each driving a *taliga* loaded with watermelons, possibly several hundreds of them in all. In their impatience to savor the sweet, juicy meat, the Rom who did not have a knife at hand slammed the watermelons to the ground where they burst open with a muffled thud, showing their bright red flesh with the glistening black seeds. From a dirty pond nearby came the discordant noises of the ducks attempting to fly at the water level, in short, noisy bursts as for a short moment they left a trace on the darkening waters. Packs of dogs prowled through the heaps of rubble and had to be chased away. As far as the eye could see there were smoky shadows moving about in the distant firelight.

Pulika let me accompany him on several trips to nearby encampments, and it finally dawned on me that the Rom were gathering for the ominous meeting of the *Kris.*

The *Kris* was a recurring subject of conversation and it was always alluded to with a strange diffidence. Throughout my stay with the Rom my fictional projection of the *Kris* and its drama had assumed awesome proportions, and in my eager anticipation it had grown into ardent and romantic imagery; the *krisatora,* the judges, had acquired legendary stature. Pulika had impressed upon me how for countless generations the Rom had survived as an entity because of their respect for the *Kris,* which enforced the restraint shown by more powerful groups among the Gypsies toward weaker parties. Pulika tried to explain to me how, in his view and that of the other Rom, the limits of the law were the limits of enforcement and the limits of enforcement were the actual limits of social organization. Without respect for the *Kris* the Rom would have reverted to savagery long ago and subsequently disintegrated as a people, for the rule of violence, or of pure power, inevitably attracted and in turn created moral inferiors.

That late afternoon, under the immensity of the sky, at some distance from Pulika's and Tshukurka's fires the *Kris* of the Lowara convened. A small group of men assembled. I knew most of them, yet something hard to define made them appear different from the men I knew. They wore the same clothes they wore every day and there were no outward symbols, no pageantry, to explain the difference except perhaps their very attitude. A hushed solemnity heightened the importance of the moment. Their voices sounded unusually subdued today; even though they moved with their customary ease, with an unaffected dignity totally devoid of arrogance, still they stood on ceremony. Most of the Rom knew each other well; many were on intimate terms and others were actually related to one another by kinship. Yet under the present circumstances they spoke with a hint of reserve and actual deference for the function each one of them filled. The *Kris* represented the collective wisdom of the Rom. The younger men, those who had not yet attained full stature in the community, stood in the background.

The Rom seated themselves in a wide circle on improvised seats: an odd assortment of crippled, disjointed chairs of all descriptions that happened to be at hand, an upturned bucket with a plank laid across it, wooden packing crates, a pile of harnesses and chains, even a battered birdcage. But in fact none of this could detract from the dignity or the repute of the *Kris*. The judges' sense of dignity reflected inner strength and vision and was not dependent on symbols of material affluence or power. The men smoked quietly and bottles of beer were passed around. After a while the conversation lagged and Pulika through his quietness demanded that attention be paid to him. He took off his wide-brimmed hat and said a few words in a low voice as if speaking to himself, and he poured part of his beer on the ground. He was deliberately undemonstrative, and if there was inherent drama in his gesture it was in the very absence of ostentation. He was offering a libation to the *Mule,* to the Ancestor Spirits, inviting them to witness the proceedings about to take place. It was a private gesture on his part and no one else followed his example.

A Rom I did not know by name was the first to address the *Kris.* After paying homage to the assembled Rom he asked in suitable form to be allowed to bring some preliminary unresolved questions to the attention of the present court. The subtlety of the argument was visibly much appreciated by the other older Rom but left me somewhat confused. I listened to the disconcerting flow of words, not knowing what to make of them or of the complexities of their meaning, until they seemed to spiral into nothingness. At first I was overwhelmed by the contrast between the ceremonial of the *Kris* and the down-to-earth everyday life of the Rom. It all seemed strangely unreal, wild and senseless. When I emerged from my reverie it was harder still to pick up the thread of the arguments.

The *Kris,* or the collective will of the Rom, was not in any sense a closed system but a structure in flux, never codified in its entirety, relying for transmission only on the accuracy of unrecorded human memory. The effectiveness of the pronouncements of the judges depended essentially on the acceptance of their decisions by the majority of the Rom. There was no direct element of coercion to enforce the rule of law. The Rom had no police force, no jails, no executioners. Even the positions of the *krisatora,* the judges, were not permanent or "professional" because of the inevitable circumstances of nomadic life. Because the Rom were forever halting at crossroads, the selection of judges depended on what qualified men were available.

A claim before the *Kris* only led to a judgment; for the actual enforcement the Rom had to rely on his own strength and that of his kinsmen. However, to cope with flagrant defiance of the law, to keep a balance between justice and power and to prevent any kind of arbitrary rule or blackmail, the *Kris* could resort to supernatural sanctions, the *armaya,* or curses. This sentencing they called the *solakh;* it supposedly left the final enforcement to the more dreaded judgment of the *Mule.*

There were a number of complaints or *bayura* before the *Kris* to be investigated. Some would be deferred, others competently arbitrated. Most cases were concerned with breach of contract. The *bayura* were presented to the judges and a sequence of procedure was established. As everybody rightly expected, Pulika brought to the attention of the court the Tshurara horde's unprincipled, lax behavior. More specifically they had broken the law of the Rom in hiding their affliction of the scabies; by neglecting to seek medical treatment they had spread it among others. Pulika asked that they be made to "pay for their shame" (*te potshinen penge lajav*). In advocating that they pay only "symbolical" damages, he asked for a very mild sentence: They should furnish food and drink for all the Rom who had assembled for the present *Kris* for three days. Pulika also asked that they furnish proof to the *Kris* that they were cured before reinstatement among the Rom was permitted. After this had been settled, Pulika bared his head and swore, *"Te loliarav i phuv mure ratesa . . .":* "May I redden the earth with my blood if, with the consent of the present *Kris,* I am not permitted to invoke the *armaya* [the conditional curse] that whoever hides the [fact that he has] scabies may remain with it for seven consecutive years." The Tshurara realized that this would be tantamount to seven years of banishment. They protested vehemently, but Nonoka answered, *"Ando gav bi juklesko shai piravel o manush bi destesko"* (In a village without a dog a man can walk without a stick).

The following *bavo* (complaint) was presented by one Punka la Anako and dealt with the dreaded concept of *marhime* or ritual defilement, one of the most strictly observed of all restrictions among Rom everywhere. The very term *marhime* was used to describe banishment, the ultimate penalty of Gypsy law. Punka la Anako accused one of Nonoka's *bora* of having purposely defiled one of his horses. There were gasps of surprise from the bystanders, for at face value the accusation sounded very serious. But with the gasps of indignation there were some chuckles too.

Nonoka rose not to defend the position of his family or to persuade the Rom of his daughter-in-law's innocence, but simply to clarify the case. He possessed a mischievous skill in debate, unlike the cantankerous and loquacious Punka. It appeared that one day Nonoka had stopped his *kumpania* on the road by Punka's camp. Nonoka and his sons had briefly visited with him, but had decided to move farther on for some reason, which Punka misconstrued as an insult. One of Nonoka's daughters-in-law, accompanied by several small children, had crossed the road and, taking advantage of the short halt, run to the camp to visit with a cousin of hers who was married to one of the young men of the other *kumpania*. Inadvertently she had walked across a chain lying half hidden in the grass. Old Punka had yelled at her angrily. Not realizing what he meant, she hastily retreated to her own wagon on the road. In doing this she had walked a second time over the chain. Tethered at the other end of the chain was one of Punka's horses, which theoretically would have been defiled "by extension." Before the *Kris* had said a word, Nonoka took his hat off, lowered his head and declared his readiness to accept the blame before the *Kris*. He would pay for his shame. It was clear to the assembled Rom that Nonoka had not only put his accuser to shame for his puerile conduct, but had also saved the dignity of the *Kris* from the ridicule of having to deliberate and reject an irrelevant case.

Punka started a passionate plea, but he was interrupted by the other Rom. Nonoka waited a few seconds, then asked Punka, in the presence of the court, in what way he intended to dispose of the defiled horse and what precautions he had taken to avoid being tainted himself. There was a ripple of soft but appreciative laughter. To atone for the ridicule he had heaped on the unfortunate Punka, Nonoka suggested that he too be made to pay for his shame. They both provided food and drink for all the Rom who had come to attend the *Kris*. They drank together all night and renewed a lasting friendship.

The case that followed was brought by Carolina, Pulika's widowed sister. She had several daughters and only one young son, which in the world of the Rom made it a peculiar, lopsided household. She alleged that a large number of gold pieces had been stolen from her and she had not even a suspicion of who could have done it. She was sure of the day it happened because she had handled the gold pieces early in the day and had wanted to change the hiding place later that same day, only to find them gone. Before bringing this to the *Kris* she had taken the understandable precaution of making sure that they had not been mislaid or, still more improbable, that they had been taken away by one of her daughters or her little son. When it happened they had been camping with only four or five other families and she had immediately brought the theft to their attention. All had been shocked at the thought of anybody's stealing from a fellow Gypsy, and all had indignantly denied guilt. It could be safely assumed that an outsider, a Gajo, a thief or a tramp, could hardly have entered the camp without being detected by the Rom. Only somebody from the camp itself could have escaped the usual vigilance or the inordinate curiosity of the small children. A theft from a fellow Rom was unheard of among the Lowara, and this had created tension and suspicion among those involuntarily implicated. Young Kalia in his usual flighty and direct way had suggested that the heads of the families sharing the campsite each contribute to replace the amount stolen from a "defenseless woman," but others pointed out that beyond restitution this did not solve the basic problem. If there was a thief among them, he or she should be found out. It was in view of this that Carolina and those who at that particular time shared her company asked the *Kris* to proceed to the *solakh*. For as the Lowara said, guilt can be forgiven but it should never be hidden.

The night before the day of the *solakh* none of those who were to submit to it in the morning were allowed to celebrate with the rest of us. Sullen, they sat by their fires. The next morning a number of men and women, walking in single file and preceded by several of the judges, left the site. Few fires had been lit yet and the entire camp was still at rest. The men were bareheaded; all were unwashed and uncombed. Carolina was among them. They were taken to a desolate wasteland a little distance away, where Pulika and several other men of consequence waited for them and also old Lyuba. Nobody smoked. A little distance behind the slowly shuffling procession a few silent dogs slinked along. Black crows alighted on a nearby field. A *diklo*, a brightly colored kerchief, was spread over a small heap of stones or rubble. On it lay a primitively made cross, several ancient and faded photographs of the dead of the group, a small bunch of wildflowers—cut flowers, which were the Lowara symbol of premature death—and a stumpy, yellowish wax candle flickering uncertainly in the morning breeze.

For a short while there still was a choice for the unknown thief to admit his guilt, and then the *solakh* began: the truth-seeking enforced by the magic power of the dead, a third degree of sorts, backed by the collective will of the Rom, part legend and part fact.

The *krisatori o baro*, the judge who would administer the

oath, made Carolina step forward and stand in front of the altar. She was grave, heaving deep sighs, and awkward. She looked disheveled and somehow unprotected. The *krisatori* was hard-faced and impersonal when he intoned his long litany: "If you know or have heard anything related to the gold pieces stolen from Carolina and you do not inform this *Kris,* may you die in horrible agony."

"*Bater*" (may it be so), answered Carolina in a hoarse, hardly audible voice.

"If in any even remote way you have had any connection with the theft of the gold pieces of Carolina, may the noxious and evil winds hit your belly and render you ill with a deadly disease."

"*Bater.*"

"If after the administration of the oath you intend in any way to have profit or pleasure or possession of the gold pieces stolen from Carolina, may God take away your strength and your pleasure; may sterility deprive you of posterity."

"*Bater.*"

The curses grew more terrible and merciless, the questions more complex and subtle. The voice of the *krisatori* had risen to a high pitch and it seemed as if the entire sentence was expelled in one breath and without any emphatic intonation, as an incantation of evil. The flame of the candle fluttered, as if tracing and duplicating the electrical impulses of Carolina's nervous system. The men and the women waiting their turn were almost breathless with emotion, sweating with anguish, apprehension and expectancy, sharing a common moment of humility, witnessing and being part of the implementation of this awesome and most powerful tradition of the Rom. What words can tell how long such agony could last? There was an uncanny, brooding awareness that, as with a game of musical chairs, the playing might suddenly stop and someone, one of them, would be left without a seat, revealing his guilt for all to see.

One after the other the Rom were interrogated and conditionally cursed. This was the *solakh.* After the Rom their wives had to submit. Under the unreasoning strain of the rite, that by its sheer weight should have brought out any latent crisis of conscience, each Rom and each woman behaved differently. Carolina had been grave, slightly awkward, somehow unprotected, her voice hoarse and hardly audible. Some had been sullen, dejected and breathing heavily. Some whimpered, a very few seemed unaffected, others had been baffled and inarticulate, but almost all of them had gone through the extraordinary experience as sleepwalkers.

The *krisatori* went on unrelentingly. There remained only one more woman to be heard. She happened to be one of the Tshurara, and all misgiving and gratuitous presumptions focused on her as she staggered toward the altar and the judge. But the *solakh* ended in a disappointing anticlimax, at least for me. Nobody had broken down and confessed, nor had anybody been struck by a thunderbolt. I was sweat-soaked, with a taste of treason in my soul. For, despite constant adjustments, my Occidental heritage had made me expect some kind of conclusive *dénouement*. For the Rom at least, the immediate suspicions were dispelled and young Kalia's suggestion was followed by the heads of households who had shared the campsite at the time of the theft, who now contributed to replace the gold pieces.

It was only much later, around the beginning of the war, that I learned about the unfortunate death of Liza, the wife of one of the Rom who had submitted to the *solakh*. On her deathbed, though she could no longer speak, she insistently rubbed her index finger and thumb in a common gesture understood by all to signify money. She would react with savage violence whenever the Rom assembled about her said to her, *"Te aves yertime mander tai te yertil tut o Del"* (I forgive you and may God forgive you as I do). It appeared to make her unhappy and she kept pointing to a corner of the wagon, until her young daughter, not daring to believe her sudden insight, investigated, and to her dismay found a large number of gold pieces that did not belong to them. Tears streamed down Liza's face and she seemed deeply relieved before she collapsed into a coma and died shortly afterward.

CHAPTER TWELVE

Before the Rom began to disperse, there were more extravagant celebrations of friendship. They lingered on endlessly reciprocating each other's lavish hospitality. Then one day the extraordinary concentration of Gypsies suddenly dissolved, as unpredictable as the wind itself. One instant the sprawling camp reminded one of a series of ancient Persian miniatures—in scarlets, magentas, crimsons, lemon-yellows and saffron and sulphur, in cobalt blues and cerulean, with ochres and sepias and gold. The next moment it resembled more a minor seismic disturbance. Wagons jerked into motion, hobbled over the rough ground and departed in opposite directions.

The camp broke up in the usual anarchistic way of the Rom. Wagons moved away, wave upon wave, like a succession of spasms. The dispersal was swift, as if the Rom were running a race. They scattered in an erratic pattern amid clouds of dust, to the thundering of wheels, the snorting of restless horses and the barking and yelping of dogs. A sense of unwarranted urgency dominated the entire scene. It was as if a floodgate had opened and spilled the water. Stragglers hastened to catch up. Some wagons drifted or changed course, intersecting others on their way, while a large number of others converged a few miles farther long. They all seemed to share the same mercurial mobility and the same restless buoyancy.

For some time after the meeting of the *Kris* many of the Rom traveled together, remaining within the same general area, and the feasting went on. The Rom lived on money earned during the previous months of intensive travel and horse trading. The celebrations were hardly disturbed, or for that matter interrupted, by the daily need to move camp; singing and drinking went on even when the Rom were actually on the road. There was hardly any need, or time, for dealing with the Gaje. The time roughly corresponded to the period of harvest, and the peasants were in an expansive mood in their own right.

Like the gentle but obsessive rustling of the cornfields, the dominating theme of conversation turned to matchmaking and marriages.

The obvious reasons for this were the unusually large gathering of Rom, which offered a wide choice of possible matches, and the desire to prolong the prevailing festive mood by finding a valid excuse for doing so. Many of the men had gathered in the shifting shade of Pulika's wagon. They drank and talked. The sun was high over the camp and hot. They talked about the marriageable girls of the present *kumpania*. In Romani the word "girl" was the same term as the one designating a virgin, and the Rom earnestly expected to marry virgins.

Among themselves the Rom appraised the girls in a direct but never a disrespectful manner. They were realists. And marriage, more than any other transaction, should be approached with undeceived realism. The most important duty of the parents was to provide their sons with suitable brides. The Lowara said that one should select one's daughter-in-law *Rode tshia bora le kanensa tai te na le yakensa* (with the ears and not with the eyes), meaning that more consideration should be given to a girl's reputation than to her looks. They also said that *Shuk tski khalpe la royasa* (Beauty cannot be eaten with a spoon). I listened, with fascination and some wonder, to the older men's sober, discerning and practical evaluations of the daughters of their fellow Rom. I was to suddenly see them under a completely new light, these contemporaries of mine and, at least theoretically, potential mates. Winsome Tsuritsa, the unmarried daughter of Dika the widow, who had married old man Butsulo, was slightly withdrawn and moody but softly sensuous. They said she was a malicious gossip. Luludja, Tshukurka's youngest daughter, was by unanimous consent the most beautiful girl among all the Lowara, but she lacked health and strength to bear many children. Besides, when she was still an infant, she had been promised into marriage to Kore. The actual consummation of their marriage was being postponed until she grew stronger.

They spoke of Dodo's two nubile daughters, Ludu and Djidjo. And I vividly remembered having been struck by their stunning combination of innocence and sensuousness, the first time I saw them, months ago on some dirt road in Voivodina. I remembered the glorious luxury of their long, black hair in braids, their dusky skin and their grace of youth not yet fully awakened to womanhood. I also remembered how Kore had to remind me of Lowara propriety before I could take my eyes off them. Ludu was too forward, the Rom said, and Djidjo too was on the wild side and ungovernable; she had been observed to be sudden and quick in anger. But their father, Dodo, had an importance in the group that amply made up for these minor defects. Both the girls would eventually make desirable matches, but Dodo refused to even consider any marriage proposal, it was said, as they still were very young. Djidjo was a strange, skittish child-woman. She sang in the rain, she feared the moon and was haunted by night clouds. I once saw her singing in the rain. She had a soft, sweet, low voice, and the water streamed down her face and neck to disappear between her breasts, slightly darkening her skin.

Keja too was discussed, but not in her father's presence. They estimated that she was strong-willed and resourceful but she was too attached to her family, and it would not be easy for a man to gentle her and gain her loyalty. Pulika would be bound to ask a high price for her, and he could afford to be choosy in selecting a future son-in-law. In discussing her marriage the Rom said that, contrary to the custom, her personal inclinations would certainly influence Pulika's decision and consequently nobody quite dared approach Pulika to ask her in marriage, at least until the omens were right, even though she was ripe for fulfillment. And so she stayed with us a while longer.

Paprika had a lush figure and she was vivacious. Her smiling face was a little too round but her eyes were soft and brown, huge and full of mischief. Her voice was caressing and slightly throaty. Her laughter was intoxicating. Her teeth were strong and white. Her brothers, however, were reputed to be hard-drinking, quarrelsome and coarse, and in turn they could become a serious liability to their future in-laws.

The Lowara speculated with great sagacity about each young girl's potential as a future wife. Aside from her family background and her personal character and temper, they considered her capability of running a household, her patience with small children, her health and physical stamina, her behavior under stress, her ability to tell fortunes, and her willingness to provide for the immediate needs of her prospective family. After these specific qualifications had been discovered, they discussed her cooking and her courtesy in dealing with guests. Lastly the Rom considered her beauty and her skills as a singer or a dancer.

Although there was no close contact between the sexes, most of the qualities and faults of the young girls were known to those interested enough to observe them, since we constantly lived at close quarters with other families with a minimum of privacy.

Girls being girls, there were bound to be some among the Rom who could be criticized for their lack of modesty or for creating a teasing impression in their dealings with the outside world. To my knowledge, however, none could be accused of sexual irregularities. The Lowara strongly believed that an unchaste woman, knowingly tolerated in their midst, brought dissension and bad luck, and because of the strict observance of sexual restrictions among their people there was a total absence of flirtation or premarital experimentation. Most of the young boys had a certain degree of experience, acquired with non-Gypsy girls by force of circumstances, but manhood was not equated with one's sexual proficiency, or with the scope or number of one's conquests; in the same way that use of obscenities was proof of manhood only for those who knew no other way to express it. When talking to young unmarried men, Pulika, warning them to beware of the cult of experience, used to say that, "*maybe* they knew something about sex but they had *everything* to learn about love."

For hours the men had discussed the subject of marriage

and, as it were, surveyed the field. Bidshika volunteered to start off the marriage proposals on behalf of the son of his distant cousin, Tsinoro. Tsinoro was not an important man nor was he affluent, and he accepted Bidshika's generous gesture without too much protest. Bidshika was thinking of asking Tsuritsa for this marriage. The girl's stepfather, Butsulo, was an old man and he would be only too relieved to see his wife's young daughter safely married. The bridal price, even if comparatively low, would be welcome. He could only gain by accepting such an alliance. The groom's relatives would be bound to give him assistance in his old age, and anyway he had no one else to rely on.

Bidshika and several of his cronies left Pulika and the older Rom by the fireside. Bidshika was an important man among the Lowara, but he retained a raw, youthful exuberance and was inclined to start mischief. He had decided to make this wedding happen. It would not be a bad match at that: Tsinoro's family was gentle and would certainly treat Tsuritsa well. At least she would not be brutalized, or starved. She would be better off living among her many young brothers- and sisters-in-law than alone with her aging stepfather and her ailing mother, even though she had a younger brother.

Shortly after Bidshika departed, another, more substantial delegation left Pulika's campsite equally bent on matchmaking. Some of the Rom were considering trying to arrange yet another marriage. It was like a fever, and the various festivities would simply overlap in one lavish, uninterrupted sequence, adding to rather than detracting from one another. For a long time to come the Rom would speak about these events. There was great merriment in anticipation of it.

Kore and I and the other young men rejoiced and slyly teased Tsinoro's young son. We embarrassed him by making supposedly appreciative remarks about Tsuritsa, the girl he was about to marry. The day after the marriage had been consummated, and proof of her prior virginity had been publicly displayed, he would move away from us to join the world of the Rom, the married men, and he would cease to be one of our companions.

Several small groups of important men crisscrossed the

encampment to visit the parents of single girls old enough to be married. Instead of walking directly toward the fire around which the family gathered, the delegation, headed by Tshukurka, circled around Dodo's wagon pretending to ignore the other more direct approach. The people sitting by the fire also play-acted total unawareness of the goings-on. The small children roared in glee as they were the only ones outside the game.

Half a step ahead of Tshukurka, Luluvo stepped toward the wagon and with his silver knobbed, ceremonial cane knocked against the wide-open door. He raised his voice to inquire if there was anybody home. Tshukurka stepped up and he too called out. Feigning surprise, Dodo slowly rose from his crouching position and majestically walked forward to greet the visitors, claiming to be greatly honored by their presence. With mock formality Dodo invited them to sit by his fire as if today they met for the first time. The youngest of his daughters-in-law, whose duty it traditionally was to assist, or on occasions even to replace, her mother-in-law as hostess, hastened to fetch old crates and empty buckets, which she considerately turned upside down for the guests to sit on. The orange silken kerchief she wore over her black hair, as the sign of her newly achieved status of married woman, was still knotted in an inexpert way. Under a modest and humble exterior she actually glowed with pride. There was a short, awkward pause without conversation as the Rom took their time to sit down. With explicit, half-completed gestures, in an exaggerated show of courtly manners, they deliberated among themselves as to who should sit where. Without having to be told, Dodo's new *bori* started brewing coffee for the newly arrived Rom. When they all were settled down, Luluvo finally broke the silence with an innocuous observation about the fair weather, the one subject the Rom never talked about under any other circumstances. They considered the weather to be too self-evident. Tshukurka looked around vaguely and commented that the Rom had survived the winter well. Nobody had perished from the cold. Spring and summer had come again, bringing beautiful, new, joyful life, full of promise.

Dodo interrupted him and begged to disagree. In turn he

spoke of the inclemency of the weather. He claimed not to see spring in the air yet; it was still too cold for it. In fact the sun was quite hot that day and the small children played and jumped about naked. Dodo shivered with comical exaggeration and he went on about the cold, the nonexistent snow and ice that threatened to engulf the Rom. Everybody was happy since this was actually an invitation to bring drinks to "warm up." In agreeing to drink with them, Dodo expressed his willingness to investigate their proposal.

Luluvo's younger brother, Kalia, who was the least important man in the delegation, promptly produced a bottle of alcohol. He had knowingly brought it along, waiting for the opportune time to open it, keeping it hidden under his jacket, which showed a suspicious bulge. The Rom passed the cups and drained them in a single draught, to chase away the nonexistent ugly cold of the dead winter. The drinking was enlivened by humoristic sparring, much joviality and a general contest of wit. These preliminaries were playfully prolonged, partly to satisfy protocol but also because the Rom were visibly enjoying it. They all were among good friends and feeling very much at ease.

Dodo did not yet know on whose behalf the delegation had come, but the identity of the various members of the present delegation dispelled his possible apprehensions. It happened that Rom from other *kumpanias* came from distant lands to arrange marriages for their sons, and since the girl's parents didn't know them well, they exercised greater caution. In this case Dodo knew his daughter would remain within the present *kumpania.* The assembled Rom were relaxed and enjoyed the situation, knowing that it was unlikely to lead to endless or bitter disputes following an insulting refusal.

After some time Kore dragged me away as no new development seemed to be in the offing. Together we ran to the far side of the camp to where old Butsulo parked his wagon. It was his habit to live and travel practically on the margin of our *kumpania,* even though he had been part of it for as long as any of us younger ones could remember. As far as we knew, he was not directly related to any one of its members, though possibly the youngish widow he had married, who was

Tsuritsa's mother, might have been. Butsulo usually was brusque and irascible and continually complaining about the noise the younger people made. He kept Tsuritsa and her younger brother away from the rest of us as much as he possibly could, even though, being old, he depended on our good will for assistance. The Rom who had come to see him, led by Bidshika, were now in a boisterous mood. Butsulo had accepted the first glass of alcohol without much protest. His narrow eyes shone with a special glint and he appeared to be slightly giddy already, to the extent that from his usual churlish self he had become rather obsequious. The marriage preliminaries were much more advanced here. They were already negotiating the bridal price and the various conditions of the union. Bidshika was in high spirits. He was enumerating the advantages and the disadvantages to both parties in rather unvarnished terms. Contrary to all logic, he alternately drove a hard bargain for both sides in a high-spirited one-man act. Butsulo was quite drunk and nodded his head, trying to appear wise and in control of things. To everybody's satisfaction Bidshika settled on a specific but very reasonable amount of gold pieces.

Butsulo insisted Tsuritsa remain present and witness the entire marriage proposal and the successive bargaining session and the settling of every detail of her nuptials. Nothing could be more humiliating to a Gypsy girl, but she submitted.

Several times other Rom present tried to spare her by pretending to send her on errands, but her stepfather was obstinate and would not let her absent herself. Aside from the fact that he was probably drunk, nobody understood why he inflicted such senseless disgrace on her. He demanded she wait on the guests, which under the circumstances was in poor taste.

Too late Bidshika realized that what he had started in good fun, even if well intended, was simply degenerating into a loud, drunken farce, and he knew this would reflect on his reputation as a man. He lost some of his swagger and belatedly tried to correct the drifting course of the events, but his drinking companions paid him no heed. They kept jesting and getting drunker until Bidshika's wife, accompanied by several other wives, came looking for them and succeeded in routing the men. Butsulo retired to sleep off his rarely indulged intoxication. Throughout the night Bidshika and his friends sang an endlessly repeated melody, which eventually rocked me to sleep.

Before falling asleep I became aware of Keja, already in bed between huge eiderdowns, which she shared with her sisters, not far from my sleeping place. She was half sitting up, propped on her elbow, intently staring at me. This had never happened before and I felt a strange, slightly disquieting feeling as if she was trying to warn me. But of what?

The next day started like any other. Taking care of the horses, fetching water and other regular camp chores kept everybody occupied. Until late afternoon it was as if yesterday had never been and nothing could be further from their minds than possible thoughts of marriage proposals.

At the outskirts of the encampment Bidshika was busily horse-trading with a local farmer. His son Nanosh stood loosely holding the sturdy Westphalian plow horse to impress the man with the animal's docility and meekness. In the meadows Tshukurka was inspecting the new gray mare, knowingly feeling her from the hip to the hoof. It briefly brought back to me how the Rom in the few previous days discussed the available maidens for the benefit of their nephews or sons, and how they had appraised them in discerning, unvarnished, long-sighted ways.

The camp was broken and moved a short distance to provide fresh grazing for the horses. When we arrived at the new location, the sky was overcast and a chill west wind was blowing. The cooking fires were built downwind from the wagons, which had been spread out in such a way as to minimize the danger of sparks or hot ashes blown in the wind.

In the gathering dusk the Rom gradually drifted to the square, low-built tavern at the crossroads a short distance away. Poetically called The Silent Rain, it was a large hall smelling of beer, stale tobacco smoke and fried bacon. It had a beamed ceiling and dark leaded-glass windows. Large, heavily embossed ornamental brass plates stood out against the dark-stained carved woodwork. In one corner the innkeeper himself and several brawny local men were playing billiards.

The Rom drank tap beer and included the local Gaje in each new round they ordered. They paid in bills of large denominations and they left stacks of smaller bills and piles of change in coins on the clean-scrubbed tables in front of them, implying that they intended to stay on well into the night and to spend lavishly. Soon some of the more restive among the women swarmed in and grouped themselves somewhat away from the men but otherwise fully joining in the merriment. When requested by either their husbands or their fathers-in-law—there were no unmarried girls present—they stepped forward into the larger circle of men to sing or dance to entertain their guests. Each dance was offered "in honor" of a Rom of mark and was specifically dedicated to him.

With each new round of drinks the toasts that were proposed became more elaborate and flowery until someone, I forget who it was, invited the Rom to join him in a toast to the new *bora*, "daughters-in-law to be, and might it be soon." This was received with joyous shouts of approval. The next general round was proposed to "the future fathers-in-law, whoever they are, and may the brides they are about to acquire for their sons bring them luck, long-lasting happiness, harmony and prosperity. May the Rom live well and long, in the company of their women and of their sons and their sons' sons. May they thrive and acquire many horses. . . ."

Tshukurka and Luluvo, who had started marriage proposals on behalf of a Rom whose identity was not yet known, but widely discussed, stood up to accept the toast as his representatives, amid cheers and the teasing chuckles of those who hoped the father of the groom would reveal himself unawares.

Bidshika and several of his drinking companions of the previous night stood up too, after a slight delay in deference to Tshukurka. There was a further moment of suspense as the Rom looked around speculating, assuming or in some cases having foreknowledge of who else among their peers was contemplating a similar step. The Rom cheered in expectation and kept cheering until a few other Rom, after hesitating, revealed their intentions. Most of the assembled men, however, were not prepared to see Pulika stand up to an ovation. It was not clear in what capacity Pulika had responded to the challenge. Was it as sponsor and champion of the prospective father-in-law or as the father of the groom? The latter seemed unlikely. Kore was betrothed to Luludja. Or had Pulika decided not to wait any longer to have the marriage vows fulfilled? On the other hand the boy Tina, who ranked in age after Kore, Tshaya and Mala, was still only a child.

Pulika merely ordered a round of brandy, then sat down. His oldest son, Yojo, had moved away from the other reveling Rom to play billiards with the innkeeper and his Gaje friends. Like his sister Keja, he was fair-skinned and tall. He was usually caustic and never very talkative. Wherever he traveled he made it his practice to dress as the local peasantry did. Only the colorful kerchief knotted around his throat gave him away, in marked preference over the flashier and more conspicuous way of dressing affected by the other men of the horde. He was present at all functions of the Rom but somehow managed to remain uninvolved, even though on several occasions he rose in the *Kris* to present a very articulate purist's point of view. Yojo played pool with the Gaje and listened to the Rom. Occasionally he vaguely informed his Gaje acquaintances of the general drift of the discussions; he told them about the imminent multiple marriages: "Tomorrow or day after tomorrow" he said, and for emphasis he added, "Gypsy style."

Fascinated by these colorful, free-spending strangers and by the prospect of seeing one or more of their weddings at close range, the landlord suggested to Yojo they stay at their present camp. He prompted Yojo to speak to the Rom, offering to approach his brother-in-law who happened to be the head of the local Gendarmerie on their behalf for permission to extend their stay. In doing this he did not overlook the windfall for his business this would represent. The Rom accepted laconically. Here or there, to them what difference did it make? Failing to understand the lack of enthusiasm with which his suggestion was received and fearing to see the opportunity slip away, he was moved to offer them a substantial amount of beer and liquor as a contribution to the wedding celebrations. To start things rolling and to confirm the arrangements, the next round was on the house. The Rom drank, talked and sang as before without paying much attention to their eager host. Only a few of the lesser members of the group deigned to join him, to flatter, coax and humor him by turns.

Nothing further was decided among the various parties planning marriages; the Rom were by now too drunk, and anyway such arrangements were by tradition not made at a tavern. The next morning, unaccountably, the encampment was in full commotion. Despite the early hour the men were visiting back and forth, actively arranging for several marriages to take place roughly at the same time or at least to succeed each other at short intervals. There was a constant flow of Gypsies going to The Silent Rain café, which was momentarily transformed into a kind of general headquarters where Tshukurka, Pulika, Luluvo and some of the more influential heads of families held court. The innkeeper, well disposed toward the Gypsies and carried by the momentum of his newly found infatuation with them, took it upon himself to be their impresario, acting as business manager, stage director, prompter and doing a creditable job of public relations. Tongue in cheek, they let him have free rein.

Bidshika and Tsinoro visited old Butsulo. Another delegation approached Paprika's father on behalf of an at first undisclosed parent who soon enough was discovered to be Yayal's father, old Bidshika. In anticipation of the coming celebrations many of the married women, indulging a reckless display of wealth, wore multiple-strand necklaces fashioned from gold pieces, in some cases representing the family's entire hoard. The responsible men walked about with relaxed, staid dignity or rushed around with purposeful intensity. Many carried heavy ceremonial walking sticks. The younger element of the camp had dressed up, but the unruly mob of small children remained strangely unaffected, exuberantly wearing their same old pitiful rags. They made a nuisance of themselves. They assailed the back door of the inn, where the kitchen maids handed them boiled potatoes sprinkled with coarse rock salt. Then they ran to the front door, playfully begging and coaxing their parents and uncles sitting inside the tavern to share with them the blackish meat of smoked hams with mustard cauliflower pickles. Occasionally an urchin managed to sneak in and remain unnoticed for a short time. Pulika had decreed that, for the time being at least, children should not be allowed to intrude or in any way irritate or interfere with the Gaje.

When the maids at the back door ran out of boiled potatoes, they handed out thick slices of freshly baked raisin bread spread with either lard or butter. Once or twice a Gypsy woman pretended to chase the children away and yelled at them to stop pestering the kitchen help, only to have the Gaje protest vehemently and take the children's side. And so everybody was kept happy.

The young men for whom marriages were being arranged by their parents acted with singular detachment and composure. The girls involved, on the other hand, were sullen and irascible, as if they resented the undue attention inflicted on their maidenly modesty, and as if they resented the very thought of marriage.

Paprika, the vivacious one with the lush figure and the infectious laughter, was pouting. She walked around dejectedly, surrounded by other young girls trying to comfort her, God only knows how. Wild little Djidjo was rebellious and intractable. She moped between fits of rage, which only endeared her more to me and made her seem more desirable still. Tsuritsa was the only one who appeared essentially uninterested but resigned.

Like so many of the camp dwellers, I too had momentarily wondered for whom Djidjo was intended. Of course there were the usual rumors and wild guesses. I thought of Tshurka, the grown-up bachelor son of Luluvo and Sidi, who was much older than the rest of us. But Luluvo had originally accompanied Tshukurka as part of a delegation. So it could not be he. There was Zurka of course. But his father Tshukurka had led the same delegation that approached Dodo. There was Tshilaba, son of Gunada. I fell to thinking of all the available girls. I thought of Keja, of Tshaya, of Ludu, of several others still. Then the thought about Keja recurred and I wondered why in fact nobody had approached Pulika about her, my sister. With bewilderment I suddenly remembered how a few nights ago Keja had intently stared at me in the half-dark. I felt the same strange, disquieting feeling. What had she wanted to tell me or warn me about? And why? Why had she failed to reach me and why had I not bothered to find out afterward?

I went in search of her, and when I approached her, at the first seemly opportunity, she stood aloof and unconsenting. In her unexpected and baffling behavior she reminded me of old Lyuba. As I insisted, she abruptly said I was not meant to live with the Lowara and I would never be able to find fulfillment among them. Presently she even spoke like Lyuba and her unwarranted rejection hit me like a cloudburst, for up to now she had shown a deep insight into my needs. It made me angry: she had never before rebuffed me. After Putzina, long ago, Keja was the person I felt the most affinity with. I admired her strength and her spirit, her self-reliance and her resourcefulness.

She said I had been cowardly in letting Pulika arrange a marriage for me.

I could not have been more astonished. Slowly the pieces started falling into place, making some kind of obscure sense. She went on saying that I would make a terrible mistake if I let this marriage happen. For inevitably I would desert young Djidjo after either three, five or nine years. There would be children, my children, and it would be Djidjo's perdition, and for my part I never would be able to forget. Or else I would stand by my choice, by both the Lowara and by Djidjo, and waste my life; and I was meant for a different kind of life. I wanted to protest, to tell her that I was innocent. Yet I knew she loved me and I also knew she was right. I no longer felt insulted, angry or rejected by her. I was reconciled, grateful, willing to take her advice. Unembarrassed, I asked for her assistance, relying on her discretion and her resourcefulness to help loosen the noose. I refused to consider flight as a solution. I had the premonition that the drama of my conflicting loyalties would recur. I was broodingly aware of the inadequacy of my love for Pulika's people.

High above in the deep blue and distant sky a flight of wild geese in arrowhead formation headed south on their seasonal migration. They were honking excitedly. Many years ago Rupa had once called me a wild goose, *vadni ratsa,* as the urge to go back would overcome me and I would leave suddenly and unobserved.

Intuitively Keja turned to Lyuba, the venerable ancient one, and I had no reason to question her judgment at that moment. She sat huddled, her knees raised, and smoked her short-stemmed brass pipe. Keja sank down in a crouch next to her, sitting on her haunches with easy grace, her small sturdy feet slightly apart. I did likewise. The old woman was imperturbable, ignoring our presence, her eyes unblinking, as she smoked quietly. And while Keja spoke to her in a low, even voice, Lyuba gazed at me rather blankly in that disconcerting way of hers. And for an instant she seemed to me to be beyond reach. Her eyes had a distant look. Not a line in her strange, expressionless face changed as Keja talked on, seemingly not sharing my impression.

Lyuba raised her hand slowly, and, like once before at a decisive turn in my life, I felt the parched touch of her fingers first on my hand, then on the back of my neck, as I bent down anticipating her gesture. I shivered and again she comforted me with a tenderness I had forgotten she could still have in her great age. Briefly she lowered the eyelids that seemed devoid of lashes. When she spoke there was no animosity in her hoarse voice. She said I should tell Pulika. She did not elaborate or explain. At Putzina's untimely death she had been the one who drew me into the fold, after originally opposing my admission, and somehow, I felt, it was she who, as it were, released me from this same bond and the demands it imposed. Once I had been accepted and I deeply felt I had now been let go, ungrudgingly but irremediably. Prompted by Keja's perceptive affection, I had faced the moment of truth and recognized my inherent unwillingness to accept total, unqualified commitment to the life of the Lowara, and to seal this by forming a union with the girl Pulika had chosen for me.

Considerately, even lovingly, I am sure, Pulika had allowed his choice to be guided by my attraction to Djidjo, which must not have escaped his observation. I had seen the luminous forbidden shore and chosen to turn aside. A serene melancholy filled me, instead of the formless and violent uncertainty of shortly before.

Unwittingly I had crossed the threshold of manhood, but in a manner Pulika could not have predicted.

I found Pulika by the meadows, and walking through the tall weeds, I went up to him. I groped for the right words as obviously I was apprehensive about his reaction to my rejection of the match, of which nothing in my behavior could have forewarned him. At the same time I knew there was no possible alternative, yet with a sense of filial disobedience I knew how inconceivable my rejection must appear to him. To the Rom marriage was the only form of initiation into the world of the Men, the Rom. Theirs was a cult of the family, and the feminine ideal was that of the mother. Celibacy was unthinkable, unnatural. I had to make him understand that it was not because of an aversion to marriage that I refused. Even less did I want him to conclude that my renunication was due to any shortcomings in Djidjo.

I started to tell Pulika how much I appreciated his generous affection and his not considering costs in purchasing me a wife. Calmly he interrupted me, answering that what I said was incongruous, that between father and son there could not be generosity and that what he did was merely due.

But my words must have rung false, for, with a profound sense of life and with the simplicity of those close to the earth, Pulika sensed my agony. It was this subtle receptiveness that led me to blurt out, breathlessly and in clumsy, ill-chosen words, what was troubling me. I closed my eyes instinctively as he swiftly reached forward. I did not know what to expect but all the same I prepared for a blow. At the same instant, and instead of this, Pulika clasped me in a forceful, conciliatory embrace, dissipating my anguish. I was silent, not knowing what to say. For a while we smoked in silence before walking back together. Pulika seemed undismayed, and with unbelievable delicacy of feeling much remained unsaid. As we almost reached the periphery of the camp, without any further elaborate deliberation but implying that we shared a tacit complicity, Pulika said I must trust him. I knew he meant he must avoid inappropriate or extreme gestures to forestall the impending marriage at such short notice. I knew he meant he must spare Dodo's honor and Djidjo's reputation. And even if Dodo were amenable—and how could one approach him in this matter?—what explanations could one offer for rejecting his daughter after she had been asked in marriage? There remained the Rom of the *kumpania* to be taken into consideration.

Coming back to the encampment, I found the festive mood and the jovial merrymaking steadily increasing. Everywhere was evidence of ample food supplies and of overflowing refreshments. The Rom were in high spirits. They were flushed and unusually lighthearted. Above the commotion rose snatches of gay songs, occasional bursts of cheering and peals of laughter. Small stark-naked baby boys tottered or squirmed through the happy crowd.

I joined Nanosh and Zurka, who restlessly roamed the campsite. They were in a playful mood. We briefly stopped at old Butsulo's fire, where, after first refusing demurely, we drained the cup of brandy they offered us. We winced and wished them good luck and Godspeed with the marriage soon to take place. Then we headed for the next place. A large crowd had gathered to drink and to watch the antics of the formalized but intentionally comic bargaining session for the bridal price.

After the initial approach to the girl's father had been favorably received or encouraged, the prospective groom's father—in this case Yayal's father, old Bidshika—joined the delegation of those who had acted on his behalf. They now pressed around him, paying court in jest to his role of king. Once or twice Paprika's father retired a short distance away, though practically within earshot, to deliberate with his advisers huddled about him. They returned to announce the number of gold pieces he would accept as the price for Paprika. The other party feigned dismay. They cajoled the prospective bride's father and flattered him in extravagant terms before making a counter offer. The style was declamatory and whimsical as the exchange went back and forth. As they were about to come to an agreement, Yayal's sponsors produced a special bottle of very good old brandy, wrapped in a bright silken kerchief around which there was a string of gold pieces. This was called the *pliashka*. The principals contracting the marriage of their son and daughter—Yayal's and Paprika's fathers—drank ceremonially. After that they embraced warmly. The drinking from the *pliashka* was in fact the most important part of the marriage ceremony. It was what in the eyes of the Rom made the union valid and binding before the *Kris*.

The union was between the young man and the girl—here Yayal and Paprika—but the formal contract was between their fathers. They had respectively acquired a daughter-in-law and a son-in-law, but the newlyweds could not, in referring to the other, use the terms wife and husband until the first child was born of their union. On the other hand their fathers would from this day on call each other exclusively and proudly *khanamik,* a term descriptive of their newly established family-in-law relationship, of which, to my knowledge, there is no equivalent in European languages.

Amid more cheering both fathers embraced and more libations followed, when suddenly the groom's side started to bargain all over again, claiming they had spent much more than they had planned to. Blessed be the bride, and her father too. She was well worth the high price that they had settled upon. And more, to be sure; since from now on she was one of theirs, but they had no money left for the wedding feast, and for them to celebrate less than lavishly would not do honor to their new *khanamik*.

This too was part of the tradition. The bride's father would relent after much supplication. Paprika's father generously returned part of the bridal price, which according to the custom was used to buy the bride's clothes, which were then bought by her future mother-in-law and the other female members of the household. Yayal's mother, who until now had remained in the background, stepped forward to hang a string of gold pieces around Paprika's neck as a symbolic warning to other men that she was spoken for. The groom was not even present.

The gathered Rom were pleased with themselves and with the progress of events. The following day, possibly even later, Yayal and his party would come to take the bride away to her new home and to the fulfillment of the first night. For the present they could eat and drink and dance.

Nanosh, Zurka and I had originally planned to join Yayal after a while at one of the other of the parties where further marriages were being discussed or on the verge of being sealed, but the surfeit of excitement and festivities dulled our appreciation and eagerness to be present at other lengthy ritual comedies, however crucial, of arguing and eventually agreeing on the bridal price.

We had eaten our fill and probably drunk more than we should have; I had completely forgotten about the scene that must have taken place at Dodo's regarding my own planned marriage to Djidjo. And I dared not even allude to it, not knowing how Zurka or Nanosh would react. We parted to go to sleep. My sleeping stead had been carefully laid out for me, and my eiderdown with the faded red silken cover waited invitingly. It had a design of large daisies outlined in black.

A huge full moon hung low. After a last drink of water from the white enameled bucket I slipped under the eiderdown and undressed leisurely. A few feet away I could see Keja in bed with her sisters. Her full face, lit by the moon, rested on her arm. Her eyes were open and she looked at me peacefully, almost lovingly. I didn't sense any urgency or distress or tension in her, and I fell asleep without another thought.

Early the next day the tavern owner drove a large party of Gypsy women into the city in his truck. They went to buy fabric for the brides' gowns and quantities of silken kerchiefs to be given to the wedding guests.

Rupa and Keja did not accompany them, from which fact I could easily deduce that my planned-for marriage was not going through. It would have been in poor taste for me to ask what had happened, but I was anxious to learn how Pulika had solved the issue. Kore avoided being alone with me and so did Nanosh. Imperceptibly he averted his eyes and said nothing. I sensed reticence, even embarrassment. And so it fell to Tshaya to break the news to me. Tshaya and I had never gotten along well. She often teased me about my Gajo appearance, my fair hair and blue eyes, and she said that "like all Gaje" I smelled sour, until Rupa told her to be quiet whenever she overheard these comments. Trying to be spiteful, Tshaya told me how I would be forced to wait to marry Djidjo. At Dodo's last night an argument had arisen. Yojo had objected to what he claimed was an infraction of the customs of the Rom: Kore and Keja, both older than I, were still unmarried, and I should wait my turn. Besides, Djidjo's sister Ludu, one year older, was still a virgin. A lengthy discussion had followed, but Pulika had not defended my cause, supposedly, with all the legal resourcefulness at his command. And so, in view of legal objections, Pulika and Dodo had agreed to accept a promise of marriage between Djidjo and myself for some unspecified future date.

I was relieved to find out how unobtrusively the matter had solved itself, or rather *been* solved. I settled down to an ordinary day.

Pulika spent most of the day at the terrace of The Silent Rain, drinking coffee and an occasional glass of white wine with the other Rom. By now the bustling traffic between the camp and the inn had become part of the daily routine. A number of people dashed about as those households where a boy was taking a wife worked furiously to prepare their feasts. By contrast, the camp appeared strangely somnolent and undisturbed. The women scuttled back and forth endlessly, carrying buckets of water, scouring the big cast-iron cooking caldrons, preparing the chicken and geese. They cleaned vegetables and mounds of onions; they fried potatoes and boiled cabbage leaves, later to be filled with chopped meat and rice and heartily spiced.

According to the traditional division of labor, the younger married men were turning the roasting spits on which whole piglets were impaled and also half a flank of beef, while others fed deal planks into the roaring fires and threw aromatic herbs into them. Young boys protesting playfully were put to work grinding enough coffee for the entire camp. At the inn the cooks, the owner's wife, several of his in-laws and the regular tavern wenches were vying with the Gypsies, boiling hams, making dozens of minced-pork pies and frying large amounts of pork chops.

After being away for hours, the truck with the large party of Gypsy women aboard finally returned from the city. There were a few last-minute deliveries of beer and additional crates of liquor. There was a last visit from the head of the Gendarmerie, who, in Romani, was declared to be a *trushalo odji,* a thirsty soul. A photographer and several newspaper or magazine reporters, who had been alerted by the innkeeper, showed up. They too happened to be hungry and thirsty.

Long, narrow, improvised tables, built on sawhorses, stood under the arbor at the back of the tavern. They were covered with red-and-white-checkered tablecloths, fastened to the tabletops with special clamps to hold them against the wind.

Toward late afternoon all was ready, or almost so, and young boys were sent out to invite the men of the camp, with due formality, to the banquet. The Rom converged, walking with great dignity, in groups of threes and fours. They allowed the older or more important men to arrive first. The others followed at a short distance, sometimes a matter of a few feet, in self-imposed order of age and importance.

There was a lavish variety of food. The long tables were heavily laden with all kinds of meat: beef and pork barbecued at the spit, the first flavored with rosemary and liberally sprinkled with cayenne peppercorns, the other flavored with just a hint of aniseed; roast goose seasoned with sage, thyme and marjoram and stuffed with currants and apples; an abundance of fried chicken. There were large bowls of lettuce and tomatoes and side dishes of cucumbers, some in yogurt and others in brine with a sprinkling of dill. There were numerous dishes of beans, some vibrant red from the paprika seasoning, cold white beans with vinegar, mashed chick peas with sesame oil, green beans with sour cream and lentils. There were plates of potato salad with chives and parsley, and plates of Bryndza cheese. There was an overflow of small containers of horseradish, of black olives, and of cold baked eggplant mixed with chopped raw onion, jokingly called the "poor man's caviar." And there were collapsing stacks of freshly baked bread, and meat balls richly spiced with nutmeg and deep-fried onion rings.

The Rom who were giving this combined wedding repast, which turned into an unforgettable display of plenty, served drinks to their guests. There was a choice of black wine mixed with carbonated water from the old-fashioned siphons, frothy blond beer from a barrel—the pressure of which was resourcefully maintained with a bicycle pump operated by Yojo —and the inevitable brandy from the numerous bottles that decorated the tables. The only thing conspicuously absent from the tables was fresh flowers, which the Rom felt should be left alone as part of nature and never cut off. Cut flowers to them were a symbol of premature death, and this was the feast of the perpetuation of life.

Yayal, Nanosh, Tsinoro's son, Paprika's brother and myself did not partake of the meal since this was "our" feast. We helped to serve the guests and to give out the new silken kerchiefs to be worn around the throat after the fashion of the Rom, to thank them for honoring with their presence the day our people took wives.

In return they gave us a donation in cash, the amount of which, multiplied by one thousand for humoristic effect, was shouted out in a loud voice. This was to help set up the new households: *das dab ka i roata le neve vurdoneski* (to give a push to the wheel of the new wagon). All this was of course accompanied by more drinking, more elaborate toasts to the groom, and more cheering to his father.

As the Rom ended their meal, a small hired band started to play popular dance tunes. It was led by a blind heavyset accordion player and included a clarinet, a guitar and a drum.

Giving the money, the Rom said, *"Mandar tsera tai kater o Del mai but te aven tumenge"* (From me a little money, but may God give you plenty). After this was done the sponsors counted the money and announced the total received.

When the Rom were seated, they lingered by the tables a little longer. They belched politely, commenting on the excellence of the food; they wiped their fierce mustaches, and cleaned their hands on the tablecloths. When they moved away, an unruly, yelling mob of women and children swarmed all over the tables like a pack of wolves. They gorged themselves without restraint, making a joyous shambles of what was left from the banquet. They ran around knocking over glasses, pulling at the tablecloths, upsetting dishes, spilling food, breaking things. Women shrieked and scolded, small children cried.

Unconcerned, the Rom leisurely walked back to the camp to witness the next event of the day: the leading home of the new bride. They had drunk lustily and were in a happy, expansive mood. It was almost dusk. As we walked away, Dodo called to me to stay close to him. With a sense of wonder it occurred to me that he had actually addressed me as *jamutrea,* or son-in-law, instead of my name. We walked side by side, his arm around my shoulders. I could feel the weight of his sturdy frame leaning heavily against me in a friendly embrace. Reassuringly, he said my turn would come one day to bring home my bride, which, among the Rom, was unheard of from any father-in-law.

The members of the bride's family kissed her, and they wept together as they symbolically unbraided her hair. They put a white satin shiftlike dress over the red one she was wearing on this day—the one exception to the rule that red was never worn by an honest Gypsy woman.

A group of playful young relatives of both the groom and the bride had gathered in the open space between the wagons, hiding the two protagonists in their midst. They were going to enact a scene of abduction. For, even though the parents had agreed upon the marriage and paid the bridal price and the union had been celebrated with a festive meal, the bride still had to surrender to her new husband.

The bride's champions, all unmarried youths, linking arms, stood as a protective wall before her. In the descending darkness there were some good-humored, exuberant skirmishes, until the groom's side either forced its way through the barrier or tricked the others to make it possible for the groom to kidnap his bride. Paprika screamed and wept and violently thrashed her head from side to side. Unalarmed, Yayal took her away and they disappeared in the night. Fifika also fought with violence. She whimpered and tore her hair. But by temperament she was less wild than her new sister-in-law.

A short distance away near Butsulo's wagon a similar scene was presumably taking place, but the harsh, piercing lament we heard from that direction hardly sounded like Tsuritsa acting out the tragicomedy ordained by the tradition of the Lowara. When we approached the spot, we witnessed a wild free-for-all that nobody could have anticipated. In the half-dark a handful of young men were trying to disentangle three youths fighting in a blind frenzy.

We were told that Tsinoro's son had halfheartedly pretended to abduct the bride, who appeared more willing to go than was proper for a virgin. She had sighed to convey alarm, but those present claimed it was almost a sigh of pleasure. Upon which her younger brother, Fonso, took offense, deeply resenting the dishonor brought by her on their family. He had seized a horsewhip—some said he had carried it with him all along—and thrashed her. The groom and his brother had vainly tried to protect her, but nonetheless she had been marked on the face and hands. She sobbed hysterically.

The Rom went back to the inn and drank the rest of the night.

The following morning, after the display of the bridal bed linen, the mother-in-law assisted the bride in knotting her kerchief after the fashion of the married women. She would never again be without it. Malicious gossip would have it that So-and-so had taken a pigeon along on her bridal night; for it was necessary that there should be blood for all to see as proof of virginity.

As there had been no wooing, so there would be no honeymoon. After their marriage the groom's life went on much as before, except that he mingled more with the married men and less with the boys. He remained within his family and with the *kumpania* in which he had grown up. Whereas in this way the men were all related by kinship ties, a bride left her group to join her husband's, with the result that the married women were all strangers to the group into which they had been brought by marriage. The new bride was taken in charge by her mother-in-law and by her sisters-in-law who had gone through the same experience before her. Some girls said, with uncharacteristic pessism, that Tsuritsa's marriage only meant "a new set of harness sores."

As a rule the bride brought with her an eiderdown and her personal belongings. The young couple lived with their in-laws, at least until the first child was born but generally much longer, unless a younger brother got married: it was the custom that only the youngest son stayed with his parents. He and his wife would eventually take care of them in their old age. In reward for this the youngest son inherited their horses, the gold and whatever other property they left.

When a young man, with his wife and children, moved away from his parents into a home of his own, either wagon or tent, he gave a feast to celebrate his acceptance as a new member of the *kumpania,* independent from his father's household.

The responsibility of the girl's parents did not end with her marriage even though they no longer had to protect their daughter's virginity. If, for example, she were repudiated for infidelity, which is rare among the Gypsies, her parents had to take her back, refund the bridal price and pay for the "shame" she had brought her husband. If on the other hand her father felt she was being ill-treated by her parents-in-law, he had the privilege of taking her away despite her husband's objections.

For a few days the new *bora* were shown off and favored by their fathers-in-law. Old Bidshika insisted that Paprika accompany him to the inn, sit by him and sing and dance at his bidding to entertain his guests, while Yayal was caring for the horses. But Yayal would not have cared to be seen publicly with his new wife. He proudly bore the welts and scratches attributed to Paprika's resistance to him the night before as proof of her chastity.

As we were sitting with Pulika on the terrace of the café, Djidjo happened to pass by on some errand. Pulika asked her to do him some small favor for the sheer pleasure of including her in our doings, addressing her, though prematurely, as *bori*. She slowly lowered her eyes, and her mouth pouted briefly, but she was grateful for the attention and unusually submissive. It struck me again that like those of most women of the Lowara, her arms looked empty without a child in them. By custom I was not allowed to talk to her or communicate with her in any way.

Enjoying the peacefulness of the moment, the Rom sat on the terrace nibbling on rarely indulged-in sweetmeats. There were fresh walnuts, which deeply stained the fingers and had a tart aftertaste, poppy-seed pastries, and pears and apricots in brandy. The fruits had been painstakingly grown inside bottles that been slipped over the flowers still on the branch so that the fruit grew inside the glass container, reminding one of ships in bottles.

Dodo, with a demonstrative gesture of affection, repeatedly made me share his brandy until I was groggy. He said to me that *kon del tut o nai shai dela tut wi o vast* (he who willingly gives you one finger will also give you the whole hand).

Shortly afterward I happened to cross Djidjo's path on her way to the river. I sensed in her an unsuspected tenderness and she flushed. She, the little wild one, was awkward in her emotions. Her nostrils quivered, she threw back some unruly forelocks, and her hips swayed gently, but she already had a willing quietness that promised eventual obedience; a disarming quality of innocence was combined with that primeval vitality which gave her, at the age of fourteen, an air of womanly mystery.

Among the Rom, cases of elopement were extremely rare. After his marriage proposal on behalf of his youngest son Inga had been turned down, old Nanosh of the so-called Norwegian Tshurara had ignominiously encouraged his son and helped him to abduct the twelve-year-old Lyuba, or Lyubitshka, daughter of Pitivo and Liza. They had lain in ambush for her as she went to fetch water at a public well and had taken her across the border where her father could not easily pursue them. After informing the *Kris,* Pitivo had taken the drastic step of reporting to the local police the abduction of a female minor. The years went by, and as the Rom said, *"Stanki nashti tshi arakenpe manushen shai"* (Mountains do not meet but people do). They met and made up their quarrel as Gypsies will. Lyuba by now had two small children and she had brought luck to both her father-in-law and her husband. Happily they paid the damages. After this they traveled together and one day chanced to go back to the country where the abduction had taken place. To their utter shock and horror, Lyuba was promptly arrested and locked up in a home for wayward girls. Her young husband managed to escape the police and they hid the babies lest they too would be taken away to be raised as wards of the state. Nanosh denounced his *khanamik* Pitivo before the *Kris* and held him responsible for the incarceration of his *bori,* now duly paid for according to Gypsy law. Their quarrel was more violent than ever before.

Her mother-in-law, posing as her aunt, visited the girl regularly at the institution run by Catholic nuns, bringing her food and news of her babies and husband. Lyuba was a little wildcat who never settled down to the routine of the place. When the nuns wanted to cut off her braids, she had fought, kicked, scratched, sworn and cursed—for among her people to cut off the hair of a woman was the punishment and the shame of adultery.

One day at dawn the caravan departed unobserved as was the Gypsies' wont. Only the two hounds belonging to the tavern owner bellowed disconsolately. These had been memorable days and the Rom had successfully established another friendly outpost in their elaborate relay where they would be welcome whenever they returned. The days of marriages were over.

PART THREE

CHAPTER THIRTEEN

In the shadows of the night that surrounded us innumerable bullfrogs croaked in monotonous unison. The skies overhead were lightening. A rooster crowed right in the middle of the camp and after a short pause crowed again, more insistent this time, with a voice clear and penetrating. It was incongruous to hear this sound at close range and in a Gypsy camp when, by association, it belonged to the barnyard. I remembered that a Rom called Ferka, who had joined us with his family the day before and had recently come from Spain, owned a pet rooster. He had to protect it against every girl and woman in the camp, threatening with dire maledictions those who might attempt to put his pet into the cooking pot.

I dressed, and after a quick, superficial wash I joined Zurka and Kore, who were already up and squatting by the newly kindled fire. Silently we ate a lump of dark bread with goose fat, staring sleepily at the thin curling smoke, waiting for the coffee water to boil. Except for a few old people already roaming the campsite, everybody slept. The previous night Pulika had asked us to go into town to buy gold pieces with the cash that was left over from the feasting of the last few weeks. Kore and I knew the hard-faced, mysterious little Armenian from whom Pulika bought gold, and we found him in one of the several cafés he patronized. The thick wad of large bills of local currency to be invested in gold was tightly wrapped up in a piece of flowery cotton and bound with another narrow strip from a different material. Tina, my young brother, volunteered to fetch the horse from the grazing plot. He harnessed the light two-wheeled *taliga* and we drove into the nearby town. We let Tina drive while Ruv, our light-eyed, rough-haired wolf dog, ran ahead chasing birds. As we passed a large farmhouse we were overwhelmed by the smell of freshly baked bread mixed with the cool scent of whitewash still damp. We stopped at the inn on the highway and broke our fast with steak and brandy. We let Tina sip from our brandy and bought him some tobacco and yellowish cigarette paper. Then he drove back to the camp, with Ruv, tired from his early morning run, sitting next to him in the flat, open cart. The tavern keeper called the local taxicab for us. We agreed on the price and paid half the fare in advance.

We felt rather lost and out of place this early in the morning in the big city, watching the crowds rush to work. We sat down at the sidewalk terrace of a café, deserted at this hour. Some of the chairs were still piled high on the tables. We drank *café-filtre* upon *café-filtre*, waiting for Monsieur Jozeph, the Armenian. After a long wait he appeared and the essential business transaction between us was quickly concluded. The gold pieces we had bought were wrapped up in the pieces of cloth and safely stowed away. There were a number of English sovereigns, French Louis d'or, Austrian Thalers and a few rare American twenty-dollar pieces. Monsieur Jozeph tried to sell us rings, old-fashioned gold watches and bracelets, but Pulika had asked us to buy a precise amount of gold coins and nothing else. Although it was only midmorning, we had another broiled steak; this was part of the expense privileges traditionally accorded those on "courier duty."

Then we went to the city's main post office to collect what we called "Gypsy mail," sent care of General Delivery. Quite often the word "Gypsy" was boldly written by hand across the envelope in addition to the name of the addressee, as one might write "Airmail" or "Registered Letter." From the postmarks I could tell that some of these letters had been lying here uncollected for months. I knew that those addressed to Pulika under the name Petalo were from close relatives. Others were addressed to him as Peterlow, Vadosh, Colombus, Korpats—names by which he was known to various persons. The name by which he was addressed on the envelope gave him at first sight a clue to the sender of the letter. Gypsies were always changing their surnames. Pulika said that only the deaf and the blind have to believe. Letters could easily lie.

They had no face, no eyes, no tone of voice to check them by. They were written by Gaje for the Rom, and hence not to be trusted. The various names were Pulika's own way to double-check the authenticity of the sender.

We called at several points of contact, or what in the technical vocabulary of intelligence operatives would be called "drops." These points were unconnected and the various Gypsy couriers knew only those places they were "lifting," and none of the others. At one we were told of a long-distance call from Paris, asking for Pulika.

By midafternoon we telephoned the inn on the highway near the camp and were told that the caravan had moved earlier in the day. We had hoped to go to see a film, but now we had no choice but to go back immediately to our last location and follow the trail, the *vurma*, the Rom had left for us, to the next temporary halting place. Toward nightfall we were back at the inn but soon realized that darkness would prevent us from seeing the tracks left for us. Rather than sleep out one night and postpone till morning our search for the camp, we decided to charter the local taxi again and try our luck. We stopped along the road and asked about the wagon train. From village to village we followed the directions given. Once we lost the trail completely. At our next stop for information nobody had seen or heard of Gypsies in the vicinity. We drove back to the hamlet where supposedly they were seen last. The taxi driver worried and became reluctant to continue this wild-goose chase through the night, and we needed all our combined resourcefulness to prevail upon him not to leave us on the open road.

The headlights of the taxi glared into the night ahead of us, violently exposing successive sections of road, disturbing wild-life and somehow isolating us even more from the world outside. At each lonely farmhouse we passed, fiendish, de-mented dogs barked frantically. In wooded sections we could see scores of glistening eyes staring at us in the dark, on either side of the road. Passing through sleepy little villages huddled around their churches, we heard the peal of church bells telling of the passing hours. It was well into the night, when stopping once more for information, that we learned to our relief that the Gypsy caravan had passed here around seven in the evening and that the Gypsies had turned into a dirt track a few hundred yards ahead, where they had stopped for the night. We treated the taxi driver to a nightcap, while Kore borrowed some cash from the innkeeper against the pledge of a small gold piece, to pay the balance of the taxi fare.

The entire camp was asleep when we finally arrived home. Tina and two or three small children, probably Yojo's little ones, had invaded my sleeping stead thinking I would not come back for the night.

The next morning I awoke early. Pulika was softly calling my name from his bed a scant few feet away from mine. I noticed that his hair was full, long and very black and suddenly realized how rarely I had seen him without his wide-brimmed, black hat. Without it he had a more youthful appearance. I told him about the previous day's errand and about the long-distance telephone call from Paris. He questioned me but incongruously attached more importance to the place where the call was received than where it had come from. The place of reception was the code by which he could not only tell the identity of the caller but also verify it.

Pulika lay back and we waited in isolated silence until the rest of the camp woke up.

It was not until many hours later that Pulika sent word for me to join him at the inn. The message was conveyed to me by one of the abundant half-naked, swarthy urchins. I had almost forgotten about the call from Paris. Pulika leisurely sipped some brandy and it was only after a long pause that he asked me offhandedly to put through the return call to Paris. Listening through the old-fashioned trumpetlike horn, I heard far-away voices intermingling with voices nearby; then far away again a bell rang insistently. The sounds overlapped, changed pitch with the ethereal confusion of an orchestra tuning up, punctuated by blank silence. Then far away again, in the gray mist, a bell rang repeatedly and a gruff voice said, "Aaloh," putting the accent on the first drawn-out syllable. Manfully I shouted back, *"Romale tai shavale akarel tume o Pulika"* (By your leave, Gypsy men and youths, this is Pulika calling you).

This was the proper and formal way to address the Rom. I was made to repeat this numerous times before the gruff phantom voice acknowledged receiving the message and, interrupting me in mid-sentence, instructed me to wait. Extraneous sounds seeped into the line and swelled suddenly to fill the void. They faded, dissolved, and the Paris telephone connection was broken off. After a few exasperating seconds, strange voices speaking in French invaded the line and intermingled sense-lessly, as if they were talking at cross purposes under water. And again the voice of an operator, nearby, cut in. From the heavy fog emerged a strong voice, unmistakably Romani. This time it was my turn to shout that he should wait, and I ran to fetch Pulika at the bar. At first Pulika strained to hear the disembodied, faceless voice at the other end. He repeated the same few words over and over again, trying to identify himself and in turn straining to hear the reply. He was ill at ease, stiff, and his speech became declamatory. Finally he handed me the telephone receiver, asking me to hold it up to him like a microphone. Pulika stepped a little to the side, and using both free hands to gesture in emphasis of his words, he spoke *to* the telephone rather than into it. Pulika usually talked in a power-ful voice, but now he even increased its volume because he was trying to reach somebody in Paris. I could sense his frustration at not being able to see the person at the other end. His burning eyes grew more intense. When he was listening to the answer from far away, Pulika's eyes narrowed visibly under the tension of catching the meaning of the distorted sounds of the other Rom's words, for he too must have been bellowing into his end of the telephone, hoping to be heard by Pulika, but the sounds of their voices only shattered into unintelligible noises. Gradually they both managed to adjust the loudness of their voices and communication started. But however much I tried, I could not follow the sense of their conversation. There were long pauses because the Rom did not talk in questions and answers but, out of courtesy, made short discourses to each other, which were answered by other more or less short discourses, not unlike the noncommittal conversation among diplomats around the conference table.

Abruptly the communication was over, after a last ritual

phrase: *"Ashen Devlesa, Romale"* (May you remain with God). Because Pulika had used the expression "remain with God" rather than "go with God," I knew he had been talking to someone in a camp that would remain stationary and we would be the ones to travel toward them.

To my eager questions Pulika answered laconically that he had just spoken to Grantsha le Yankosko of the Zingareshti group. They were self-styled Russian Kalderasha, or coppersmiths. And he had also briefly talked to Djordji, the oldest of old Tshompi's three sons.

One or two days later we were peacefully traveling along a tree-shaded country road. There were several wagons ahead of ours. As we drove by, I saw Bidshika standing at the side of the road waiting for us to catch up. Putting his foot on the spoke of the revolving wheel, he pulled himself up and climbed into our wagon. He was clean-shaven and dressed up. A little farther ahead his wife jumped out of their wagon, which was traveling in front of ours; she waited for us to pass and she too clambered onto our wagon. As we went we picked up several other people. This in itself was not unusual. What was unusual was their spruce appearance and the fact that the women carried small bundles wrapped in cloth. I was still wondering what it was all about when Pulika asked me if I felt like going along with them on this trip. The tone of his voice told me he did not expect an answer. This was a *fait accompli.* Rupa gave me my still-valid Belgian passport and a bundle of bank notes, and tied two small gold pieces in the corners of my *diklo,* which was knotted around my throat. Unthinking, Pulika must have assumed I knew all I had to know about the trip, which, I rightly guessed, was connected with the telephone call to Paris of a few days ago.

Kore sprinkled some water on me and brushed off the downy fluff clinging to my clothes from the feather bed, and Keja sewed on one large button—cut off Yojo's old sport jacket— to substitute for the three missing from mine. The only thread she had available happened to be white, and she first darkened it with a piece of coal. From the unusual fuss I guessed it must be an important trip I was going on.

After these sudden and frantic preparations several hours

passed without further developments. Then as we passed through an overgrown village that had developed as an outgrowth of its railroad junction, we jumped off. The Gypsy wagon train traveled on without slowing down for one instant, to disappear at a turn in the road.

The group consisted of Bidshika and his wife Terom, one Milosh and his wife Tshaya, their little daughter Mozol and myself. The two men carried heavy walking sticks with curved heads and ornamented with silver inlay, which they hung nonchalantly from the crooks of their left elbows. Milosh's Tshaya carried a huge round loaf of bread wrapped in a frayed piece of faded vermilion silk tied together by the corners. A hole had been dug in the bread and was filled with butter. There was also some cold roast meat that made grease stains on the material, some hot peppers and sour gherkins. Another bundle held tightly wrapped goosedown pillows, called *sheranda,* covered in gay, flowered material. Nobody carried anything even resembling a possible change of clothes. After several more hours of waiting we boarded the train to the capital, from where, with more delays in between, we caught the Mittropa overnight train to Paris.

Because we had not made reservations, the seats we found were widely scattered. The other men and I went to the dining car to drink, while Terom watched over our scant but colorful belongings, Tshaya and twelve-year-old Mozol (her name meant Black Currant) roamed up and down the narrow corridor where Tshaya joked with male passengers, stared inside other compartments or told fortunes to pass the time away.

Bidshika and Milosh wore what once must have been expensive double-breasted business suits; they were not too well pressed and the trousers were a shade too wide to be fashionable. Both men were athletic, if a little heavyset, and vividly healthy compared to most of the other passengers.

When we returned to our individual scattered seats after consuming many lager beers, we peered, not always too discreetly, through various compartment windows and were not surprised to discover that our women had managed to switch places and were now together. I was struck by the loudness of

Tshaya's voice, even though she was not speaking in anger, and then it occurred to me that we, the Gypsies, all spoke with voices louder than those of the people around us. I wondered if this could be due to the open-air life we led and to our having to cope with wind—and sheer distance, for that matter—to communicate with one another. Little Mozol sat in the corner of the compartment facing forward and nearest the corridor. Her eyes were closed, her head leaning back, and she breathed gently. Her hands, demurely folded, rested in her lap and she looked touchingly young and pure. There was a slight fullness in the way the ample, faded lilac skirt and the low-cut yellow blouse were draped about the well-rounded but still slender shape of her young body, which I had never noticed before. Somehow it was the first time I had ever paid any attention to her at all, even though we lived side by side in the same *kumpania*. In her colorful if ragged and faded dress she struck me incongruously as a tender Gypsy Madonna, as seen in a dream. She sat tightly squeezed in by a generous-looking, middle-aged woman, who could have been a small shopkeeper's wife. She kept staring with pity at Mozol and alternately delivered heated, disapproving comments to Tshaya who sat squarely opposite, patient and unconcerned. With insistent Romany courtesy Tshaya gave her seat to Bidshika and joined us outside in the corridor to smoke an elegant, gold-tipped, Turkish cigarette she had begged from one of our fellow passengers. Once in a while I looked in our compartment, finding it hard to resist staring at sweet little Mozol. Both she and Bidshika sat back with their eyes closed, obviously to avoid conversation with the Gaje. They had not moved in more than half an hour. Then, with her eyes still shut, Mozol gently but persistently started scratching herself. At first with great modesty and restraint she rubbed her knee through the many ample skirts; then after a pause she scratched the back of her slender neck; then again, reaching inside the loose-fitting blouse, she scratched her bare right shoulder. When the middle-aged woman sitting next to her moved away, apprehensive about the scratching, I began to understand. After a period of more subdued scratching, the woman, by now purple-faced and angry, finally got up, cast a last look at the little Gypsy girl, and left her seat, taking her luggage with her. She didn't return.

We all sat merrily together. The suggestive scratching had ceased and there were no Gaje left among us. Not suspecting the ruse, they had fled before the implications of vermin. Milosh reclined comfortably on the goose-down pillows, which were once again in full view.

At the border our compartment was invaded by customs and immigration officers, but Bidshika must have obtained French passports for the inspection was soon over. I had known Bidshika for many years and traveled with him before, and I seemed to remember his using his identification papers as a stateless person. But I was sleepy and in no mood to pursue my initial curiosity about this. He and his family must have been selected for this particular trip because they possessed the necessary French papers, making it possible for them to travel by train instead of being forced to move in a clandestine way. It was obvious why I had been sent along: besides possessing a valid passport, I could write and thus would be able to summarize the situation for Pulika more clearly than letters dictated to a Gajo by a Rom would do.

The train rushed on through the night with a hypnotic, repetitive noise of wheels hitting the ridge between the sections of rail. The electric lights overhead were dimmed. Outside daybreak was nearing. Villages flashed by, bathed in the ghostly light, followed by meadows that made me think of our own horses grazing lazily somewhere far behind. More villages.

The train stopped and I went to look out the window. I could not distinguish the name of the place. Mozol joined me at the window. The cold night air washed our faces. It smelled of coal fumes, water that had boiled too long and machine grease. On the quay stood a man with a lantern; as the train started moving, he waved at us, swinging it several times in a wide arc.

Tshaya fetched us some coffee. It was burning hot but tasteless, since we were used to a much stronger brew, Turkish coffee, which was supposed to be "black as sin, hot as hell and sweet as love." Mozol ate lumps of sugar she soaked in our coffee—for the fun of unwrapping them from their tiny envelopes, I suspected. We ate the loaf of bread and the cold meat Terom had brought along. After that we stayed awake watching the new day being born, until some hours later we arrived in Paris. Bewildered by the traffic and confused about what bus would take us where we wanted to go, we settled for a taxicab to the poorer section, at the outskirts of the city. I believe it was the Porte de Chignon court. Bidshika, who had been here before, told of the night life and the many renowned eating places where gourmets came to savor their great specialties: frogs' legs. To the Gypsies frogs were the most repulsive creatures in the whole universe, and for some unexplained reason they were considered to be the very image of the Devil, *Beng*. We stopped at the *Marché aux Puces,* the flea market, where most diversified and disparate articles were bought and sold, ranging from old worn shoes, cheap cotton dresses and plain old junk to expensive antiques and Persian rugs. This was a section of narrow, tortuous streets, some of which had improvised canvas awnings stretched across them, as much to protect the merchandise as to accommodate the clients. This gave one the impression of being in the native quarter of a North African town. This impression was reinforced by the large number of Algerians, with their narrow, distrustful eyes, who lived in this *quartier*.

We walked about and ate fried potatoes at an open-air stall and drank some of the cheap young wine they called *pinard*, soaking in the atmosphere. The sun was already setting when we met several Gypsy women and girls hurrying past, wearing exceedingly high heels. Their clothes were very different from what our women wore. They favored shiny dress materials and showed a preference for blues and greens. They wore long sleeves and instead of tucking in their blouses, they wore them outside and over their skirts, with imitation gold and silver belts. Otherwise they looked cleaner than we did and definitely urban. When they spoke, their speech was nasal compared to ours and the tempo was faster. They also had a tendency, at least in our presence, to giggle, in a silly but suppressed way that struck us unpleasantly.

Terom and Tshaya talked to them, as it would have been

unseemly for us, men, to do so under the circumstances, and after a few minutes we followed them through the narrow, winding alleys. Bidshika, Milosh, Mozol and I walked a short distance behind them.

The air rang with a resonant cadence of hammers beating on metal. At close range the steady, quick hammering became ear-rending and stunning. Two of the willowy, high-heeled Kalderasha girls, dressed in shades of blues and greens, abruptly broke away and ran off, holding hands. They disappeared inside a doorway and we followed them through a dark passage that led into a courtyard. We soon found out they had only run ahead to announce our coming, the coming of unknown Gypsies who were not Kalderasha. Excited murmuring replaced the hammering. Several short, heavyset middle-aged Kalderasha men met us with welcoming smiles that showed flashing gold teeth. They wore dark-colored sport shirts and light ties, in contrast to our own *diklo* and navy-blue pin-striped, double-breasted, rather conservative suits. Their hands were stained an unpleasant, shiny, greenish black from handling metal. The place itself reeked of a pronounced, sourish chemical smell which, as we later learned, came from the *zalzaro,* a special kind of acid they used in their tin-plating process. There were many women of all ages and they stood neatly in a line facing us. At first sight they looked thinner, possibly more elegant, than the Lowara women.

In the open yard three large tents had been pitched. Each one was easily twenty by twenty-six or twenty-seven feet, made of heavy brown-and-dark-red canvas. The largest of the tents was open on three sides. It consisted of a canvas roof slanting down on two sides from a central ridge going from front to back, supported by tall tent poles decorated with spiraling metal foil. The back of the tent was closed off, and against it huge feather beds were piled high. On the three other sides the canvas walls had been rolled up and were kept in place by strings. At one side of the yard there was a pile of brass and copper caldrons, vats and basins. In a pit in the ground a coal fire was burning white. A pair of small bellows, their outlets buried underground and connected to the open pit, kindled the blaze, snoring viciously. It was operated by hand by a thin, sweating youth. Several greasy mats lay on the floor, on which our hosts had been kneeling when we came, industriously at work. Strewn about on the floor there were long tongs, sundry hammers, bits of coppersmiths' solder, small dishes containing *zalzaro* acids, and singed rags. With an emphatic show of good manners the middle-aged Kalderasha men invited us inside the larger tent, which, we were informed, belonged to one Petsha. "May your names remain the lucky ones they have been until today," they said. We replied, "And may God remain with you and with your sons and with your sons' sons. May you all remain in good health, in good cheer and at peace with the world."

We were invited to sit down in a wide circle facing the entrance of the tent. The next moment something happened for which none of us had been prepared. Two young Kalderasha girls rolled a wheel about six feet in diameter into the tent, moving it along with short, continuous, self-assured movements as they walked. The huge wheel stood in front of us, blotting out the view. There was a split-second hesitation before it flipped over toward us. Without moving from their sitting position next to us, the Kalderasha men stretched out a helping hand and the wheel lightly fell into its intended position, and to our astonished eyes it was revealed to be nothing stranger than a large round table. The short extending legs had been on the opposite side from where we sat and consequently hidden from our sight.

Another young woman brought a heavily ornate silver samovar with yellowed ivory handles, which she placed on a silver-plated triangular tray. During all this time not a word was exchanged; the atmosphere had the solemnity reserved for a ritual. Other young women milled about bringing tablecloths, heavy metal trays with slices of raisin cake, baklava, *rahat lokum* and various jars of jams and jellies.

I saw one of the young girls standing outside the tent violently whirling around some strange contraption from which flew sparks. Later on, having been exposed for a longer period to the ways of life of our hosts, I learned that this receptacle with a protruding handle was made from wire and was used to make charcoal incandescent after it had been lit.

Anka lifted the cover of the samovar and filled it with water, then she put the glowing brazier inside a pipelike miniature furnace as the core, which heated the water, so to speak, from inside out. On top of a small chimney protruding from the samovar she placed the teapot in which she brewed a black, almost poisonlike tea, which was afterward diluted to taste with boiling water from the tap extending from the front. As the water boiled, the samovar gave forth a soft, pleasant, reassuring gurgle. In front of us Anka carefully washed each glass in a dish of boiling water that also served to catch the drip from the tap. The glasses of tea sitting in deep saucers were passed along in an orderly manner until everybody was served. Together with the tea the host passed along several dishes containing berries, bits of apple, slices of lemon and lumps of sugar. We watched the host and did as he did. The berries or apple bits plus the lemon were plunged into the hot tea, which was then poured out into the saucer, from which it was drunk. The sugar was held between one's teeth and the tea sipped through it; thus it melted inside one's mouth rather than in the teacup. We nibbled sweetmeats and raisin cake and wondered how it was that some Gypsies could be so different from others. Young men and young women came to look at us from a respectful distance and spoke in hushed tones.

From everywhere older Kalderasha men came by twos and threes until there must have been at least thirty of them assembled in Petsha's spacious tent. The samovar was refilled several times and more cakes and sweetmeats were brought in by the girls. Many questions and answers were exchanged, as Gypsies were wont to do when they met, but little warmth developed. The conversation remained polite and subdued. At times we had difficulty understanding their pronunciation of certain words and some of their idioms. Aside from their adopting the use of the samovar, they seemed to have absorbed a certain amount of borrowed Russian words, which we of the younger Lowara generation did not understand. Pulika and most of the older men of our *kumpania* had lived in Russia at one time or another and still spoke Russian after a fashion.

An important-looking older man invited us all to visit the tent of his older brother, Grantsha le Yankosko, after obtaining permission from our host to take the newcomers away, bowing to him from the waist while remaining seated. Petsha and several older Kalderasha followed us. Petsha's brothers declined the invitation, saying that they were not dressed for the occasion and that they had to finish the work they had interrupted. We thought this certainly would not have been the Lowara way of doing things. Petsha insisted that Terom, Tshaya and Mozol remain behind with the women of his own household where, he added, they should feel at home. We knew we could not protest even though we were reluctant to see our small unit split up so soon. The implication, of course, was that Petsha considered us his houseguests and that he cleverly took this precaution to maintain his "ownership" over us. We would certainly not move in with some more important Rom if our women were staying with him. He, Petsha, was the first Rom we had met in Paris, and to him fell the duty, but also the honor, of giving us hospitality.

Our group walked slowly through the winding alleyways, some of which had open sewers running through the middle of them. This was what in French was called Bidonville. It was a nightmarish no-man's-land, depressing, shabbily ugly, fringing on grim slums and industrial suburbs, but worse than both combined. It was the last refuge of those living on the outskirts of hope. Taken in tow by the friendly Kalderasha, we strolled through these ghettos of human flotsam, interspersed with wastelands of garbage and piles of junk smelling of decay and urine. The Kalderasha seemed oblivious to the surroundings. We walked in a slow procession. Every now and then a group would stand still and the others ahead waited for them to catch up again. It reminded me of a scene I had witnessed many years ago near Cluj, the capital of Transylvania, where Hasidic Jews, clad in their long, black caftans and fur hats called *shtreimels,* wearing flowing beards—not a few of them reddish —and sidelocks, *peyesin,* slowly made their way through the wretched, shadowy passages, celebrating the presence in their midst of the venerated, charismatic leader, the *Klausenburger Wunder Rebbe,* the *Tzaddik.*

We finally arrived at the tent of Grantsha le Yankosko, the man Pulika had talked to. He was an impressive barrel-chested man of dark complexion who welcomed us heartily, and made it a point to inform us that he knew Pulika well and was familiar with the peculiarities of the Lowara. He purposely used Lowara words and expressions, and typical Lowara greetings. We felt more at ease at Grantsha's. The low round table was already in place and the samovar was bubbling. While we were sitting down, a young woman, our host's daughter-in-law, lifted up the heavy samovar and took it outside the tent where, to our amazement, she let the boiling water pour out. After doing this she poked out the fire and shook the cinder grate through some holes at the bottom of the samovar. Anticipating our surprise about this strange Kalderasha custom, Grantsha explained that among his people it was the tradition that when honored guests came from afar the entire samovar procedure should be started afresh for their benefit, the charcoal fire rekindled, the water allowed to boil anew. With a broad genial smile, revealing an impressive number of gold teeth, and with sweeping gestures, he said that perhaps this was the moment we all had been waiting for, the one rare moment when there would be no Kalderasha tea available and we could, without being criticized for it, change to something more potent and less filling to drink. "Lowara style," he emphasized. Even though he was a Kalderasha himself, he, too, occasionally welcomed something more manly than tea. At this suggestion an older woman brought a crystal decanter and several tiny metal goblets on a tray. After he proposed an eloquent toast, almost in the spirit of the Lowara, he closed his eyes, threw back his head and gulped down the drink in one swallow. We did the same, but to our surprise the drink was sticky, very sweet, more like some kind of not unpleasant medicine than alcohol. When the water started boiling in the samovar we went back to drinking tea. The table was set with a profusion of pleasantly decorated dishes of thin toasted bread with black caviar, hard-boiled eggs with bits of raw, pink onion, small pieces of dark bread with only a tiny rolled-up anchovy in the middle, some sardines, herring in sour cream, but no roast pigs, no geese, no chickens. We learned the Kalderasha saying *Kon khal but, khal peski bakht* (He who eats much, eats away his own luck), but we violently disagreed with it in private.

Grantsha's tent was lit by a single bare bulb burning with a yellowish, wavering, underpowered light. In another tent some young Kalderasha girls were giggling. They had cranked up a gramophone and were playing synthetically emotional Russian folk songs. Oppressively alien sounds flooded the tent camp. They came from the shacks and tenements everywhere around us, pouring forth from blaring radios, from drunken quarreling couples. It was not the noise in itself that seemed objectionable but rather the fact that the Gaje were violating *our* privacy for a change.

The floor of Grantsha's tent was covered with several layers of deep-piled Oriental rugs. He was well disposed toward us, but his artificial mannerisms irritated us, and listening to the oratory of his people, I could not imagine their indulging in anything more extreme than verbal violence.

Their girls were quite attractive, but their amorous glances and surreptitious flirting made me ill at ease, as if I were being treated as a Gajo, to be deceived or tricked. They smelled of cheap perfumes and brilliantine, and they wore lipstick.

On the following days we explored the vicinity. We went to the horse market of the Rue de Vaugirard and met more Kalderasha, a few Tshurara and numerous Sinti, or Manush—musicians who all claimed to be related to Django Reinhardt, the famous jazz guitarist and co-founder of Le Hot Club de France. One day at Grantsha's tent, where we dutifully made our daily call of respect in expectation of I don't know what, we met several coppersmith Gypsies who had come from Poland by train, like ourselves. They referred to themselves as Shoshoyara, which in our language meant rabbits, but we never found out why. Whimsically Bidshika said it was because they ate rabbits, which we Lowara considered taboo. The Shoshoyara wore bushy unkempt beards, and their long curly hair hung down to their shoulders. They affected soft felt hats with high crowns and narrow sloping brims. They looked much like Kotorara we had run into, who lived in tents in the

Carpathian forest and at the foothills at the edge of the Ukrainian plains, although the Shoshoyara claimed they lived in large wagons not unlike our own. They looked wild and extravagantly out of place in the present setting. In turn they made us self-conscious about our own appearance, only slightly less wild than theirs. That afternoon Bidshika, Milosh and I had our hair cut at a neighborhood barbershop that was the meeting ground of the Spanish Republican refugees of the Civil War and the headquarters of their inevitable softball club, but we were disinclined to take off our colorful and distinctive *diklo*.

I was seized by a sudden sadness. I achingly longed for the restless erratic pace of the Lowara I had become attuned to. I longed for the woods, for nature, for the smells, colors, tastes, sights and sounds that made life lyrically sweet. I longed for the seasonal pattern of growth—yes, I even longed for the earthy peasants I had hitherto scorned: the earthy peasants with their capacities limited to the slow, heavy, archaic tilling of the soil, who lived and slept and bred and died in dark, smelly holes close to their cattle and the earth. I longed for the farmyards with their huge dunghills where geese and piglets played in the dark brown pools that formed around them. Gradually, even though belatedly, I had discovered another side to them too: their patient, tenacious courage, their sense of purpose and duty to the land, their uncomplicated loves and joys, their sorrows, their fears and uncertainties about supernatural life, and their inarticulate emotions.

After the refugees from Spain had come, those from Poland, Austria, Czechoslovakia and Germany followed. France had called a general mobilization and, together with Britain, declared war. I was sixteen, going on seventeen, and I suffered from *Weltschmerz*. I longed to be again among the Lowara, with Pulika. I longed for Rupa, Keja, Kore, and for Djidjo and what might have been.

One day, as simply and unpredictably as one long-distance telephone call had wrenched me away from Pulika's *kumpania* and miserably changed my life, I was once again reunited with Pulika's people. Grantsha le Yankosko received a call from an unidentified youth who left a message for me to stay close to home for the next day or two because "they" wanted to be able to reach me at their convenience whenever "they" reached the city. Bidshika and Milosh kept me company in my vigil, drinking white wine at the *bistro du coin*, watching the eternal crap games.

A dust-covered, dilapidated Rochelle-Schneider limousine, packed with disheveled, intense, wild-eyed, noisy Rom, stopped halfway down the alley. Next to the driver sat Mimi, Tshukurka's white-haired wife who had never left the wagon side under any circumstance, and next to her sat Keja. Zurka and Laetshi, Tshukurka's sons, were the first ones to jump out. They all looked tense and fatigued. Then came Luluvo and some others. In the back of the spacious car Tshukurka lay prostrate on his feather bed. His eyes looked extinguished and his skin had a dull gray cast.

It appeared that shortly after Bidshika, Milosh and I had left the *kumpania* to come to Paris—on a mission the purpose of which still escaped me—Tshukurka had a collapse, which might very well have been brought about by the inordinate libations and excess of rich fare he had indulged in day after day, night after night, from the end of the *Kris* through the inexhaustible *patshiva* and to the consummation of the multiple marriages. In the night the Rom had frantically searched for a doctor. The one they finally found had been frightened to follow them to their camp, but eventually had relented. He had diagnosed acute diabetes with complications, and he had returned later to give Tshukurka injections, while the women lamented and wailed and the small children cowered. A few days later Pulika had rented a car with a driver and had taken his brother Tshukurka to Germany to see "the Professor," who supposedly was the greatest medical authority in this field. They had bargained with him, offering him an ever-increasing number of gold pieces for restoring Tshukurka's health. The Herr Professor had vainly tried to convince them that there was no miracle cure available. The patient would have to observe a strict diet and take four daily insulin injections for the rest of his life. The more he explained, the more convinced were the Rom that he was only driving a shrewd, if unscrupulous, bargain with them, and accordingly they increased the pile of small gold pieces they were stacking up in front of him on his desk. Finally he had called upon the orderlies to throw out the uncomprehending *Zigeuners*. From one of the minor hospital clerks they had heard about a charlatan miracle maker and promptly drove to see him. At a bar one night they met César, a footloose jack-of-all-trades who had seen service in the French Foreign Legion. He must have been in his late thirties, had slightly protruding eyes, and was fleshily handsome. He could have been played quite well by Jean Gabin. Ever since the night they met he had taken a strong liking to the Rom and had tried to make himself indispensable to them. He liked to relate his allegedly scabrous adventures in the Tonkin, which at that time was still part of the French colony of Indochina. He professed a savage contempt for government and for clergy but at the same time, inconceivably, had advised the Rom to take the ailing Tshukurka on a pilgrimage to Lourdes. He was a competent driver and the owner of a Rochelle-Schneider that had seen better days. And so one late afternoon they had left together for France and ultimately for Lourdes at the foot of the Pyrenees mountain range. Luluvo and one of Tshukurka's sons were to accompany him, but at the time of leaving, Mimi, his wife, had suddenly insisted on going with them. In her distress at being refused, she had first ripped open one of their large feather beds, and the goose down, after whirling about, had settled down on everything in sight. It was inconceivable that Mimi would travel alone and consequently Keja had been invited along on the spur of the moment. Several other relatives had insistently offered their good services and joined the expedition. As a result, the sick, loudly moaning Tshukurka had been badly crowded, and suffered more discomfort than pleasure. Half a mile away from the camp Laetshi, Tshukurka's other son, seeing them drive away, had stood in the road and insisted he would not let his sick father go away "alone." Huffily Mimi repeated that whatever César might say about Lourdes, she had never heard of it. The place to go, she said— unaware of the difficulties of going there because of the tense international political situation—was Czestochowa in Poland, about which in her youth she had heard great things said.

Unwillingly César was cast by circumstances as the apologist for Lourdes. The glowing accounts given by this open anti-clericalist were tinged by chauvinism. After the first two days of driving, Luluvo had called Paris and decided to take me along if I happened to be there or anywhere near. Events, as in the past, had a perverse way of turning out well for me.

Every morning César carefully studied the road maps, priding himself on knowing the shortest road straight through the heart of France. The Rom were used to wandering in wagons, and had no idea of the distances we were covering. Repeatedly Tshukurka had César stop the car in the middle of nowhere so he could step out "to breathe." The Rom fed him lukewarm champagne by the spoonful. A few times he emerged from his torpor, growing angry at the length of the trip.

Stopping for the night in small French provincial towns, we had difficulty in finding lodgings. Even money did not help. But César was resourceful and soon discovered that in every city there were places that would not refuse us: the brothels. We paid the *tarif* and dispensed with the services usually included in the price. The Rom all gathered in one room. They pooled the mattresses and slept together on the floor, after having removed the white sheets as they would not sleep in "shrouds." In the middle of the night Mimi and Keja joined us, fearful of sleeping alone among strangers. Here we usually were treated not only correctly but kindly. A few times we were bothered by bedbugs, which I had never been exposed to among the Rom. Luluvo said he had known them before, in prison.

Lourdes itself, when we finally arrived there, was an anti-climax. Deceived by the picture that César had painted of it—he had been carried away, possibly because he had never been there—the Rom had expected a "new Jerusalem."

In Lourdes I stayed with the other Rom at the local brothel on the outskirts of the city, while César took Tshukurka, Mimi and Keja to the church and to the crypt. We drove away the same day and I never heard much about what had happened. No miraculous cure had been effected, and Tshukurka felt worse than before. He lay prostrate, moaning constantly.

When Keja gave him his lukewarm champagne he quietly spilled some of it on the ground with an apology addressed to his ancestors, the *Mule,* for having come to Lourdes to appeal to the Blessed Virgin of the Gaje, instead of simply relying on the *Mule* of the Lowara tribe. "But," he added in a low murmur, still addressing them, "if it had worked it would have been another welcome opportunity to trick them, the Gaje."

We drove away through a drizzling rain. The windshield wipers broke, but our undismayed César leaned out of the side window and, slowing down, drove on, peering ahead with eyes narrowed, his brow deeply furrowed and dripping with rain. Tshukurka had an obsessive wish to return to his wagon, to die among his people.

The sun broke through and there was a splendid rainbow. César said it was a good omen. The landscape was mist-shrouded and the Rom were getting restless. César took the Rom to the place they had left from, and they parted good friends.

CHAPTER FOURTEEN

A number of wagons stood in a single row along the lonely, tree-lined, paved country road. It drizzled, with occasional downpours. Inside the wagons it was hot and humid; the rain drummed incessantly on the arched wagon roofs low overhead and babies cried. After a short while we left Tshukurka and Mimi's wagon. Keja and I ran through the rain to find our own wagon. The night fell early, its intimate protecting darkness blotting out the outside world. Rupa took the lid off the stove and let the leaping, dancing flames light up the wagon. They moved capriciously, full of life, joy and mischief, as they lit people's faces with a red glow. The flames seemed teasingly to try to jump beyond the confines of the old blackened stove with its top left off. In rapid sequence they licked the hot metal rim and made puffing, crackling and explosive little noises. We were quiet, loving the fire after seeing so much rain. In a corner a young mother suckled her baby, shading its eyes with her dark hand to avoid the distraction of the leaping fire. The baby made gurgling sounds of deep contentment. Before going to bed we adjusted the army blankets and shifted the pieces of tarpaulin to try to keep the horses as warm and as dry as possible. All night long we heard the sounds of horses' hoofs scraping the pavement or shifting position. The animals were tied at the backs of their owners' wagons, feed bags of oats tied at their necks.

The following day it rained again and nobody left the wagon train. The moment the rain stopped, the Rom began to disperse even though it was already late in the day. There was only another month ahead, or at very best two, to roam the villages to trade horses before the big rains would come and the autumn mud set in. And after that the snow and the frost would come, imposing on the Rom a time of paralysis. Tshukurka's health was declining rapidly. He was short of breath and lay motionless on his eiderdown. His eyes now shone with fever and he moaned softly day and night. When he emerged from his isolation, he expressed to those around him regrets for his shortcomings as a Rom. They in turn would moan and protest and begged his forgiveness for their possible offenses to him. A hushed spell dampened the spirits of our *kumpania*. All the Rom who could be reached with the news of Tshukurka's state of health, not to say his impending death, came to visit with him. They squatted at his bedside and repeated to Tshukurka and he to them, *"Te aves yertime mandar, te yertil tut o Del"* (I forgive you and may God forgive you too) in a ritual exchange of forgiveness. For it was not good for a Rom to depart to the other world without having settled his conscience. No secret resentment or envy should remain, no unspoken reproach.

Pulika and Yojo traveled to nearby villages to procure food and drink for the many people who came to see Tshukurka, as it was the family's obligation to provide for them under these circumstances. We limited the the radius of our travel to remain within easy reach in case of emergency.

Tshukurka's wagon was taken to a vast camping spot near a village at the bottom of a valley where a doctor lived, whose sympathy and concern for the Gypsies was well known. Two or three times a day we checked with his house by telephone. Tshukurka's condition seemed grave but for a time it remained stationary. The doctor was distressed that he refused to be hospitalized. The Rom knew his days were limited and they wanted him to spend them among those he loved rather than in the confines of a hospital. All they wanted from the kind but distraught doctor was that he help extend Tshukurka's life span by a few more days to allow just a few more of the Rom to come and say goodbye to him.

Tshukurka received daily insulin injections and other medical treatment at his wagon, which smelled like a pharmacy. Several weeks had passed without much improvement or change but without emergencies, when Pulika chose to go back to Tshukurka.

To reach the valley we first had a long climb, which became increasingly steeper. When we finally made it to the hilltop, we waited to let the overheated horses recover their wind. The twilight deepened around us and we could see the campfires flare up far down in the valley ahead of us and we could hear the crackling of burning wood. We put long, sturdy poles through the wooden spokes of the rear wheels and with all our might held the wagon back to prevent it from rolling down too fast. Unassisted, the hand brakes would burn out. The hoofs of skidding horses made sparks in the dark. The descent was slow, long and tense. Pulika yelled encouragement and instructions over the general din. One wagon at a time was allowed to slide down the slippery road. My bare feet hurt from the unaccustomed straining against the hard pavement. The wagons were brought down without mishap, and after a short drive we entered the sheltered camp area. The horses were streaming with sweat and many dogs were barking. In contrast to the usual reception when newcomers arrive at established encampments, only a few small children came to meet us. Around the burning fires there were only younger women with small children. Men and older women were conspicuously absent. I could sense that death was near and consequently I was reluctant to absent myself, but nonetheless I volunteered to take our horses to pasture while Kore stayed close to his father and the other men who had just arrived with us. Other young boys took the other horses of our caravan to the meadows. In the dark the boys and I, out of sheer habit, appraised the horses of the Gypsies who had arrived before us. There was plentiful grass, and a small stream flowed nearby. We lingered for a while, smoking, sprawled on the grass. The familiar sounds of grazing horses all around us added to the feeling of peacefulness. At the distant camp the many family fires echoed the stars in the sky above in a minor key. The women would still be cooking, and until the evening meal was ready there seemed no pressing reason to go back. I was surprised when we reached the camp to find that no food had

been prepared at all. Then Keja told me in tears that Tshukurka had died tonight shortly after our arrival. She directed
me toward the section of the camp where Tshukurka's wagon
stood.

The men had all gathered there. A large canvas roof had
been improvised, extending from the top of the wagon and
supported on the other side by ten-foot poles set at a sharp
angle and maintained by the tension of pieces of rope attached
to stakes driven in the ground. There were no walls or enclosure, just a sheltering canopy. In front of this large makeshift tent a fire burned. The Rom crowded around it more
subdued than I had ever seen them before. Some were prostrate near where the body lay. Seven tall candles, placed
unevenly, fluttered restlessly at the side of the downy pillow
covered with a gay flowered pattern on which Tshukurka
rested. Several police constables and the doctor were about to
leave the tent and discussed formalities with one of the
younger men.

To me *Nano* (uncle) Tshukurka looked as he had when
alive, but his eyes were closed. His hands, covered with
massive gold rings, lay alongside his body. Both his heavy
cane with the curved head and his favorite horsewhip were
near him. He looked as if he were only lightly slumbering. I
had the uneasy feeling of violating the Rom's privacy. Overhead the canvas awning quivered in the unquiet breeze, and
the night was full of whispering sounds.

Sudden bursts of loud wailing, howls of pain and fury
alternated with violent, rebellious phrases expressing disbelief
in Tshukurka's death. When they talked this way they addressed themselves only to Tshukurka, who lay in state before
them. During this first night of the wake people were oblivious
of life and of other Rom around them. They often repeated
soothingly in what almost seemed a ritual, *"Te aves yertime
mandar,"* yet unspoken, the formula included the hope, the
prayer, that the dead also may have forgiven them. When one
left for the Nation of the Dead, all emotional ties with the
living should be consciously severed over a period of time,

including unspoken or half-forgotten jealousies. It was also bad to think of a departed person with bitterness, regret or contempt.

Tshukurka's wife sat at his feet, weeping softly and rocking herself disconsolately. She was surrounded by Luludja and two of her daughters-in-law crouched in a dark huddled mass. The dawn was misty. At daybreak several young women brought hot black coffee but most mourners refused it, turning their heads and looking away in an absent fashion. They did not even reply to the women's insistent coaxing. That morning nobody washed or shaved; none of the women or girls thought of combing their hair. No food was prepared all day long, and again the small children cried, protesting their desire for hot food instead of the dry bread, cold chicken and raw bacon they were given.

Tshukurka was never left alone. His immediate kin spent the nights and their entire days by his fire or under his tent. The other Rom and their families took care of their horses, provided firewood and drinking water for the entire camp. It was also they who saw to it that the news of Tshukurka's death spread to all the Gypsies traveling in the vicinity, a great many of whom joined us for the funeral.

The second and third nights of the wake everybody grew more dejected and brooding. The men had not eaten or slept all this time, but had drunk steadily and with a grim determination. Their eyes were red and bloodshot, their faces drawn and unwashed, showing several days' growth of beard. Many of the older men had ripped off the buttons of their coats, vests and shirts in sign of mortification. They continued their intemperate drinking as if to demonstrate their disbelieving bewilderment. The women sobbed and wailed continuously and an old one softly sang a dirge.

A hired Gajo brass band played military marches and preceded the coffin, followed by the local priest, the widow and her children, and the other mourners, to the burial grounds. They were followed by a disorderly mob walking in a total haze from sorrow and hunger and lack of sleep. As the procession entered the cemetery, the Rom suddenly emerged from their numbness and wailed and shrieked savagely. Some women tore at their hair and had to be restrained forcibly by relatives to prevent them from doing themselves harm. They ripped their clothes, tossed their heads back, bared their teeth in horrible grimaces, their faces stained by uninhibited tears. The village priest and the choirboys were intimidated by this undignified behavior and their faces showed traces of fear. The band was not allowed to stop playing until the coffin was lowered. The priest started to say the benediction in Latin but was interrupted by a violent scuffle at the graveside, as several Gypsies tried to prevent Mimi, Tshukurka's wife, from throwing herself into the open pit. Protesting in a hoarse voice about their lack of generosity toward the dead, she was led away by relatives.

Before the grave was filled, the Rom one by one threw gold pieces on the lowered coffin. Some threw handfuls of silver change. They repeated their forgiveness to the dead, praying him to forgive them also. Then they walked away rapidly and said, as they had done long ago at Putzina's burial, *"Akana mukav tut le Devlesa"* (I now leave you to God).

At the camp an abundant meal had been prepared and was awaiting the returning Rom. This was the *Pomana* meal. It was the first food most of the Rom had eaten in days. In true Lowara fashion there was mountains of geese, chicken and beef, and wine and brandy to drink. Tshukurka's immediate kin did not participate. Sitting down to the meal and rising after it, the Rom said, "May this food be before you, Tshukurka, and in your memory, and may it profit us in good health and in good spirit" (*Te avel angla tute, Tshukurka, kodo khabe tai kado pimo tai menge pe sastimaste*).

This *Pomana*, or feast for the dead, was repeated after nine days, and again after six weeks, after six months and at the anniversary of death. At each *Pomana* certain relatives publicly declared their decision to end their particular period of mourning, which corresponded to their degree of kinship, and renounced the restrictions this imposed on them. Again they would comb their hair, wear jewelry, buy new clothes, dance, sing and get drunk. But black as a sign of mourning was never worn by the Gypsies.

Beyond the period of one year no one was permitted to

mourn. Life must go on. As it was important for the peace of soul of the dead to be made aware of the affection and loyalty of those he left behind, it was equally important for his sake not to sorrow exceedingly as this would make the dead want to come back to them to console those he loved. After an appropriate period of adjustment he should be allowed to continue his way in the new life. Hence the ritual saying at the end of the time of mourning: "I open his way in the new life again and release him from the fetters of my sorrow" (*Putrav lesko drom angle leste te na inkrav les mai but palpale mura brigasa*).

The night of the first *Pomana* for Tshukurka the camp was noisy until dawn. Early the following morning small bands of wagons started to leave in all directions. We stayed till early afternoon and were among the last to leave the open, desolate, flat camping ground.

Pulika had helped his brother's widow to burn the tent under which Tshukurka had died, the pillow with the gay flowery pattern and the rugs on which he had last rested. They had destroyed the plates from which he had eaten, the cups and the glasses from which he had drunk. Nothing should remain in use that had been used by him and that he had been attached to. When we broke camp his wagon had been thoroughly ransacked; only the shell of it remained intact. Tshukurka had died under the open sky, lying on rugs close to the earth instead of on the soft feather bed, not to prolong existence needlessly. Had he died inside the wagon that too would have had to be destroyed by fire. For a whole year his widow or his children would not be allowed to prepare food.

I felt relieved when our wagons slid off silently from this place of death where, together with Tshukurka, it seemed we had buried all joy, exuberance and zest for life. In dramatic contrast to our mood, the day was hot, the meadows were yellow masses of flowers, birds sang and insects buzzed persistently.

The Rom had no articulate concept of the Hereafter. They were certain there was neither Hell nor Heaven. Life after death went on much as before but on a different plane. They rarely talked about it and failed to grasp the Gaje's curiosity about it since "Everyone will go there and then will know beyond any doubt."

The belief was not uncommon among the Lowara that the dead may return to haunt the world of the living. Evil or sinful people returned in vain search of forgiveness, or those who had died a sudden death, or those who died before their time. The likelihood of a dead one's return was in direct proportion to his inner drive during his lifetime and his relationship to the people he cared about. The Rom yearned for what they called "a great death," for which they could prepare and which they could share with their households, relatives and friends. They feared most that kind of death which came when one was unprepared.

The *Mule,* the ancestors, the "souls" of the dead of the tribe, did not have eternal life. They somehow weakened with the years until at the death of the last person who had known them the "old souls" conceivably died once more. To questions of what might be beyond this the Rom shrugged their shoulders. Why should anybody seek comfortable illusions in a search for the unfindable?

After Tshukurka's death we traveled away from the main body of the *kumpania* and only joined with them at long intervals for the celebration of the *Pomana* meals. We could not impose on others our own restrictions imposed by mourning.

Staring ahead at an empty windswept spot, Pulika would say, "Tshukurka is still with us." These statements used to upset me as I would vainly strain my senses to experience what he did. Every time Pulika was reminded of his brother's liking for certain foods or drinks, he would casually approach the first stranger he came upon and invite him to accept a meal or drinks. At the yearly horse fair he bought a large number of the best horsewhips available from an invalid peddler who was a regular feature of the establishment. He distributed them among the startled Gaje horse dealers in silent offering to his dead brother whose appreciation of a good snapping whip was well known among the Lowara. In the same frame of mind a Rom would buy a new suit of clothes, shirts, shoes, overcoat and hat to give away to the first Gajo he met, in memory of a particular member of the family who had died recently. No explanations were ever given.

As his last specific wish Tshukurka had asked that nobody mourn for him longer than "through the coming winter," as he had said he was impatient to set out to travel again, when we would, which would be at the first signs of spring.

And so it happened that one day, after the last *Pomana* meal—which, contrary to custom but in accordance with his wish, was held after a period of only six months—we joined the main band of the *kumpania* again. Because of his solicitous consideration in abbreviating the restrictions of mourning for him, we were possibly more conscious of his absence each time we dressed up, drank, sang or danced, and we never neglected to dedicate to his memory whatever joyful thing we did, saying, *"Te avel angla tute."*

CHAPTER FIFTEEN

The winter that followed Tshukurka's death seemed interminable, the most lonely one I could remember. Because of our mourning there were no feasts to relieve the monotony of the shabby deprivations we shared with the Gaje poor among whom we lived; for the time being, we existed at the subsistence level, as they did. We lived in the confined space of our wagons, where the air became unbreathable. The rare Gaje we came into contact with were pessimistic and bored, cynical and defeatist. They were frustrated by a general mobilization that lasted too long. There were wild rumors and political unrest.

Pulika was restless. He repeatedly called Bidshika in Paris, at Grantsha's place, and he visibly chafed at the bit. It was after one such frustrating telephone call to Bidshika that I had an opportunity to gain a more explicit understanding of what Pulika was up to, and why he had originally sent Bidshika, Milosh and myself to France. He wanted to seek closer contact with some of his relatives in Spain. He wanted to be able to join them but only as a step toward going *perdal l paya*, beyond the waters, to the Americas, as Loiza la Vakako had managed to do only recently. Grofo had also gone there straight from Germany; and so had old Tshompi, if the rumors could be believed.

To the north, in Holland, there was the *kumpania* of Baba Tshurka, who possessed passports of Guatemalan nationality and who often spoke of going away. Also the horde of the four Tshurara brothers from Norway, Pani, Nanosh, Popoy and Gunari, had tried to go to Spain in the traditional semilegal Gypsy way. They had boldly but foolishly tried to bluff their way across the international bridge at Hendaye and were stuck between France and Spain, both of which refused to admit or readmit them, until finally, after much hardship, they were deported back to Norway.

The previous summer a very rich and important Gypsy had come with his family from South Africa. He was called Stevo o Africano but among the Gaje he liked to be known as Diamond Jim. He had taken as his *bori* one Valentina, daughter of Honko, and he had promised her father to help his new *khanamik,* or co-father-in-law, to emigrate to the United States. Another distant cousin of Pulika's, Marko, had left Yugoslavia for Italy. As if by common instinct the Rom everywhere were becoming restless and were on the move in search of fresh havens. Several of the younger and more impatient Rom of our *kumpania* had already traveled ahead to join Bidshika in Paris. After some heedless words they had provoked friction with the Rom who "owned" Paris at that time, Stevo la Gulumbako, who was an extravagantly ambitious and ruthless person, brutal and quarrelsome. Among the younger Gypsies who had joined Bidshika was his nephew Mertshak, the oldest son of Luluvo. He was powerfully built and popular, but gentle and easily influenced. Away from the *kumpania* and the restraining influence of their elders, he and several others became involved with the underworld of organized crime. He made a small fortune and lived in conspicuous luxury; but as the Rom claimed, *O low tai o beng nashti beshen patshasa* (Neither money nor the devil can remain in peace). He was eventually arrested, condemned, and jailed for life for his association with an international gang of counterfeiters.

One chilly early spring evening we sat with several local horse dealers, from whom we had bought a gray mare, warming ourselves over the glowing embers of a fire. We had exchanged stories about ghosts and freak accidents and compared notes on the various ways of treating equine ailments. Because of the presence of Gaje at our campfire the young women sat slightly away from the circle of firelight so as not to draw attention to themselves. They observed the activities of the men, Rom and Gaje, from the discreet protection of the half-dark. For lack of interest in the company most of the children were asleep. Already standing up and on the point of leaving, one of the horse dealers, a ruddy-faced, robust and zestful man, casually remarked that a colleague of his had bought several horses from a large band of Gypsies. They had inquired about the location of other Gypsies in the land. Unhurriedly the older Rom asked questions, but hid their keen interest. With the right shade of indifference they pretended not to be surprised at all and on the contrary to know "them" quite well. Early the following morning a score of young Lowara men left the roadside camp, driving in *taligas*. They traveled together for many miles in the same direction before splitting up in search of the newly arrived Gypsies reported the night before. As Kore and I let our new gray mare trot, we could see Yayal and Nanosh and others still driving more or less parallel with us, far off. They sometimes disappeared in the landscape and later would show up again farther away beyond the bend in the road. Sometimes they clattered down steep slopes or slowly made their way back up a hill. Some of them we could see standing upright in their *taligas*, legs apart, driving like Roman charioteers. They cracked their long, thin whips through the air for effect and let out wild, eerie yells. These were mostly the very young. Others encouraged their horses with low guttural cries that were hardly audible at this distance. For a long while Kore and I traveled at a leisurely pace watching the exulting skylarks dizzily soaring into the deep blue sky till, having exhausted their strength, their breath and their rapturous enthusiasm, they glided once more down to earth. As the sun climbed the sky we stopped now and then for a glass of beer at a wayside inn and once at a blacksmith's workshop, where in conversational tones we asked discreet questions. After hours of travel we telephoned to the tavern near our big camp to find out from those who stayed at home whether any of the other scouting parties might have reported better luck than we and possibly had found the reportedly large band of "new" Gypsies, *Rom neve*. At sundown we made another call, this time to ask if we should turn back and join the main body tonight or if we should instead camp here on the spot more easily to resume our search tomorrow. No news had been reported yet and so we decided to spend the night away from our people. We traveled a few more miles and stopped at the first tavern, where we spent part of the night drinking after a hearty meal of peasant food. When the tavern closed we took to the road again insisting that we had to reach the city before morning. We harnessed the mare and hitched her to the *taliga* and drove off into the night.

In fact we left the road only a few miles beyond the tavern and at random drove the *taliga* across a shallow ditch across some deeply plowed farmland and hid it in a clump of brushwood, where we also tied the mare to some branches. We lit a small fire, taking precautions to make it as little noticeable as possible from the main road. We stretched out by the smoldering wood fire, settled down and listened to the night. Nocturnal birds filled the air with their mystery-filled sounds of unexplained apprehension. Alone with Kore under the darkened, expansive, Prussian-blue night sky, I felt that the very meaning of the night had changed. The moon looked unreal and small. From the semidarkness where they sat we were watched by the big, wondering eyes of wild rabbits and other animals all about us; they were fascinated by the glow of the fire and unable to tear themselves away.

When we woke up, the fire was almost dead, with only a thin, spiraling thread of white smoke rising in the cold morning air. The wide-eyed rabbits were gone. The sky overhead had a strange luminescence; it was almost daybreak. Slowly the ground mist lifted in pearly, semitransparent milkiness. Our limbs were stiff from sleeping unprotected, and our eyelids felt heavy. We contented ourselves with tightening our belts before harnessing the horse. We patted it on the nose and rubbed its mane and drove away in moody haste and without unnecessary words. The two-wheeled cart rattled along the road at a mad speed while we gradually woke up to the new day. At a brook we washed ourselves, and the ice-cold water brought back our cheerfulness and manly good humor. Again we could joke. We cleaned our teeth with salt, which was the only thing we had carried with us. We stopped at the first roadside inn, where we had coffee and cognac and resumed our scouting. Toward noon we telephoned the camp. The police had broken up the encampment and forced the Rom to

move on, but Pulika and a few other men had come back by
taliga to coordinate the incoming calls from the scouting
parties and relay them to the next clearing post, the inn near
the new encampment. There was still no news from the
supposedly large Gypsy group we were seeking, but information the other parties had gathered so far was shaping into a
definite pattern. We were told we could stop the search if we
felt like doing so, and by traveling cross-country we would cut
into the route of the main group. Instead of doing this we
decided to go in the general direction of where the other group
was reported to be. It was early yet and we wanted to share in
the excitement. We drove at a mad pace, stopping at inns
along the road mainly to let the mare rest. Off a dirt track we
saw three wagons. They were smallish, garishly painted and
their bodies seemed clumsily perched on too high wheels.
There appeared to be only two horses, rather decrepit-looking.
A little to the side a group of swarthy youths played the fiddle,
the guitar and bass viol. They were Sinti. We greeted them
with a sweeping gesture but drove on. Farther up the road we
met some Sinti boys with their ebullient mongrel dogs, returning from what looked like a successful hedgehog hunt. We
bought a pair of little animals from them, and for an extra
handful of small change they gladly killed and cleaned them,
and roasted them for us over the open flame of a small fire.
Our salt provisions again came in handy. It was the wrong
time of year for hedgehogs as they were skinny from their
hibernation. The gamy, slightly charred hedgehog meat made
us thirsty and we stopped once more at an inn, where we also
bought some bottles of local beer which had a sourish aftertaste. For the rest of the day we drove through dense silent
pinewoods. We followed a roughly marked sand track, which
greatly slowed down our progress. The silence, the smell of the
pines, and the penumbra of the woods evoked distant echoes
in us. High above us the treetops rustled, humming softly in
unison, with an undertone of whispering wind and sudden
deep sighs. The scent made our nostrils quiver and our lungs
expand, this sweet, full-bodied smell of pine resin and the
musty odors of fungi. We easily succumbed to the spell of the
woods, trusting the gray mare to take us out of the enchant-

ment and into the open plain with expanding horizons. We hardly traveled any faster than at walking pace through the bluish-gray shade of the tall, close-set, singing pine trees. At sundown we suddenly emerged from the woods. Kore snapped his whip and forced the horse into a sharp trot, and we rushed at full speed right into the setting sun. From a delicate mauve, in strong contrast to the dark green shade we emerged from, the sky slowly turned a translucent turquoise with the tint and delicacy of the eggshell of certain wild birds. Ahead of us a golden-yellow horizontal stripe many miles long slanted from right to left in a vast sweep that turned blood-red as the sun sank down. The light had an indescribable quality. It subtly changed the shape and density of every object and mysteriously modified perspective; measurable distances seemed not to exist.

Suddenly we became aware of a long line of Gypsy wagons a great distance ahead of us, slowly moving in wide lazy curves like a languorous and fat summer snake. We stood up in the *taliga* and like demons urged the mare on. We drove on at a crazy speed for a long while. The horse slowed down and our encouraging shouts lost their gusto. The air smelled strongly of the sun-heated dust of the road. The sky lost its opalescence and turned leaden-gray and heavy as only a narrowing, flaming vermilion line still emphasized the horizon which was rapidly melting away in the descending dusk. A lonely dragonfly hurried past. The caravan ahead of us seemed to move forward slowly, but the distance between us remained exasperatingly the same whatever efforts we made, as if we were under a powerful magic spell which, although giving us the sensation and illusion of speed and action, kept us immobilized on one spot. Darkness increased and with it sounds seemed to gain in emphasis. We hurried on for fear of losing the caravan of newcomers in the darkness. After another spurt of speed the wagon wheels suddenly ground loudly in the quiet evening as we hit a stone-paved road. Parallel to the road we followed ran a telephone line, and every hundred yards or so, and with frightening repetition, a huge wooden pole jumped forward at us out of the deepening darkness to recede again as we hurried past. Overhead the wires hummed and sang as the wind touched them. The crescent moon was shaded by haze.

Then we suddenly found ourselves in the middle of a roadside encampment. The heavy wagons were lined up a few feet off the road and on both sides of it. We had actually rattled past the first few wagons before we realized that this was the camp we were searching for. With effort we stopped the skittish horse and looked around, dazed by the unexpectedness of it. In the semidark we saw some of the men pick up burning sticks and hold them over their heads while others poked the fires to make them flare up, and, shading their eyes with their other hands to pierce the darkness, they stepped forward to identify us. A young barefoot boy had already grabbed the halter to prevent our horse from moving forward. From everywhere dark, intense eyes observed us. We stood upright in the *taliga* but waited to jump down. Because they had to look up at us the whites of their eyes showed. Kore and I loudly shouted, *"Na daran Romale wi ame sam Rom tshatshe"* (Do not fear, you Gypsy men, for we too are Gypsies). Out of the darkness many men's voices shouted back, *"Devlesa avilan"* (It is God who brought you), to which once more we shouted *"Devlesa araklam tume"* (It is with God that we found you). We jumped down and followed the torch-bearing men down the road to a campfire lit between two wagons which hid it. We let the young boy take care of the horse. Most of the numerous men had assembled by the fire and we were put through the customary and lengthy procedure of official greetings, followed by a check on each other's genealogy and a further long period of questioning. Then food was served and drinks flowed profusely. This was the *kumpania* of Milosh, Pulika's younger brother. As soon as cooking was over, the fires were put out to avoid attracting the outsiders' attention. That night we shared the sleeping stead of Milosh's youngest son Kalia. Our cousin Kalia was about our age but he was already the father of two small children by a gentle girl called Marona. Later we learned that they had been betrothed early in life and that at her father's untimely death in Spain both she and one of her brothers had been taken into Milosh's household.

Kalia and Marona had grown up together, knowing that by the law of the Rom they belonged to each other and that one day they would be husband and wife. Rumor had it that they did not wait until the proper time, but secretly took it upon themselves to consummate their marriage vows. It was from Kalia that we learned many tricks, such as how to roll cigarettes with only one hand.

In the morning we led the newcomers back the way we had come the day before, in order to intersect Pulika's route and then follow the *vurma*, the trail, he must have left for them and for us.

We spent the first few hours of that day wagon-hopping, chatting and drinking coffee, as we gradually worked our way down from the front to the rear of the line of rolling wagons. We slid off the last wagon and unobserved crept into the manger full of hay extending from the rear of it. I felt dizzy from drinking too much coffee and not eating, also from lack of sleep and too much talking. For hours we lay dozing in the hot sun, overwhelmed by a gentle nausea from the constant rocking and the combination of smells of tar from the newly built road and the dusty, dry sweet hay. Swarms of small insects, attracted by our perspiration, hovered over us. We pulled some hay over our faces and abandoned ourselves to formless daydreams. We had at least a full day's journey ahead before catching up with our *kumpania*. Somewhere in the underbrush an unseen cuckoo repeated its mysterious call at regular intervals. From different directions other cuckoos replied in such subtly varied tones that at first I thought it was the same one moving about. They all called with precise clocklike regularity.

Shortly before nightfall we reached Pulika's encampment, and the newcomers settled down amid great rejoicing and cries. Pulika and Milosh had not seen each other in nearly seventeen years and they were deeply moved. The night that followed was one of excitement and joy, with endless songs and toasts and anecdotes from the Rom's youth, punctuated by ecstatic embraces.

The following day we broke camp with a joyous, competitive hurry and we wondered where Pulika planned to find safe shelter for as large a band as the present one, where we could worthily celebrate our reunion before separating again into small traveling units for safety's sake. As far as we could remember, none of us had ever been to the site Pulika took us to. The *taligas* shuttled back and forth as the members of our *kumpania* prepared for a *patshiv* so lavish that it would become a legend of hospitality and brotherly love among the Rom.

The Milosheshti, as we called them, were conspicuously clean and looked well-fed. It was strange at first to find out how similar we were despite their long separation from Pulika's own people: almost like a reflection in a mirror. They told wondrous stories about their escape—I never found out from whom or from where, but I guessed it must have been from Czechoslovakia or German-occupied Poland. They had paid a huge sum in gold pieces, and had been allowed to charter several open railroad cars onto which their own wagons had been lashed down for the long journey across Germany. After being sidetracked and stalled, they had arrived in Holland, where they were allowed to enter. They had remained there for a short time before traveling illegally across the border in search of Pulika. They spoke of the war and of the urgency of moving farther west, away from it.

Many of their men wore leather caps and bulky navy-blue or black sailors' sweaters. Something in the way their women dressed was disturbingly different. I later discovered that the printed cotton fabrics they wore were batik sarongs from Java, Celebes and Bali; they had recently bought them in Holland.

By nightfall the lavish *patshiv* meal was ready, and it lasted well into the night. The Milosheshti lent us beautiful silver beakers for the occasion and they also provided silver spoons, forks and knives, but these were mostly for display; the Rom were more used to eating with their fingers. The Milosheshti also contributed a large amount of Dutch gin in brown earthenware bottles.

Unsolicited, a wild, exultant song burst forth, disturbing and strange in its unexpectedness, and it brought a sobering note to the long-drawn-out indulgence in food and drink and merrymaking. The young boy of the Milosheshti sang an epic song of sorrow and hardship, and the Rom listened to the words and slowly shook their heads from side to side and repeated the significant words in low voices. The mood grew intensely contemplative. Milosh himself first joined in and then took over the singing. He sang to his brother Pulika in a deep, strong voice with a slight quavering that underlined the emotional impetus of the words. He sang for a long time and tears flowed freely over his mature and manly face. The crescent moon rose over the woods. The Rom seemed to be in a trancelike enchantment as if sharing in some ancient and sacred rite. When Milosh ended his song, he and Pulika embraced and kissed each other on the mouth as Gypsies do. The spell of the last chanted phrase remained with us with the pervading effect and glow of a sustained concluding note. Around us the woods sang and insects chirped, hummed and screeched exultingly. The Rom drank to each other and wished each other countless blessings; these wishes were extended to all those present, to those at large, to those still to come and to the dead ones too. They drank to Tshukurka who had died before the last winter, and they slowly spilled the libation on the dark earth which absorbed it. Milosh and Pulika addressed Tshukurka in a low voice as if he were present. They explained things to him as if talking to a convalescent, unhurriedly. And they told him of their gratitude for his understanding and for his granting them leave to drink together and be merry so soon after he departed. Their words were simple, direct and sincere.

Then Lyuba slowly walked out of the night that surrounded us. Her unanticipated presence among the celebrating Rom brought them out of their rapturous moment of bliss. Unseeing, she walked among them and her ancient lips quivered. She coughed drily a few times. Then suddenly she broke out in a lament for the dead, a *mulengi djili*. Her voice had a penetrating, unfathomed, metallic quality the like of which I had never heard before and which stirred me in a way I cannot forget. I was too shaken and enraptured by the singing itself and by the total impact of what was happening to remember the precise tenor of her words beyond the general scope of what she said. She sang of experiences shared in common that bound the living and the dead, and how through their lives and past deeds the dead contributed to and inspired the living, how they lived on in the hearts and memories of those present. She humbly begged them, the dead, to give us the strength to live as they had lived and to die as they had died, as generous, true Rom. The old woman stood upright and seemed to be gaining in strength, stature and presence. Her voice grew more powerful, her eyes filled with pride and authority. I wondered at the strange metamorphosis in the silent, slow-moving old Lyuba with the dark, wrinkled face, and I realized this was as she must have been long ago and as the legends about her portrayed her, when Yojo, Pulika's father, and his brother Duntshi were alive, when Tshompi made and spent fortunes in Spain, Mexico and North Africa, and when the Kalderasha first went to the Americas. She belonged to those legendary days. She talked to the dead and for a while they and their times lived again in the present, as a vision for all of us to see. She sang and talked of them intimately. Some of the events she told about had happened so long ago that only the very old people remembered and wondered about them. Pulika thanked her and gave her a silver beaker of brandy, but she went on singing, more and more inspired. Milosh took her hand and tried to kiss it and soothe her, to distract her and make her end her lament. The Rom were afraid of the aftereffects of the exhaustion and strain she was subjecting herself to. But she sang on. With a sweeping gesture of her long, thin arms she rejected all their devoted attentions, while her voice still grew in volume, drowning out all objections, interference and blessings. Her singing surged, as irresistible and powerful as a spring tide. Long afterward we wondered how such power and inspiration could pour forth from so ancient a woman. She talked to the old ones, the dead, about the present generation; she exhorted and she censured. It was as if she wanted to give herself completely in one lavish and powerful last breath. Eventually she collapsed and fell to the ground, surrounded by all her kinsmen and descendants. The distant look in her large old eyes told that she was no longer with us in heart and mind. For a short period she would remain with us, to quietly depart one day leaving for us her own unmistakable trail and a timeless inspiration for all the trail-blazing still to come.

EPILOGUE

I t was the hour before sunrise, and the large troop of horses massed together was growing restless. I woke up and heard a faint purr overhead in the paling night sky, followed by the rumble of distant thunder, and then I saw a black column of billowing smoke arise and the sky was burning. The soft, not unpleasant, purring grew ominous as wave upon wave of planes passed over us. The horses panicked, neighing frantically, and stampeded. Terrified but fascinated, we watched the slow flight of enemy bombers. One by one they tipped their wings and fell from the sky like black falcons, plunging headlong into the abyss of fire, and the earth itself seemed to blow up with devastating intensity. As the planes fell, they screamed in a high pitch. This was repeated endlessly and the earth shook. The purring drone grew faint again, ending in a soft, faraway rustling, and all nature about us became oppressively silent. The day was sunny and bright. It was May 10, 1940, the beginning of the angry years.

The Rom were momentarily possessed by a primeval terror but equally astonished to be alive. Then came the shouting, the weeping and the frenzied tears.

Sirens wailed mournfully like wounded animals.

The Gajo population fled away from the advancing German armies. Soon all the roads were clogged with trucks and buses and private cars. There were hordes of bicycle riders and some who pushed their bicycles laden with blanket rolls and mattresses and bulging suitcases tied with ropes. Some pushed wheelbarrows piled high with their possessions; others wheeled invalid relatives. Small merchants dragged pushcarts with their entire stock of shoes or other wares. A tattered

251

multitude flooded all roads south and southeastward. Enemy fighter planes swooped low over the crowded roads and machine-gunned the fleeing crowds.

There was no choice for the Rom but to join the exodus. The bombing continued and rumors were rife about German paratroopers and about the infiltration everywhere of the "fifth column." There were frequent manhunts through fields bordering on the roads we were following, and there were summary lynchings, probably of innocents, as frustration-bred violence and homicidal hysteria spread. We passed through deserted localities charred, shell-torn and bullet-spattered. There were dead lying by the roadside. The crowds lamented loudly. Some prayed aloud, others cursed bitterly, others yet were mute in their grief-stricken distress. There occurred some fierce scuffles, and lawlessness spread as fear turned into senseless vindictiveness. There was an unavoidable shortage of food, and drinking water was hard to find. After the first few days we began to find abandoned private cars and trucks, still laden with belongings. They had run out of gasoline, and in the total chaos none was available. There was even an abandoned hearse, which had been turned over in a ditch to clear the obstruction it had created on the road. All along the roads were hedges of abandoned suitcases and other private belongings as the fleeing populace grew tired and more concerned with saving life than property, with the exception of a pathetic few who preferred to collapse from exhaustion rather than give up what was theirs. The crowd of automatons moved forward inexorably. Unthinking, panic-stricken, the people reverted to near savagery.

Used to similar emergencies in their daily struggle for survival, the Rom moved with a clearer sense of purpose, with greater dignity. Numerous Gaje limped from blisters, unused to walking great distances. They were haggard, unwashed, unshaven, uncombed, glassy-eyed, tired and hungry—looking, probably, much worse than Gypsies ever looked under any circumstances. Day after night the bombings continued. Most nights the skies were red and the smell of burning never left us.

The Germans caught up with us at the Somme River and our exodus was forcibly halted. There was sporadic fighting between the French (supported by some British and Moroccan units) and units of the Waffen SS. France signed the armistice. Most of the refugees started moving back to where they had come from, with the exception of a small band of hard-core cases who pressed on, hoping to reach unoccupied French territory and freedom. There was chaos in the land. Administration and law enforcement had been disrupted by the desertion and flight of the officers in charge.

The German soldiers treated the Gypsies well at first, and for a while the Rom roamed the occupied territories at will. Prior to the German invasion whenever Gaje objected and remonstrated about Gypsies' wrongdoings, the latter had replied, *"C'est la guerre."* Now they simply replied in German, which did not endear them to the local population. At the same time, and with an inconsistency typical of the Rom, they often gave temporary shelter to British pilots shot down over German-occupied territory and to escaped prisoners of war who turned to them for help. This was due to the Gypsies' deeply ingrained tradition of compassion for the hunted. This subsequently led them into the organization of "escape routes" for Allied personnel, but it was the gradually mounting pressure put on them by the Germans that led to a fuller cooperation with the various local resistance movements.

Before the Blitzkrieg, the French government had proceeded to intern many nomadic Gypsies, along with undesirable aliens and political refugees. After the German invasion many of these prisoners were handed over to the Gestapo and deported to extermination camps in the East. Like the Jews, the Gypsies became *Rassenverfolgte* (racially undesirable), enemies of the Reich, and were legislated out of existence. But unlike the Jews, the Gypsies were difficult to seize because of their elusiveness, the relative smallness of their widely scattered groups, and their mobility.

Soon alarming rumors reached us about wholesale massacres of Gypsies by the Croatian Nationalists. There were outbursts of killings by Ukrainians in the forest of Wolyń in Eastern Poland. There were endless other instances of random exterminations. But never at any time was an overall effort made to liquidate the gypsies. These fitfully recurring campaigns of murder flared and subsided and flared again, inexplicably. There were equally inexplicable oversights and inconsistencies to which many Rom today owe their lives. There were long intervals of peace followed by sudden raids by the SS or the S.D. (*Sicherheitsdienst* or security police). Between 1939 and 1945 nearly half a million Gypsies died in more than two thousand camps that were scattered throughout German-occupied Europe.

At first the Rom, like the local populations, had grown accustomed to the goose-stepping soldiers in their black or *Feldgrau* uniforms. After the parachutist psychosis and the hysterical Germanophobia waned, people were relieved that "the war was over," and that the hated enemy appeared less ferocious than had been expected. They were polite; they looked clean; they appeared to be average middle- and working-class men, and they sang beautifully when they marched. But this did not last. Requisitions started. Collaborators sprang up everywhere. Food was rationed and there were severe shortages. All the good horses of the Rom were taken away. The blackout had been imposed since the war started, but the people had been lax about it. Now it was strictly enforced. The German soldiers simply shot at burning lights whenever they saw them.

Most of the soldiers of the defeated nations who had surrendered were in prisoner-of-war camps. There were few young men around, and those who remained or had escaped were rounded up and deported to Germany as slave labor. The persecution of the Jews followed, and the hunting down of members of leftist organizations. People whispered and learned to fear.

Pulika and the other Rom from our *kumpania,* after some hesitation, had nevertheless registered for their ration cards, since without them no food could be obtained. With the additional rations of their numerous children the Rom did well. They traveled, avoided making themselves too conspicuous, and also registered in different localities under the various identification papers they possessed. This ruse went undetected, and consequently they lived in comparative affluence. Because of the shortage of food, an extensive black market promptly developed. The farmers who managed to withhold produce from government requisition sold their surplus in the black market at inflated prices, or in exchange for silver and gold. Besides affording luxury for the affluent, it also made it possible to feed those living in illegality, individuals of military age living in hiding and provided for by relatives, and various other elements wanted by the enemy. After at first trading in their fairly numerous additional bread coupons for meat and fat, some of the Rom sought ways to gain ever-larger supplies of ration cards. Somewhere along this path they came into contact with members of the fledgling resistance movements. Soon supplying illegal ration cards became a Gypsy monopoly. Driven by the exigencies of the times, the Rom were persuaded to undertake armed holdups and burglaries of ration-card distribution centers.

Because the Rom had lived all their lives in a "twilight zone," forever aware of tactics of survival, they were well prepared and became willing instructors in the secret war. They had lived on the borderline of the criminal underworld, and some of the Rom had maintained friendly, if superficial, contacts with certain of its members, which made it easier for them to obtain their collaboration in the wholesale manufacture of false identity papers. They had experience which the resistance movements as yet lacked. Thus the Rom were able to recruit and employ an expert safecracker, whom they paid by the job, until he too volunteered to work without compensation in the common fight. In the beginning the Rom had obtained their weapons and ammunition from the underworld, but later these were supplied by the Allies.

The Gypsy women and children mostly stayed out of sight in well-hidden havens. Since they were adequately provided for, they refrained from fortune-telling, begging or petty thievery, which in turn lessened the danger of their being discovered.

The Rom from our *kumpania* were actively engaged in resistance activies until mid-1943, when many of them were caught by the *Geheime Feldpolizei*. Some escaped, and certain of the younger men of the Lowara and a few of the Tshurara group took up arms against their persecutors, though the old people said that this was the disease of the Gaje and that only the sick liked war.

One day the war ended and the survivors regrouped and started life anew. Yojo lost his family and remarried Tsura, of the Tshurara, who had lost her husband and children. Kore survived the concentration camps but died only a few weeks after the liberation, either from ill treatment in the camp or from the aftereffects of starvation; so did several others.

Only quite recently I found out that Keja is alive, as is her husband Tshurka, Luluvo's youngest son. They have eight children. The oldest son, now twenty-three years old, is called Pulika. The youngest is only five years old. Tshaya, Djidjo, and Yayal and Paprika live, and they all have gone back to the old ways, no doubt forming a new *kumpania*, kept fluid, scattering and regrouping, like the flowing of water, adapting itself to all circumstances, endlessly remodeling itself but forever remaining true to its essence, the eternal Rom.